LLEWELLYN'S

2 0 1 8
HERBAL
A L M A N A C

© 2017 Llewellyn Publications is a registered
trademark of Llewellyn Worldwide Ltd.

Cover Design: Kevin R. Brown
Editing: Lauryn Heineman

Interior Art: © Fiona King

You can order annuals and books from
New Worlds, Llewellyn's catalog. To request
a free copy, call 1-877-NEW WRLD toll-free
or visit www.llewellyn.com.

ISBN 978-0-7387-3780-5
Llewellyn Worldwide Ltd.
2143 Wooddale Drive
Woodbury, MN 55125-2989

Printed in the United States of America

Contents

Herbs for Health and Beauty

Herb Crafts

Herb History, Myth, and Lore

Moon Signs, Phases, and Tables

Introduction to
Llewellyn's Herbal Almanac

More and more people are growing, gathering, and study-ing herbs for their enlivening and healing properties. Whether in the form of weedy first aid, easy seasonal decor, or a new favorite jam recipe, herbs clearly can enhance your life.

In the 2018 edition of the *Herbal Almanac*, seasoned writers offer tips, recommendations, helpful resources, and personal anecdotes to inspire your own herbal practices. With sage ad-vice appealing to novice gardeners and experienced herbalists alike, our experts tap into the practical and historical aspects of herbal knowledge—using herbs to help you reconnect with the earth, enhance your culinary creations, and heal your body and mind.

The thirty articles in this almanac will teach you every-thing from planning an herbal seed-sowing calendar to xe-riscaping in arid climates. Featured plant profiles include rosemary, dandelions, and yarrow, offering a host of history, growing tips, remedies, and recipes. You'll also learn a holistic dentistry routine, how to safely forage for wild berries, which repurposed materials make a great miniature greenhouse, and kid-friendly steps for creating a butterfly box using native plants.

May your garden grow tall and your dishes taste delicious!

Growing
and
Gathering
Herbs

How to Grow Milk and Eggs in Your Garden

⪼ by Monica Crosson ⪻

If you asked my father, he would tell you the secret to growing eggs in the garden is to plant chicken feathers gathered from the coop at midnight in large circles around your mother's tomato plants. At least this is what he believed when he was six.

I was fifteen years old when he told me this story. I had been gathering eggs from our own chickens, a sassy mix of Rhode Island Red and Barred Rock hens who you knew were gossiping about you as soon as you left their coop.

"Yeah," he said. "You should have seen your grandmother's face when she looked out the window and saw all of those chicken feathers sticking out of the ground." He took another sip of his coffee. "You'd think she'd seen an alien spacecraft."

"Did you tell her it was you?" I asked.

"Of course." He smiled. "I was proud of what I had done. I thought I was going to grow a whole new crop of chickens."

"Oh, Dad!"

"Did I ever tell you about the time I tried to milk our steer?" He wore a mischievous expression.

"I think we've heard enough of your farm stories," my mom said, placing a plate of hash browns in front of him.

"That's gross, Dad." He winked as he shoved a forkful of hash browns into his mouth.

I grew up surrounded by farm animals. Our array included Holstein cattle, chickens, horses, sheep, and goats. They provided us not only with pleasure, but meat, eggs, milk, and fiber as well. In return, we provided them with love, shelter, and a healthy diet to keep our working animals at their peak. The majority of their food needs were grown on our farm. Hay was harvested from rich, green Timothy fields. Sprouted grains and cover crops provided our chickens with a nutrition-packed alternative to grain, and garden waste and unwanted leaves, stems, and vines added much-needed vitamins and protein for our milking goats.

The Backyard Farmer

The most recent recession caused many people to reexamine what was important in their lives and to truly grasp the idea that you can't buy happiness. The quest for a simpler life has taken us back to our agricultural roots—growing and raising our own food, food preservation, wild-crafting, and arts and crafts such as spinning, knitting, and quilting have all made a resurgence as of late. Urbanites have gotten in on the act with rooftop or balcony gardens. And suburbanites who have embraced modern homesteading have added small-scale farm animals on residential lots.

The most popular farm animals for the modern homesteader are backyard chickens and dairy goats, both being small and relatively easy to care for. Chickens lay one egg per day, when conditions are right, and a single dairy goat can provide a family with a gallon or more of milk per day for drinking, cooking, or making into yogurt and cheese. Raising backyard livestock is a great way to get reconnected with nature and provides exercise and food security for your family.

Fussy Feeders

The problem for most people without acreage is providing their backyard livestock with healthy forage. Just as a chicken cannot thrive on cracked corn alone, a goat will not flourish on only hay or commercial grain.

Goats are browsers, so setting them free in your front yard to "mow" down the grass probably isn't going to work out for you. They may nibble at the grass, but they will also devour your prized rose bush. Goats are also ruminants (they have a four-chambered stomach and chew their cud), whose digestive system is best suited for forage, hay, or grass. Contrary to popular belief, goats cannot literally eat anything. A drastic change in feed or too much commercial grain can cause the sometimes-fatal ruminal acidosis.

Chickens are omnivores. I saw one of my little ladies eat a baby mouse once. I have to admit it was kind of horrifying. Chickens naturally prefer a varied diet that includes insects, worms, seeds, greens, and grains. If your chickens are free-range (raised in natural conditions), that's easy. But if you must keep your ladies in a coop due to space restrictions or predators, just feeding them laying pellets or a cracked-corn diet will not allow them to flourish.

Yard and Garden Clippings

Adding forage to your working animals' diets will help keep them happy and healthy and can save you a lot of money on feed costs. One way to do this is to feed them clippings from your garden. Sunflowers, for example, are a great source of quality protein, vitamins, and minerals. Once the flowers have bloomed and the heads are covered with seeds, clip them off for your goats or chickens.

Letting your chickens scratch and peck in the compost pile helps boost microbial decomposition. You provide your hens with free, natural feed, they move your compost heap around for you, and their droppings add nutrients for earthworms and nitrogen to help create amazing soil for your garden bed.

Comfrey is another great plant that can be clipped down several times over the growing season. Comfrey is low in fiber and high in protein and contains vitamins A and B_{12} and calcium. Be warned—this herb is a voracious grower and can easily take over a garden bed, so I suggest planting it in pots or, if you have the room, in a space that is well separated from your flower and vegetable beds.

Herbs are also beneficial to your animals, providing them with antioxidants to help boost their immune systems. Other great garden clippings include kale, mustard greens, lettuce, sweet potatoes, carrots, squash, beets, turnips, cabbage, melons, and cucumbers. As you enjoy the fruits of your summer harvest, pick a few extra for your barnyard crew. You can store the extra in your barn or garage for use later in the season.

Your Backyard Feed Store

The key to feeding less grain is keeping good quality forage to add to your stock's diet. Growing your own forage as part of your vegetable garden will guarantee happy and healthy working animals. Here is a list of fruits, herbs, and vegetables that your animals will love:

The Goat's Garden

Black Oil Sunflower Seeds: Black oil sunflower seeds contain vitamin E, zinc, and selenium. They add butterfat to your goat's milk and give them a wonderfully shiny coat. Try 'Black Peredovik' or 'Red Sun'. (Also great for chickens.)

Mangel Beets: Mangels were grown extensively as livestock feed on small-farms for generations, but usage dropped as large-scale farms became the norm. They are starting to make a comeback with modern homesteaders and hobby farmers. And why not? They are easy to grow, weigh up to twenty pounds each, store well, and pack a nutritious punch. Try 'Red Mammoth Mangel' or 'Giant Yellow Eckendorf' varieties.

Broom Corn: What I like about broom corn is that you can use the tops for making your own brooms and feed the grain and stalks to your backyard stock. Broom corn is actually a type of sorghum that will grow wherever corn grows. It is a good energy source for working animals, and goats enjoy the leaves and grain. Try 'California Golden' or 'Evergreen Dwarf'.

Carrots: Both the roots and leaves are edible. Carrots offer more minerals and less fat than corn while providing the same amount of protein. Carrots also provide beta-carotene, which aids disease resistance, vision, lactation, and reproductive health. Larger varieties overwinter better than small varieties. Try 'Danvers' varieties or 'Saint Valery'. (Also great for chickens.)

Cowpea: Originating from Africa, the cowpea is high in protein and dietary fiber, as well as a good source of vitamin B_9. Your goats can eat the vines, pods, and peas. Try 'California Blackeye' or 'Queen Anne'.

Greens: Mustard greens, swiss chard, beet tops, lettuce, collard greens, corn salad, broccoli, and cabbage leaves all supply much needed vitamins and minerals to our backyard friends. Feeding them the unwanted leaves left over from harvesting and damaged or pest-ridden leaves cleans up your garden space and is good for your goats. Try 'Dutch' corn salad, black mustard greens (Brassica nigra), 'Georgia Southern' collard greens, 'Bloomsdale Long Standing' spinach, 'May Queen' lettuce, or 'Ruby Red' swiss chard. (Also great for chickens.)

Pumpkin: Both the vines and the fruit can be fed to your goats. Pumpkins provide your animals with good protein, dietary fiber, and fat content. They store nicely and the seeds can be used as a natural wormer. Cut up the pumpkins before feeding them to your stock. Try 'Connecticut Field'.

Sweet Corn: After you enjoy fresh corn on the cob, feed the stocks to your backyard critters. Though corn stocks are relatively low in protein, goats love the green leaves, where most of the nutrients are stored. Try heirloom varieties like 'Stowell's Evergreen' and 'Country Gentleman'.

The Chicken's Garden

Apples: Planting an apple tree supplies your flock with a low-fat, vitamin-rich treat. Remember to core the apples before giving them to the hens—the seeds contain trace amounts of cyanide, and it's better to be safe than sorry. Try your favorite standard variety grafted onto dwarf rootstock like 'Gala', 'Yellow Delicious', and 'Fuji'. (Also great for goats.)

Broccoli: Known as one of the superfoods, this member of the cabbage family is packed with vitamins and disease-fighting phytochemicals. Break the florets up and use them to make a "salad" for your chickens along with sliced cucumber and mixed greens. Try 'Arcadia' or 'Spring Raab'.

Cucumbers: Cucumbers make a nice, refreshing treat for chickens on a hot summer day, and with the added benefits of potassium, manganese, and vitamins B, C, and K, your chickens will thank you. Try 'Greensleeves' or 'Raider'.

Nasturtiums: We love these peppery gems in salads. They look lovely in the garden, but they are also great for your chickens with their natural antibiotic properties. Try 'Double Dwarf Jewel Mix' or 'Alaska Mix'.

Sprouted Grain: Sprouting grain such as wheat, spelt, or lentils takes very little time and can be done in containers all year long. Your little ladies will enjoy the benefits of improved enzyme content and chlorophyll and beta-carotene for rich, orange egg yolks.

Squash: Hold out a few squash blossoms for your backyard chickens. They are packed with calcium, iron, and vitamin A. Calcium is an important mineral for egg development.

If your chickens are laying soft-shelled or no-shelled eggs, they need more calcium. Store squash for winter feeding. Remember to cut them up before feeding them to your little ladies. Try winter varieties for better storage: 'Blue Hubbard' or 'Waltham Butternut'. (Also great for goats.)

Strawberries: Chickens love berries. They pack a vitamin-packed punch, and it seems chickens know not only what's good for them, but what tastes great, too. Strawberries are easy to grow, and if you chose an everbearing variety, you will have healthy snacks for your feathered friends all summer long. Try 'Quinault'.

Watermelon: What a wonderful summer treat for your chickens. Watermelons are 92 percent water, so they really do a great job of hydrating your girlies. Also being rich in vitamins, minerals, and antioxidants, watermelons will definitely enhance your chicken's diet. Let the melons fully ripen on the vine so your flock can get the best nutritional benefits. Try 'Garden Baby' or 'Cole's Early'.

Nature's Vet Kit

Here are a few beneficial herbs and weeds that you may have on your property or that you could purchase through any herbal supply company. For overall general health, slip a few sprigs in with your backyard stock's regular feed.

For Goats

Basil: Antibacterial and helps support the immune system.

Blackberry: The leaves, roots, and berries can be fed to your goats to help remedy scours (diarrhea) in goats.

Garlic: A natural wormer and disinfectant.

Marshmallow Root: For increasing your doe's milk production.

Raspberry Leaf: Should be fed to your doe just before, during, and just after her pregnancy. This cleansing herb is important to female reproductive organs.

Sage: Helps promote general health and is an antioxidant.

Slippery Elm: Soothes and coats a goat's sensitive digestive track, treating both scours and constipation.

To improve the quality and taste of goat's milk, try these herbs: lavender, rosemary, thyme, borage, fennel, or dill.

For Chickens

Bee Balm: Antibacterial and also used to clear respiratory problems.

Lavender: With its stress-reducing qualities, this aromatic herb can be placed in nesting boxes to ease your laying flock. Also a natural insect repellent.

Marigold: Plant these golden beauties around your chicken coop as a natural insect repellent.

Oregano: This natural antibiotic supports the immune system.

Parsley: This highly nutritious herb is also a laying stimulant and aids in blood vessel development.

Purple Coneflower: Both the seeds and the flowers are great for respiratory health.

Red Clover Blossoms: A very nutritious yard weed that is both an antioxidant and a blood purifier. This powerhouse plant also contains calcium for your egg layers and a host of other vitamins and minerals for overall general health.

Thyme: Another great herb for respiratory health. Thyme is also antibacterial and has antibiotic properties.

Poisonous Plants
(or What Not to Feed Your Barnyard Crew)

Goats are browsers and, for the most part, are pretty savvy about what their plant needs are. I've watched my own goats nibble willow bark and completely skip over bracken fern or foxglove (both deadly to them). Chickens, too, will typically leave alone what instinct tells them may be harmful, but if you throw dried rice into your chicken's feed, your flock isn't going know that it can swell in their gut and potentially kill them.

Here is a (partial) list of foods to avoid when feeding your barnyard crew: avocado, azalea, boxwood, bracken fern, citrus, curly dock, fixweed, foxglove, fuchsia, holly, horse chestnut, horseradish, hyacinth, ivy, larkspur, lilacs, lily of the valley, lupine, milkweed, monkshood, nightshade (anything in the nightshade family, including the leafy portions of potato and tomato plants), oleander, onions, rhododendron, rhubarb leaves, tulip, water hemlock, and moldy, salty, or sugary foods.

Chickens Only

Dried rice (can swell in their gut), dried beans (contain hemaglutin that is toxic to chickens; cooked or sprouted is okay), and apple seeds.

Goats Only

Wilted wild cherry, elderberry, and plum or chokecherry leaves (fresh and dry leaves are okay).

Remember, never make big changes in your animals' (especially goats') feed all at once. Ruminants such as goats need a gradual change so as not to throw off the bacteria in their rumen. Introduce small quantities and watch them carefully.

I can't imagine a life without goats and chickens in it. And though they are not traditional pets, like a cat or a dog, strong bonds can be made with your working animals. Goats are curious, loving, intelligent, and affectionate creatures that provide wonderful companionship. I don't know how many times I have turned around in my home to find a goat has made it through an open door, bleating for a treat behind me. "Come on, Mom!" they seem to say. "I saw Chloe with an apple. Where's mine?"

Our chickens, too, have funny personalities. Some chickens follow us around the property, while others don't want anything to do with us, unless it involves food. I have one sassy chicken who will follow me as I work in the garden, pulling up whatever I plant. She's sneaky about her work. If I turn to catch her, she darts behind the nearest shrub.

So whether you already have an established backyard farm or are planning to try your hand at animal husbandry, remember that these working animals are giving their all to supply our families with eggs, milk, meat, or fiber. So why not repay them with love, a clean, dry shelter, and the best possible food that we (and nature) can provide?

Resource

De Baïracli-Levy, Juliette. *The Complete Herbal Handbook for Farm and Stable*. 4th ed. New York: Farrar, Straus and Giroux, 1991.

Monica Crosson *is the author of* The Magickal Family: Pa-gan Living in Harmony with Nature *(Llewellyn, 2017). She is a Master Gardener who lives in the beautiful Pacific Northwest, happily digging in the dirt and tending her raspberries with her husband, three kids, three goats, two dogs, two cats, many chickens, and Rosetta the donkey. Her garden was featured on Soulemama .com's 2016 virtual garden tour. She has been a practicing Witch for twenty-five years and is a member of Blue Moon Coven. Mon-ica is a regular contributor to Llewellyn's annuals, calendars, and datebooks. She also enjoys writing fiction for young adults and is the author of* Summer Sage.

Xeriscaping with Herbs

⤜ by Jill Henderson ⤛

Herbs are the perfect xeriscape plants. Not only are they beautiful, naturally disease resistant, edible, and medicinal, but most also happen to be incredibly heat and drought tolerant, which means they don't need a lot of water to thrive.

Herbs are also naturals at attracting hummingbirds, butterflies, and a whole host of beneficial insects to the garden while repelling bothersome browsers like deer, groundhogs, squirrels, and rabbits. Naturally xeric herbs also make stunning additions to perennial gardens and take a fraction of the time and water to maintain.

What Is Xeriscaping?

Merriam-Webster defines xeriscape (ZEER-a-scape) as "a landscaping method developed especially for arid and semiarid climates that utilizes water-conserving techniques (as the use of drought-tolerant plants, mulch, and efficient irrigation)."

For tens of thousands of years, humankind has lived off the land by gathering wild plants and cultivating subsistence crops such as grains, corn, beans, and squash. But very few had the kind of technology and manpower needed to bring large quantities of water to their crops. Some may have used skins or pottery to carry water to seedlings, while others may have gone so far as to divert runoff to a specific area through the use of shallow berms and trenches. But in general, the majority of our ancestors simply cultivated crops that could produce food with whatever amount of rain came directly from the heavens.

Over time, we humans learned to channel and control water not only for irrigation, but for everything else we do in our modern-day lives. We have become so accustomed to water on demand that we have forgotten how precious it is. Most people don't realize the conundrum our world is in. Water is becoming harder to find, more expensive to use, and at times questionable in quality and quantity. For those living in dry or semiarid parts of the world, water conservation has become the new battle cry. Take the Colorado River for example. This behemoth of a river used to run 1,450 miles across seven US states and two Mexican states before flowing into the Gulf of Mexico. But in most years all of the water is pumped out before it even gets close.

When it comes down to it, water is the ultimate elixir of life, and some people believe that we are running out of it—and fast. There's even talk about future, and maybe not so future, water wars. So when we talk about water conservation, it is realistic not only to address our excessive water consumption, but also to find ways to reduce it. In 1980 the Denver Water Department developed a detailed system of landscaping that severely limited the use of irrigation. Playing off of the Greek word *xeros*, which means "dry," the creators dubbed this dry landscape the "xeriscape."

Experience Is the Best Teacher

I have one steadfast rule for nonfood plants in my garden. It's a simple rule: if a plant doesn't grow well on its own with little help from me, it doesn't grow in my garden. I know that sounds a little harsh, but with all the other chores I have to do on my forty-two-acre homestead, coddling pretty plants is not high on my priority list. But don't get me wrong, I love my gardens and work hard at making them beautiful to look at. In fact, I have loads of gorgeous plants growing throughout the multiple gardens on my place. And while many of them, such as the irises and grasses, are purely ornamental, most are there to feed or heal my family or to improve biodiversity in the landscape by attracting beneficial insects and pollinators. Many do both and more.

But here in my Ozarks zone 7a garden, where the "soil" is primarily red clay and rock, things I can always count on in the middle of summer are heat and often prolonged periods of drought. And when you're gardening in clay, there is little room for forgiveness: it's either completely waterlogged or bone dry and hard as a rock. Those kinds of conditions are almost guaranteed to be a death sentence for the average perennial. And unless there are some major interventions, such as bringing in load after load of topsoil, rotted manure, and compost and constantly watering during the summer months, most plants just won't make it. Or will they?

When we first moved to this farm six years ago, about two acres immediately surrounding the house were a denuded red clay moonscape lavishly dotted with rocks and boulders and complete with two-foot-deep erosion gullies that ran for hundreds of yards down the driveway. That was in late August. By the time spring rolled around, we had the hillside mended and mulched and the erosion completely under control. We turned to friends and those who were caring for our old gardens for cuttings and divisions of plants we had left behind.

Since we didn't have much time left to amend the soil on either the terraces or in the vegetable and herb gardens, we just picked the driest days we could to loosen the clay before planting directly into it, thinking we'd deal with it later. I cringed when my husband began digging into the clay right beside our front deck and proclaimed that this is where the herb garden would start. In went the precious divisions of bronze fennel, mint, sage, oregano, marjoram, and thyme, punctuated by small tufts of grassy garlic and onion chives, Siberian irises, daylilies, and 'Autumn Joy' sedum. Those were soon followed by basil seedlings and the direct sowing of dill, parsley, and fennel along with vegetable seeds and starts for the food garden. After each planting, we covered everything with a thick layer of oak leaves and prayed for a miracle.

Over the next six years I would learn a thing or two about water (and the overabundance and lack thereof), proper drainage, and clay, in that order. I would also learn that if you get the timing and location right, mulch like mad, and have just a little patience, good things will happen. That first summer was a bear, with temperatures hovering in the 100° Fahrenheit range and almost no rainfall from mid-March all the way through September. It was all we could do to keep our little vegetable garden from withering away and not drain our well or burn out the well pump trying to keep it alive. The herbs and ornamentals became low priority in the watering department. But much to our surprise, they and quite a number of hardy ornamentals hung in there and even grew in size with little more than a passing gesture from the hose every now and again. I was very encouraged.

Herbs Thrive in Harsh Landscapes

Of the many plants that we have attempted to grow in these harsh conditions, the herbs have been the ones that continually reward us. Not only did our herbs grow that summer, but they thrived in ways we never would have imagined. To this day, our herbs are the most beautiful aspect of our gardens as a whole. They have been carefree, undemanding, and incredibly abundant year in and year out. The herbs don't require much, if anything, in terms of fertilizer or pest control, and they never beg for water.

Since those first tenuous days, the herbs have been divided many times and transplanted to the dreaded terraces and other forlorn places in the yard, where they act as hardy ornamentals that always seem to bloom when nothing else is blooming and provide us with more quality spices, seasonings, tea, and medicinal herbage than we can possibly use in a year. And all the while, it is the herbs that attract the most butterflies, hummingbirds, bees, and other pollinators, along with praying mantises, spiders, and parasitic wasps that help us keep our vegetable garden free of pests.

Not all gardeners who are interested in reducing water consumption have to deal with conditions like mine. Some are even worse, while others are much better. Sandy soils are particularly difficult to deal with, especially in areas that receive little rainfall. Although sandy soil is airy and allows roots to dive deep, sand drains and dries out very quickly. And if the earth is more sand than soil, it may be naturally low in plant nutrients, as well. To top it off, what nutrients that are in or have been built up in sandy soils are notoriously prone to being flushed out by heavy rains and overwatering. And like clay, sand is prone to erosion.

For tons of great resources on xeriscaping, check out the Colorado WaterWise website at http://coloradowaterwise.org/page-645744.

When you set out to do further research on xeriscaping methods, keep in mind that the original xeriscape system was developed specifically for gardeners living in Colorado and other southwestern states, where extreme drought conditions naturally exist. This system is intensely focused on dryland plant species and minimal to zero irrigation, which may not exactly suit your desires if you live in an area that suffers only occasional or seasonal drought. For example, here in the Missouri Ozarks—a place not well known for being drought-stricken—I can grow plants that gardeners in Colorado can only dream of. And I can also grow those plants with little or no direct watering because this area naturally gets more rain than Colorado does, even in a summer drought. So, if you live in an area like mine, where rainfall is adequate much of the year, you may not need to follow the strict guidelines called for in the original xeriscape system. Using what is sometimes referred to as "low-water" or "controlled irrigation" landscaping may be more akin to your situation. Either way, by reducing and concentrating irrigation, you not only conserve water, lower your water bill, and reduce stress on private wells, but you also go a long way to protect our natural waterways and aquifers for future generations.

The Wonders of Mulch

Obviously, not every gardener lives in a climate with perfect weather. Some have longer or shorter growing seasons, some have harsh winters, and others can only grow certain crops during the cooler winter months. In all soil types and climatic zones, mulch is the singular key to a successful xeric garden. I can't stress this enough. Organic and natural mulches, be they straw, hay, deciduous leaves, grass clippings, bark chips, sawdust, or even rocks or gravel, help to protect the soil from the harsh forces of nature and reduce water consumption.

Mulch prevents evaporation of moisture, keeps roots cool in summer and warm in winter, ends the destructive cycle of freeze-and-thaw heaving of plants, and eliminates the loss of topsoil and added amendments like compost. Mulch also attracts worms, toads, and burrowing insects whose tunnels not only "turn" the soil, but also add nutrients to it while simultaneously creating avenues for water to dive deep into the soil where plant roots need it most. Mulch also encourages beneficial fungi and microorganisms to take up residence in the soil around plants, creating and digesting organic matter that improves overall soil tilth and fertility. In short, a three- to four-inch layer of natural mulch can make or break the xeric garden, no matter the type of soil it covers. One final benefit of mulch is that it can easily hide ugly soaker and drip irrigation hoses, which can be an integral part of successful xeriscaping.

Herbs for the Xeriscape

Let's take a look at some of the herbs that will not only survive but thrive in a xeriscape garden. Some are easy to guess, while others may leave you scratching your head, but all have the ability, and the genetics, to survive with very little water. Note that plant names inside parentheses whose genus is followed by the word "species" indicates that there are multiple species within that genus that are useful in the xeriscape garden. For example, "agastache" is both a genus and a common name that is used indiscriminately to describe multiple species within the genus. Texas hummingbird mint (*Agastache cana*), licorice mint (*Agastache rupestris*), and giant hyssop (*Agastache foeniculum*) are different species within the genus but are commonly referred to as agastache. So, wherever I mean to indicate that there are many species within a genus that will work in a xeriscape garden, I give the genus name followed by the word species. It is then up to you to do further research into the various species available in that genus.

Aster/Daisy Family: Asteraceae (Compositae)
>   Artemisia (*Artemisia* species)
>   Coneflower (*Echinacea* species)
>   Costmary (*Tanacetum balsamita*)
>   Mugwort (*Artemisia vulgaris*)

Roman chamomile (*Chamaemelum nobile*)
Sagebrush (*Artemisia tridentata*)
Santolina (*Santolina chamaecyparissus*)
Sunflower (*Helianthus* species)
Wormwood (*Artemisia absinthium*)
Yarrow (*Achillea millefolium*)

Mint Family: Lamiaceae

Anise hyssop (*Agastache foeniculum*)
Basil (*Ocimum basilicum*)
Bee balm (*Monarda* species)
Cat thyme (*Teucrium marum*)
Catmint (*Nepeta* × *faassenii*)
Catnip (*Nepeta cataria*)
Clary sage (*Salvia sclarea*)
Germander (*Teucrium chamaedrys*)
Hummingbird mint (*Agastache cana*)
Hyssop (*Hyssopus officinalis*)
Lamb's ear (*Stachys byzantina*)
Lavender (*Lavandula* species)
Lemon balm (*Melissa officinalis*)
Marjoram (*Origanum majorana*)
Mint (*Mentha* species)
Oregano (*Origanum vulgare*)
Rosemary (*Rosmarinus officinalis*)
Russian sage (*Perovskia atriplicifolia*)
Salvia (*Salvia* species)
Savory (*Satureja* species)
Thyme (*Thymus vulgaris*)
Horehound (*Marrubium vulgare*)
Motherwort (*Leonurus cardiaca*)

Parsley Family: Apiaceae

Angelica (*Angelica archangelica*)
Bronze fennel (*Foeniculum vulgare* 'Purpureum')
Dill (*Anethum graveolens*)
Fennel (*Foeniculum vulgare*)
Lovage (*Levisticum officinale*)
Parsley (*Petroselinum crispum*)

Miscellaneous Families

Baptista (*Baptisia australis*), Fabaceae
Bay tree (*Laurus nobilis*), Lauraceae
Comfrey (*Symphytum officinale*), Boraginaceae
Epazote (*Dysphania ambrosioides*), Amaranthaceae
Evening primrose (*Oenothera* species), Onagraceae
Garlic chives (*Allium tuberosum*), Amaryllidaceae
Green ephedra (*Ephedra viridis*), Ephedraceae
Hops (*Humulus lupulus*), Cannabaceae
Lady's mantle (*Alchemilla* species), Rosaceae
Mallow (*Malva* species), Malvaceae
Mullein (*Verbascum* species), Scrophulariaceae
Rhubarb (*Rheum rhabarbarum*), Polygonaceae
Rue (*Ruta graveolens*), Rutaceae
Salad burnet (*Sanguisorba minor*), Rosaceae
Sweet woodruff (*Galium odoratum*), Rubiaceae
Yucca (*Yucca* species), Asparagaceae

To find out more about the various species within a genus, including height, bloom time, and flower color, Internet search engines are invaluable. Start by typing the genus name into your search engine. Let's continue using the genus *Agastache* as an example, which would make the search term "agastache species." This search should pull up multiple references to the various species within that genus. I also like to look through the image results of a search like this, which is basically all of the images that came back as having those search terms associated with them. Doing this really helps narrow down the color and structure of plants I'm looking to add to my garden. Once I find one I like, I follow the link associated with the image and try to track down the specific variety (common name) and the Latin botanical name of that particular plant.

Remember, the key to xeriscaping is not to adapt your watering schedule to your plants, but to grow plants that are naturally adept at growing with less water. In addition to common culinary herbs, look for edible, medicinal, and dye plants that are native to your area. Many native plants are not only drought tolerant, but beautiful and useful as well. If you are gardening and using conventional watering schedules, you should be prepared to either lose those plants that cannot adjust to the xeriscape or move them to a special area reserved for water-hungry plants. I think you will find that switching over to a pure or modified xeriscape in your yard will result in less work, less water, and more beauty year round.

Resource

"Xeriscape." Merriam-Webster.com. Accessed November 23, 2016. http://www.merriam-webster.com/dictionary /xeriscape.

Jill Henderson *is a backwoods herbalist, author, artist, and world traveler with a penchant for wild edible and medicinal plants, culinary herbs, and nature ecology. She is a long-time contributor to* Llewellyn's Herbal Almanac *and* Acres USA *magazine and is* *the author of three books:* The Healing Power of Kitchen Herbs, A Journey of Seasons, *and* The Garden Seed Saving Guide. *You can find more of Jill's work at* Show Me Oz *(ShowMeOz .wordpress.com), a weekly blog filled with in-depth articles on gardening, seed saving, homesteading, wild-crafting, edible and medicinal plants, herbs, nature, and more. Jill and her husband, Dean, live, garden, and attempt to herd three furry felines in the heart of the Missouri Ozarks.*

Living Juicy:
An Introduction to Succulent Plants

❧ by Natalie Zaman ❧

While visiting family in Tucson, we drove out to Mount Lemmon for pie. To get to the café perched atop the mountain, we traveled through a patch of the Sonoran Desert, a sandy flatland speckled with *Carnegiea gigantea*, better known by its common name, "saguaro."

Eventually the mountain loomed, and as we climbed, the temperature dropped and the environment changed, the cacti magically morphing into pine trees. The pie, for the record, was pretty awesome (and unfortunately no longer available, as the Mount Lemmon Café has closed), but it was the cactus that won the day. Later, when I got to stand next to one—tall, majestic, prickly, and deep

jade green—well, let's just say that nothing compares to seeing a living thing growing wild in its natural habitat.

Cacti or Succulent?

Cacti are succulent plants, poetically and literally. Succulents are (for the most part), as their name suggests, plump and juicy. They're the camels of the plant kingdom, storing the moisture that will keep them hydrated even in the most arid conditions (although there are varieties that thrive in tropical and temperate climates). So cacti are succulents—but not all succulents are cacti. The difference? Areoles.

Look closely at a cactus and you'll see small knobs of flesh from which hair or spines grow. These little nubs of evolution (cacti spines serve a protective function to help them survive in harsh environments) are the single differentiating characteristic between cacti and other succulents.

Succulents are classified by group and then by Latin and familiar names. For example, *Agave* is a genus made up of several plants such as the hardy *Agave utahensis*, the tree-like *Agave stricta*, and the *Agave tequilana*, used for distilling liquor and other consumable treats. What follows is a sampling of succulents that you may have encountered in your travels. Some are for looking, some are for cultivation, and some just might surprise you.

Fruiting

Most fruits are succulent—but some are true succulents. **Saguaros**, which can only be found in the Sonoran Desert, grow their first arm (if they grow any at all) at 75 to 100 years and reach their full height (about 70 feet) at 200 years. They start flowering at about 40. The flowers, which bloom in April, only open for approximately 24 hours. If the local bats, bees and birds do their job, then the flowers will produce fruit that ripens in June and July.

Watch out for that teddy bear—he'll get you every time. He looks cuddly, but even the slightest brush against his furry sides will leave you stuck with pins. Teddy bear (Cylindropuntia bigelovii) is succulent, but his spines make him a cactus!

It's illegal to pick saguaro fruit, as it's an essential part of the diet of many desert fauna, but the Tohono O'odham Nation can collect fruit from cacti outside the Sonoran Desert National Monument (national park). The saguaro harvest signals the start of the highly anticipated monsoon season. After a prayer is sung, the first fruit is picked and then split open. A bit of the juice and flesh are rubbed over the heart as a blessing, and then the rind is then left out and pointed toward the sun to pull down the rains.

Luckily there's a similar fruit that's more plentiful and easily accessible for everyone to enjoy. *Opuntia ficus-indica*, or the **paddle cactus**, produces yellow, white, and red prickly pears. Even if you don't grow this cactus at home, the fruit is quite common in grocery stores. The Aztecs cultivated another species of *Opuntia*, the *coccinellifera*, not for its fruit, but because it was (and still is) a nutrient-rich habitat for the cochineal beetle. Harvested year round, the cochineals were boiled, dried, and then crushed to make a red-purple dye. Spanish settlers continued the practice when they came to Mexico in the sixteenth century, using cochineal dye to tint papal and royal vestments.

Cochineal farms are still active today, producing natural coloring for textiles, cosmetics, and sometimes food.

Perhaps the most common—and arguably the most succulent succulent—is the **pineapple**. Pineapples resemble another succulent, the yucca, in both appearance and moisture storage; water is saved in the plants' leaves. After flowering, the fruit forms, like the leaves that keep it hydrated, in a geometric, rosette pattern. Although they flourish primarily in tropical environments, pineapples can be grown successfully indoors.

To grow a pineapple, you'll need a whole fruit with its leaf-top intact, some potting soil, and a large pot. Cut off the top of the pineapple, leaving about an inch or two of meat base below the leaves. Plant the top in a soil-filled pot, leaving only the leaves exposed. Keep the soil damp but not soaked. Depending on the size of your pot, you may need to transplant; pineapple leaf clusters have a spread of up to five feet. Next, be patient. It can take a few years before your pineapple produces fruit.

Healing

If you've ever purchased a "natural" skin lotion, there's a good chance that one of the ingredients is *Aloe barbadensis*, or **aloe vera**. This variety of aloe yields a clear sap that is a primary ingredient in countless skin care products. The sap, accessed by splitting one of the plump, stalk-like leaves, can be applied straight to the skin to sooth scratches, burns, and cuts. (Check with your doctor before applying any plant sap to your skin, injured or not.)

Aloe and agave look similar; both grow in rosette formations and have variations that thrive in a wide range of climates. However, aloes mature more quickly, producing flowers every year, while slow-growing agave can take up to forty years (or as little as five years) to flower. And where the leaf of the aloe vera contains its potent sap, it's the heart of the agave, specifically the *Agave tequilana,* that possesses intoxicating as well as healing power.

Hearts of *Agave tequilana,* also known as *agave azul* or **blue agave**, are fermented and boiled to make tequila and the lesser-known but equally potent *pulque.* Nectar from these same hearts is extracted to produce a syrup that is sweeter than sugar but is absorbed more slowly by the human body, providing a natural sugar option for those who are challenged by hypoglycemia and diabetes.

Blessing

My poor **snake plant** (*Sansevieria*) has been knocked over more times than I can count and has spilled completely from its pot at least once—and yet it's still here. Perhaps it's the resilience of this thick-leafed plant that's made it a symbol of prosperity in China. According to Taoist and feng shui practices, placing a snake plant at or near the entry of your home will ensure that the Eight Immortals bless you with their virtues: longevity, prosperity, wisdom, beauty, art, poetry, health, and strength. Potting it in a vessel with a dragon motif bestows further fortune; according to the Chinese zodiac, the snake is the "little dragon." Easy to care for, snake plants need water when their soil feels dry, and they like to be turned occasionally for even sun exposure. Should your snake plant meet with several unfortunate accidents, as mine has, resituate it and chances are it'll bounce back pretty quickly!

Also known as "Jupiter's Eye" or "Jupiter's Beard," **hens and chicks** were planted by the front doors of ancient Roman houses to attract prosperity (hence the link to Jupiter). In England hens and chicks at a home's entrance encouraged virility and were called "welcome husband." With petal-like leaves that grow in a swirling spiral, hens and chicks spread quickly in dry, sandy soil, making them excellent ground—or roof—cover. Charlemagne capped his palace with hens and chicks, *Sempervivum tectorum* ("always living on the roof"), to keep away lightning.

Jade plants are evergreens with thick, juicy leaves that resemble coins, so it's not surprising that they're also called money, joy, luck, and dollar trees. At Chinese New Year, a jade plant is often placed on top of stocks in the hope that its energies will be absorbed by the investments. For luck with money, place a jade plant in the southeast corner of your house. Easy-care jades will let you know when they need attention; when a jade's leaves start to pucker and lose their shine, it's time to water!

Changeling

You didn't imagine it—the plant that was gray-blue yesterday can and did turn pink. *Graptopetalum paraguayense*, or **ghost plant**, is like a mood ring, though it's not telling you if it's happy or stressed out when it changes hue. The amount of heat and light to which a ghost plant has been exposed will show in the color of its plump, petal-like leaves. Full sun will cause them to take on a yellow hue, and in the shade they are blue-gray. In extreme heat the leaves turn pink. The ghost is a hardy succulent, surviving on little water, with broken and damaged stems, and even in the cold.

Threadbare *Tillandsia usneoides*, **Spanish moss**, drapes trees all over the South and parts of the southwestern United

States. Part of the same family as the pineapple, space- and shape-shifting Spanish moss is, surprisingly, a succulent. The gray-green scales that cover the plant's stems and leaves store moisture absorbed through humidity—rain, fog, and mist. Neither moss nor Spanish, its common name was bestowed by French settlers, who called it "Spanish beard." Spanish moss only grows in trees, spreading via wind and wildlife to catch on new branches, which expose it to sunlight. Buds at the ends sprout new growth and lengthen the strands. Spanish moss has been used as a mulching compound because of its ability to absorb moisture, but it also repels insects and other critters. Hunters and fishermen would wrap themselves in Spanish moss to repel mosquitoes, and only up until 100 years ago it was used as a stuffing for furniture.

Collecting and Cultivating

Cultivating succulents is a work of patient appreciation. Visit CactiGuide.com for tips on selecting plants as well as growing and caring for them. The Cactus and Succulent Plant Mall provides a listing of properties in the United States that offer delicious displays of these juicy plants that are open to the public (http://www.cactus-mall.com/gardens.html).

Resources

Baldwin, Debra Lee. "Why I Love Ghost Plant (Graptopetalum paraguayense)." *Gardening Gone Wild*, January 2, 2013. http://gardeninggonewild.com/?p=22817.

Felsher, John. "Spanish Moss Remains the Stuff of Legends Throughout the Deep South." *Voice of NC*, October 25, 2010. http://voiceofmoorecounty.com/2010/10/25/spanish-moss-remains-the-stuff-of-legends-throughout-the-deep-south/.

Hewitt, Terry. *The Complete Book of Cacti and Succulents: The Definitive Practical Guide to Cultivation, Propagation and Display*. London: Dorling Kindersley, 1993.

Nightlight. "Snake Plant—Perfect Houselant." Quiet Corner. May 30, 2016. http://www.quiet-corner.com/garden-ideas/snake-plant-perfect-houselant/.

Owen, T. S. "The Meaning of a Jade Plant." Garden Guides. Accessed July 10, 2016. http://www.gardenguides.com/120475-meaning-jade-plant.html.

Shaw, Sarah. "Cochineal: Bug Juice from Oaxaca Makes Natural Red Dye." *Wander Shopper*, October 2, 2013. http://wanderlustandlipstick.com/blogs/wandershopper/2013/10/02/cochineal-bug-juice-from-oaxaca-makes-natural-red-dye/.

Troy. "Herb of the Week—Hens and Chicks." *DTL Herbs*, December 11, 2010. http://dtlherbsltd.blogspot.com/2010/12/herb-of-week-hens-and-chicks.html.

WondersoftheWest. "Saguaro Fruit Harvest." YouTube video, 7:42. July 20, 2007. https://www.youtube.com/watch?v=YjsvGg5kAgM.

Woofboy111. "How to Grow Pineapples." Instructables. Accessed July 15, 2016. http://www.instructables.com/id/How-to-Grow-Pineapples/?ALLSTEPS.

Natalie Zaman *is the author of* Magical Destinations of the Northeast *and coauthor of* Color and Conjure *and the Graven Images Oracle deck. A regular contributor to various Llewellyn annual publications, she also writes the recurring feature Wandering Witch for Witches & Pagans Magazine. When not on the road, she's busy chasing a flock of free-range hens around her magical back garden. Visit Natalie online at http://nataliezaman.blogspot.com.*

Rosemary for Remembrance

❧ by Elizabeth Barrette ❧

Among the most popular of Mediterranean herbs is rosemary, now grown throughout much of the world. Most cultivars produce a beautiful, bushy little plant with narrow leaves. Although vulnerable to frigid temperatures, it flourishes in pots, so almost anyone can grow it.

This herb has many applications. It can be trimmed into interesting shapes, harvested for cooking, and used in crafts. Rosemary symbolizes remembrance, and its piney scent can refresh memory. Let's take a closer look at it . . .

Cultivation

Rosemary (*Rosmarinus officinalis*) belongs to the family Lamiaceae. It typically grows one to three feet tall.

However, prostrate rosemary may only be a few inches high while trailing much longer along the ground, and some bush forms may reach up to nine feet high. In general it grows larger in climates where it can be evergreen and perennial. In cold climates, rosemary dies with the frost and thus performs as an annual herb. Many cultivars tolerate salt, making it a good beach plant. It can even be trimmed into a topiary.

The plant puts out bushy stems covered with narrow, needle-like leaves. They resemble pine or spruce needles and smell very similar. They tend to be dark green above and grayish-green to silver underneath. In early to mid-summer, racemes of tiny blue or white flowers appear. These attract bees and other pollinators, making it an excellent choice for an insect garden. All of the plant's parts—stems, flowers, leaves—emit a fragrance that is aromatic, resinous, and sometimes camphoraceous. For this reason it is popular in sensory or healing gardens.

Rosemary grows best in light, well-drained, alkaline soil. Although it prefers full sun, it needs shelter from blustery wind. These factors make it well suited to an herb spiral or other rock garden. It also thrives in containers, keyhole gardens, or up against a stone wall. Position prostrate forms where they can trail over the edge of a pot or down the wall of a rock garden.

To grow rosemary from seeds, start the seeds six to twelve weeks before planting time. They germinate slowly and have a low success rate. This may be improved by soaking them for several hours before sowing. Fill a tray or pots with potting mix, and then plant several seeds in each space. (If more than one germinates, you can snip away the extras to leave the strongest plant per space.) Mist until the potting mix is damp. Cover the tray. Place it in a warm place or on a heat mat to reach 75° to 85° Fahrenheit (25° to 30° Celsius). When seedlings sprout, remove the cover. Move them to a sunny spot and mist gently. They are ready for transplanting at three inches tall.

Plant rosemary in the spring when the weather and soil have warmed. In zone 8 or farther south, you may also plant it in fall, early enough that the roots have time to establish before winter. Space seedlings two to three feet apart. They grow slowly the first year and then gain speed in later years if given a warm climate.

Water rosemary evenly and generously, but allow the soil to dry out between watering times. Ideally, choose a raised bed or pot where you can water it until the drain holes at the bottom begin to leak. The low water requirement makes rosemary a good choice for xericulture in dry climates.

If necessary, apply a slow-release fertilizer at planting and each spring. Be careful not to overfertilize it, though. As with most Mediterranean herbs, too much plant food will get you lots of gorgeous leaves but little fragrance or flavor.

In warm maritime climates, rosemary is robust and tough. In humid regions, it's prone to powdery mildew and root rot. To avoid this, maximize drainage and air circulation. Whiteflies, spider mites, scales, and mealybugs all like to munch on rosemary. Organic pest control is best for controlling them. In zone 8 or southward, the plants need no winter protection. In zones 6 to 7, winter cold may kill the tips of the stems. Plant rosemary in protected spots, such as against a south wall, and mulch it to protect the roots. Farther north, ice kills the whole plant, so bring potted rosemary indoors.

Varieties

'Albus' is a bushy plant that reaches four to six feet high. It bears large white flowers and is a repeat bloomer. It grows in zones 7 to 11. It is a flashy specimen plant, especially alternated with a cultivar that blossoms in dark blue.

'Arp' has a round, open habit that reaches four feet tall and wide. Pruning makes it denser. It has gray-green leaves and bright blue flowers. Among the hardiest rosemary cultivars, it can survive down to -10° Fahrenheit. Remember, you can buy yourself an extra zone by using microclimates and other protection.

'Baby P.J.' is among the smallest cultivars, a prostrate plant only reaching four to six inches high and twelve inches long. It bears minute leaves and lavender flowers. It is prized for bonsai, fairy gardens, and other miniature gardens.

'Boule' grows three feet tall and wide. Easily trimmed into a sphere, its name actually means "ball" in French. It is an excellent choice for formal gardens.

'Joyce de Baggio' may be sold as 'Golden' or 'Golden Rain' rosemary. It changes color with the seasons. The leaves begin as bright yellow in spring, turn dark green in summer, and then return to yellow in fall. It can be trimmed into a Christmas tree shape. Fantastic accent plant.

'Majorca Pink', or Spanish rosemary, grows two to four feet tall. It has thinner, shorter leaves than most others and lovely pink flowers. It comes from the Balearic Islands in Spain. It is deer-resistant and hardy to zone 6. This cultivar is good for hedges, potpourri, and cooking.

'Miss Jessup's Upright' stands four to six feet tall and two to three feet wide. It has slim, airy branches with pale blue flowers. It works well in a formal herb garden or confined spaces and has nice flavor for culinary uses.

'**Portuguese Red**' is a vigorous, upright grower reaching two to three feet high. It has dark green leaves and deep pink to light red flowers that make it a fine specimen plant. It is best suited for zones 8 to 10.

'**Prostratus**' reaches two feet tall and four to eight feet wide. It has pale blue flowers. It is a good bushy ground cover and also nice atop walls.

'**Santa Barbara**' is a prostrate rosemary. This vigorous grower can reach lengths of three feet or more but doesn't get very high. It is good if you want to cover a wall or make garlands.

'**Spice Islands**' produces a potent flavor. It grows as an erect shrub reaching four feet in warm climates. It blossoms with dark blue flowers from late winter to early spring. Ideal for culinary uses or scented crafts.

'**Tuscan Blue**' is an upright shrub reaching six to seven feet tall. It bears wide, intensely aromatic leaves and dark blue flowers. It is a popular landscaping plant and the favorite culinary variety of many chefs.

Harvesting and Storage

When grown as an evergreen perennial, rosemary may be harvested throughout the growing season. Snip off the top few inches of each sprig, which may be used whole. On a bush of any significant size, they won't even be missed. For peak flavor, harvest just as the plant begins to bloom. Take care not to cut off too much as winter approaches, or the bush may not have time to recover.

When grown as a tender annual, rosemary may be harvested more vigorously. You can take whole branches because they don't have as much time to get tough, and simply strip off the leaves. Just before frost, it's possible to cut the whole plant, tie a string around the base, and hang it to dry.

Rosemary retains its resinous flavor for a long time when dried. Harvest in late morning after the dew has dried. Cut branches or whole plants depending on growing conditions. Suspend the rosemary in a dim place with good air circulation for about two weeks, until crispy.

Hold each bundle over a baking tray. Rub your hands along the stems to remove the needles. The dried leaves may be left whole, or chopped, and stored in glass jars. The woody stems can be burned as incense or used as skewers in cooking. Keep dried herbs in a cool, dry, dark place, such as a pantry.

A faster method requires an oven. Remove rosemary needles from their stems and chop into small bits. Spread these bits on a baking tray and put them in the oven on the lowest setting. Dry for three to four hours or until crumbly. Funnel into a glass jar and seal tightly.

Rosemary may also be frozen. An easy way to do this is to strip off the leaves and chop them. Pack into an ice cube tray. (A little rosemary goes a long way, so choose a tray that makes small ice cubes.) Fill the remaining space with water, broth, or a fat that freezes well, such as butter. Freeze until solid. Pop out the rosemary cubes. Store them in a plastic bag in the freezer. These are fantastic for making batches of soup, gravy, or sauce or for cooking things in a crockpot.

Cooking

Rosemary leaves may be used fresh or dried. This spice retains its flavor exceptionally well over time. Whole tender sprigs may be used if harvested before the stems become woody.

The woody stems make excellent skewers for shish kebabs. Note that it's not a great idea to bake or roast whole rosemary needles, because they turn hard in the oven and can easily pierce tender mouth tissue. Chop them instead. Whole needles or sprigs are fine as a raw topping or in wet cooking methods.

Rosemary combines well with beef, pork, lamb, and turkey. It also works with grilled fish such as salmon. Its sharp, piney flavor stands up well to dark, robust flavors. For this reason I also like it with game meat such as venison, elk, and bison. In side dishes, rosemary goes well in bread, potatoes, white beans, corn, tomato sauces, and poultry stuffing. It's a great addition to marinades and rubs. Try it fresh in salads or dried in soups. It complements tart fruits such as apples or figs and can be infused into a sugar syrup for use in a citrus salad.

Rosemary harmonizes with many other herbs, including bay, black pepper, garlic, juniper berries, lavender, marjoram, mint, oregano, rose, and winter savory. The famous combination "parsley, sage, rosemary, and thyme" makes a delicious rub for a pork roast.

Here are some recipes to try:

Rosemary Vinegar
Begin with a bottle of apple cider or wine vinegar. Pour off ¼ to ½ cup to make room for the herbs. Stuff several sprigs of rosemary into the bottle. You may also wish to add other robust herbs such as peppercorns, juniper berries, or sage. Top off the bottle with the reserved vinegar, saving any excess for another recipe. Seal tightly.

Place the bottle in a sunny window. Once a day, gently shake the bottle to circulate the vinegar and blend the flavors.

At the end of two weeks, move the bottle to a place out of direct light. These things look quite nice on a kitchen counter. Use rosemary vinegar in marinades, in salad dressing, on meat or poultry, and anywhere else you like a robust vinegar.

Rosemary-Infused Oil

Pick a large handful of rosemary sprigs. Separate them from the stems to produce ½ cup of individual leaves. Chop the leaves and put them into a ceramic bowl. Gently warm 1 cup of extra-virgin olive oil in a saucepan. Pour the warm oil over the rosemary. Stir with a wooden spoon, pressing the rosemary against the sides of the bowl to crush it. Add another cup of olive oil. Stir again. Allow to cool. Pour into a glass jar and seal tightly.

Place the jar in a sunny window. Every day, shake it gently to combine the flavors. Wait 2 weeks. Then strain the oil through cheesecloth to remove the rosemary bits. Pour the oil into a clean bottle, add 1 or 2 fresh sprigs of rosemary, and cap snugly. Use rosemary-infused oil in marinades, salad dressings, and sauces. It keeps up to 6 months in a dark pantry.

Rosemary Herbed Butter

First take a stick (8 tablespoons or ¼ pound) of unsalted butter and set it on the counter to soften. Next, add 2 tablespoons of minced rosemary. (You may wish to add other herbs such as thyme or sage, but keep the total amount at 2 tablespoons.) Either fold the rosemary into the butter by hand or use a food processor to puree everything.

Herbed butter may be served immediately. You can form it into decorative shapes by pressing it into a butter mold and refrigerating it. Another method is to put the butter into an ice cube tray or mini-muffin tin and freeze it. Then pop out the frozen cubes or disks and store them in a plastic bag in the freezer. To make a butter log, scoop the butter onto waxed paper and roll it into a cylinder. Twist or fold the ends closed. Refrigerate or freeze until solid. This way it can be unwrapped and sliced into pats. It tastes great with savory toast, baked or mashed potatoes, and other vegetables.

Roasted Potatoes with Rosemary

3 roasting potatoes

⅓ cup fat

Salt

Pepper

½ teaspoon dried rosemary

Preheat oven to 400°F. Clean and chop the potatoes. Choose a flavorful fat such as olive oil, chicken fat, or real butter. Melt the fat and rosemary together in a small saucepan.

Into an 8 × 11-inch baking dish, put half the potato chunks. Dust with salt and pepper. Drizzle half the rosemary fat over the potatoes. Add the rest of the potatoes. Season. Add the remaining fat. Stir until coated. Cook at 400°F for one hour, or until potatoes are browned outside and tender inside. Serves 3 to 4 people.

Nutrition and Other Health Benefits

Rosemary offers the benefit of many phytonutrients, anti-oxidants, and essential acids. It contains phenolic antioxidant rosmarinic acid as well as numerous health-benefiting volatile essential oils such as alpha-pinene, borneol, bornyl acetate, cineol, and camphene. These help prevent disease and promote health.

This herb is also rich in vitamins. It is highest in vitamin A—just a few leaves per day would meet the typical need.

Vitamin A supports vision, mucus membranes, and skin. It also helps the body avoid lung and oral cancers. In the B-complex group, rosemary provides folic acid, pantothenic acid, pyridoxine, and riboflavin. Folates are vital to the production of DNA. Fresh rosemary leaves provide plentiful vitamin C. Add a few sprigs to green smoothies. Vitamin C prevents scurvy, strengthens the immune system, and removes harmful free radicals. It's also essential for making collagen, the body's structural protein.

Rosemary is a mild emmenagogue, encouraging menstruation, and it also stimulates uterine contractions. This benefits women with an unreliable cycle and generally helps flush out old tissue from the womb. For this reason, people who wish to be pregnant should avoid using rosemary.

Rosemary also furnishes minerals and trace elements. Among these are calcium, copper, iron, magnesium, manganese, and potassium. Iron allows the hemoglobin in blood to carry oxygen. Potassium contributes to cell and body fluids, relevant to heartbeat and blood pressure.

Medicinal Uses

Rosemary has many health benefits. It is antiallergic, antifungal, anti-inflammatory, antiseptic, astringent, diaphoretic, rubefacient, stimulant, and tonic. The essential oil has the carminative qualities of other volatile oils and is an effective stomachic and nervine, helpful in relieving both stomachache and headache. Rosemary tea is used similarly for soothing effects.

This herb is also used in hair care products to stimulate growth and create a pleasant smell.

Both as a live plant and essential oil, rosemary uplifts the mind and stimulates memory. It's very popular in aromatherapy for those reasons. The dried leaves may be added to incense, or the essential oil may be used in a diffuser or added to floor washes, to obtain these benefits. You can also grow rosemary as a houseplant and touch it gently to release the fragrance.

Crafts and Miscellaneous Uses

Beyond culinary and medicinal purposes, rosemary has many applications. Traditionally, the leaves and flowers have been used in festivals and wedding ceremonies. They decorate banquet halls during celebrations. This works best when growing rosemary as an annual because more of the branches remain soft and flexible, so you can easily turn them into crowns or miniature wreaths.

For long garlands that hang along tables or doorframes, it helps to have rosemary grown as a perennial because the stronger branches hold together better. Smudge sticks can be made with either annual or perennial sprigs, but the latter often have more fragrance. Combine two parts sage to one part rosemary, tie them together with cotton string, and hang until dry. These burn with a sweet, spicy scent that is said to keep away negative influences.

Similarly, rosemary has been used as a strewing herb. These were scattered on floors or tucked into thatch to discourage vermin. In modern contexts, people sometimes sprinkle a mix of flower petals and herbs for festive occasions. Outdoors you may want to use petals and leaves that will easily disappear into grass. Indoors, larger sprigs are easier to clean up afterwards.

Herbal sachets make lovely gifts. For hidden use, the bags can be made of plain muslin; if they will be seen, cotton calico is preferred. If you want to use lace, put it over muslin or a solid-colored cotton because otherwise the dried herbs will leak out through the mesh. Combine dried rosemary leaves with other herbs such as bay leaves, citronella grass, lemon balm, mint, pennyroyal, sage, thyme, or wormwood. You may also want to add orange peel, small pinecones, cedar chips, anise, chipped cinnamon bark, or cloves. Include chopped orris root or calamus root as a fixative to preserve the fragrance. Sachets may be sewn closed for security or tied with a ribbon if you want to reuse the pretty bag after the contents have worn out. Herbs naturally lose their scent over time, although the sachet can be refreshed with a few drops of rosemary oil or other essential oil.

Rosemary also makes a beautiful, living Yule tree. A small one will fit where pine trees won't. These usually won't support a string of lights but can hold tinsel and very lightweight ornaments. If you have a larger shrub that you bring indoors during winter, then it might be able to hold lights, but take care not to damage the branches. Lightweight ornaments are still a better idea than heavy ones. Touch the leaves gently to release their piney fragrance.

Selected Resources

Bremness, Lesley. *Herbs: The Visual Guide to More Than 700 Plant Species From Around the World*. London: DK Publishing, 1994.

Cohoon, Sharon. "The Right Rosemary for You." *Sunset*, November 2001. http://www.sunset.com/garden/flowers-plants/right-rosemary-for-you.

Grieve, M. "Rosemary." *A Modern Herbal*. London: Jonathon Cape, 1931. Electronic reproduction by Botanical.com. http://www.botanical.com/botanical/mgmh/r/rosema17.html.

"Growing Rosemary." Bonnie Plants. Accessed December 2, 2016. https://bonnieplants.com/growing/growing-rosemary/.

"Herb Guide—Which Herbs Go Well with Which Foods?" Living on a Dime. November 25, 2015. http://www.livingonadime.com/herb-guide/.

Kowalchik, Claire and William H. Hylton, eds. *Rodale's Illustrated Encyclopedia of Herbs*. Emmaus, PA: Rodale Press, 1987.

Krohn, Elise. "Rosemary." Wild Foods & Medicines. January 7, 2016. http://wildfoodsandmedicines.com/rosemary/.

Preserving Your Harvest. "Rosemary." 2009. http://www.preservingyourharvest.com/Rosemary.html.

"Rosemary." Food Facts. Accessed December 2, 2016. http://foodfacts.mercola.com/rosemary.html.

Rudrappa, Umesh. "Rosemary Herb." www.nutrition-and-you.com. Accessed on December 2, 2016. http://www.nutrition-and-you.com/rosemary-herb.html.

Steph. "DIY Herbal Home: 12 Fresh-Smelling Recipes & Projects." Web Ecoist. *Momtastic*. April 1, 2013. http://webecoist.momtastic.com/2013/04/01/diy-herbal-home-12-fresh-smelling-recipes-projects/.

Elizabeth Barrette *has been involved with the Pagan community for more than twenty-seven years. She served as managing editor of*

PanGaia *for eight years and dean of studies at the Grey School of Wizardry for four years. She has written columns on beginning and intermediate Pagan practice, Pagan culture, and Pagan leadership. Her book* Composing Magic: How to Create Magical Spells, Rituals, Blessings, Chants, and Prayers *explains how to combine writing and spirituality. She lives in central Illinois, and her public activities feature Pagan picnics and science fiction conventions. She enjoys magical crafts, historic religions, and gardening for wildlife. Her other writing fields include speculative fiction, gender studies, and social and environmental issues. Visit her blog,* The Wordsmith's Forge *(http://ysabetwordsmith.livejournal.com/), or website, PenUltimate Productions (http://penultimateproductions.weebly.com).*

Cultivating Your Own Hybrid Tea Roses

✿ by Estha K. V. McNevin ✿

Regardless of all the Valentine's hype and at willful risk of cliché, hybrid tea roses are, hands-down, my favorite choice of flowers. Although it may take a careful green thumb, the art of rose gardening is truly enchanting. As a child of summer, roses adorned many of my birthday cakes and are still among my favorite flowers to cultivate, harvest, and preserve. Above all other varieties, I favor the English hybrid tea rose for its northern, hardier constitution and sweet hips. So many of my most cherished recipes call for rosehip honey, rose petal jelly, or rosewater. Learning to hybridize and graft my own roses has been a rewarding exercise in patience and genuine horticultural fervor.

Putting that Couture Pollen in the Air

Hybridizing roses is easy-peasy but about as predictable as a bridesmaid on her fifth shot of tequila. The color, fragrance, and character of the host rose are widely and wildly influenced by pollination. Intentionally developing a new flower can take generations. Breeders strive to achieve a particular color, petal type, disease resistance, and fragrance combination using ancient and meticulous techniques. Many rose gardeners collect or purchase pollen that is harvested from their favorite flowers for this purpose and are ever eager to document the breeding habits of their roses.

Introducing new pollen requires a careful genealogy record of the mother and father plants as well as some kind of isolation to ensure the best results. Documenting your favorite mother plants and paternal pollens in a rose journal will help you keep track of the geological qualities of each type of rose that you cultivate. In the last century, many rose breeders have had great success matching wild rose pollens like that of *Rosa rugosa* with other hybrid and tea roses that are still hardy but are varied in all the right ways. For a first and favorite cross-pollination, try using the hearty hybrid tea rose 'Fragrant Cloud' as your mother plant and any wild rose plant that you favor from your local area.

The only special equipment required is tweezers, long cotton swabs, and equal-sized sample vials to keep them in. These are easily available at campus bookstores, science lab supply providers, and various online retailers. To collect pollen, the wild blooms must be only half open and healthy. Using a new cotton swab, gently rub the pollen sacs found on the stamen, hidden deep within the rose bud. Give your best bumblebee impression as you roll the cotton tip all around the anthers, coating it in pollen. Place this in a glass vile, then use tweezers to remove the anther nubs and place them in the vile as well, affixing the screw top. Label each sample with the species name and the date that it was collected.

Tea roses are best planted with other annual flowers like strawberry, lavender, sage, tulsi (holy basil), and thyme. Such neighbors will do roses many a favor by enriching the soil, detouring pests, and improving the color and fragrance of the flowers.

Samples are best when used after resting for twenty-four hours but will last for a year or more if carefully stored in the coldest part of the freezer. Many rose breeders make seasonal notations to help distinguish qualities that new hybrids may have, like "bloomed in drought" or "autumn at its most aromatic." When the mother rose shows blooms that are nearly open, it is the ideal time to pollenate. Begin by removing all of the outer and inner petals, down to the core of the bud. Using tweezers, strip off the anthers filled with pollen from the mother rose. Let the naked pistils rest for six to eight hours. Remove the swab from its vile. The anthers within the vile should have released even more powdery pollen while resting. Gently roll the swab all around the pistil of the mother rose bud. Repeat the process a day later to ensure the best results.

Once you've documented your roses genetics, wait and watch the hips grow. Hybrids are sprouted from seed, and the mature hips will contain anywhere from twelve to thirty seeds, uniting the genetic material of both parents and creating a whole new rose variety. Harvest the hips in the early autumn, after the first light frost when they turn bright orange. Remove the outer fruit pulp to reveal the seeds within. Store the seeds wrapped up in a paper towel. Keep them in the fridge over the winter and plant them out in spring. If you live in a mild region, you can store the seeds in an airtight plastic bag and keep them in the freezer for seven weeks before planting them out in the greenhouse.

Grafting

Once you overcome the anxiety of just keeping your roses alive, the next level of rose cultivation is working to develop strains of your own. The goal of grafting is to create a broader range of colors or bud types on one plant and to introduce to the garden the classical rose fragrance from more fragile old-world roses using a hardy wild or hybrid host. Every temperate region will favor different types of roses, but selecting flowers for root and stock strength, petal formation, or color are just the beginning. Learning to graft and hybridize roses allows even the newest gardener to create a localized variety of roses to call one's own. Helping evolve the *Rosa* gene pool produces stunning wonders like 'Abraham Darby', a rose developed by David Austin in the 1970s. By selecting deeply-cupped China tea roses and hybridizing them with wild English roses, one of the most fragrant English 'Cottage Rose' roses was born.

Taking "Stalk" of Stem Anatomy

Like all flowers, roses have a double-chambered phloem structure indicative of dicots. The primary stalk is overgrown and incorporated into the secondary phloem as a plant matures and prepares to flower. These two median layers protect the tender pith tissues and give fibrous structure to the plant. This allows water and nutrients to pass through the xylem wall up through the stalk. This is the heart of the vascular system and contains parenchyma tissue supporting the life and health of the plant. This central region cannot be disturbed without causing harm to the rose. Grafting must never penetrate this cortex region and is a delicate epidermal introduction of a scion plant to a host plant or rootstock.

The benefit of grafting roses is all in trait selection. Tea rose stalks are often prized for their strong cortex layer, which takes to grafting more easily than others in the rose subfamily. Strong, healthy roots are a must, and the thicker and longer the stem of a plant is, the more strength its internal fibers will have. Host roses allow more fragile or finicky scion roses to thrive in extreme climates or less-than-ideal conditions. Many nursery roses are a classical Alba or Damask rose that survives grafted onto a hardy tea hybrid or wild rose.

Surgically Grafting Roses in Seven Easy Steps

This easy guide will have you experimenting like a Victorian horticultural enthusiast in no time. Take care to bleach or otherwise disinfect all the equipment that you intend to use. Gardening scalpels are a wonderful tool and are made especially for detailed jobs like grafting. They are extra sharp and made of surgical stainless steel so that they can be boiled for twenty minutes, ensuring disinfection. To ensure sterilization I add a few drops of pure essential tea tree oil to the water.

Clean hands and sterile equipment will guarantee that no bacteria or disease are introduced through grafting. Any soil or plant material, household soaps, and even oils from your hands can prevent the graft from taking. If untreated, contaminations can kill both the host and scion roses. Do not graft if you see any signs of disease, black mold, powdery mildew, or white mildew. Such infections render the plant unfit for grafting and will quickly spread disease in the garden.

Getting everything ready a day or two beforehand will ensure quick and careful grafting when the time is right. Work late in the afternoon for the best results. Nighttime moisture and lower temperatures can help the scion rose, which is more susceptible to higher temperatures and rot because it has been cut from its own root system.

1. Begin by selecting a hardy stock rose. Pick an ideal host with a mature and healthy root structure of its own, such as the beloved 'Cottage Rose'.

2. Prune the host rose of all buds and most leaves, leaving the top two sets of leaves on each stem. Select a mature stem onto which you intend to graft a scion, and trim the leaves from the middle section of the stem.

3. For the scion rose, select a more fragile tea rose such as the hybrid 'Moonstone', an exhibition gem hybridized from wild and heirloom roses. At a 45-degree angle, cut a single 8- to 12-inch section of intact stem with intact leaves and bud eyes. These will appear as small spots near the stipules at the base of a leaf stem. Trim all the leaf and bud eyes except for the top two; this will promote future flowering. Apply honey to the cuts and place the clipping, submerged and weighted, in water for 24 hours. Such is the scion's creative power that when left standing upright in water or potting soil, the clipping will develop roots in a matter of weeks, creating a whole new plant.

4. Using a rose scalpel or very sharp knife, make a small, thumbnail-sized incision into the epidermis of a thick and mature host rose stem. Always graft at a trimmed leaf section break on the middle of your chosen mature stem. Begin by making a cut that is ½ centimeter long, revealing the fragile cambium within the stem.

5. Carefully wedge the rose scalpel into the incision and make a shallow downward cut to form a T shape, peeling a ½-centimeter strip of epidermis tissue down the stock, without cutting into the cambium of the cortex or disturbing the internal tissues of the stock. This will create an epidermal incision into which the scion cutting can snugly fit.

6. Trim one end of the scion to match the host stem in width and size. Implant the scion into the epidermis tissue flaps so that the core of the scion stem fits flush against the stem of the host rose.

7. To keep the grafting site free from fungi and infection, brush or mold hand-warmed grafting wax onto the wound and secure it tightly with a 4 × ³⁄₁₆-inch grafting rubber band.

Harvesting and Preserving

Roses will bloom from mid-summer to mid-autumn and are best harvested in the cooler hours of the morning, just after watering. It is common knowledge that roses will give you hassle in ways that you never dreamed such an unassuming beauty would. For example, if they are not trimmed at a down-sloping 45-degree angle, water will be blocked from the cambium of the flower stem, and it will wilt in a matter of hours.

Hips appear after the first frosts of autumn and are ideal when they turn bright orange or red. In our yard, we are hard-pressed to get to them before the deer. Rosehips are beloved by many rural creatures and children alike. Sow the seed back into the ground in the spring and use the fruity skins for breads, fruitcakes, jams, jellies, and teas. They provide a wonderful dose of sweet and tart flavor because they are rich in citric acid. Highly prized for their medicinal uses, rosehips can prevent scurvy and treat mange as well as heal bacterial skin infections when the fruit pulp is pulverized and applied to yeast rashes.

Flowers That Will Power On

A bit of the following mix, when added to a fresh gallon of cold water, will keep cut flowers alive for weeks longer. I mix it ahead of time and refrigerate the excess nutrient-rich water to refresh vases later. When roses are stored overnight in the fridge or kept in a cool and shady area on the north or west side of the home, then they will have a longer vase life. Cut flowers should always be displayed out of direct sunlight to avoid vase rot, bud drooping, and petal loss. To keep roses looking fresh and smelling like heaven, flower vases must always be bleached before each use to prevent bacteria from forming on the fresh-cut flowers. Vase water can brew bacteria quickly and should be completely replaced every two days.

To prepare roses for the vase, recut them underwater. The cutting wound is a sensitive location on any harvested rose. The three core layers of the stem can only be cleanly cut with a razor-sharp gardening scalpel or a pair of rose secateurs. A box cutter or a pair of dull scissors will damage the plant and prevent the stem from taking up water as the dull blades pinch the capillaries of the stem cortex.

Flower Chow

- 3 tablespoons baking soda
- 3 tablespoons cream of tartar
- 2 tablespoons citric acid
- 1 tablespoon Himalayan pink salt
- 3 tablespoons honey powder

Mix together in a small canning jar. Place ring and lid on the jar when done, and store in the fridge for regular use. When your roses are in bloom, add 1 teaspoon of flower chow to one gallon of cold water and shake vigorously until dissolved. Use this in vases to keep flowers fresh longer, and store in the fridge between uses.

Resources

Burnie, Geoffrey, ed. *The Practical Gardener's Encyclopedia.* San Francisco, CA: Fog City Press, 2000.

Damrosch, Barbara. *The Garden Primer.* New York: Workman Publishing, 2008.

Elpel, Thomas J. *Botany in A Day: The Patterns Method of Plant Identification.* 6th ed. Pony, MT: HOPS Press, 2013.

Griffin, Judith. *Mother Nature's Herbal: A Complete Guide for Experiencing the Beauty, Knowledge & Synergy of Everything That Grows.* Woodbury, MN: Llewellyn, 2008.

McHoy, Peter. *The Complete Book of Practical Gardening.* London: Hermes House, 1997.

Montagné, Prosper. *Larousse Gastronomique.* With Joël Robuchon. New York: Clarkson Potter, 2001.

Seymour, John. *The New Self-Sufficient Gardener*. New York: DK Press, 2008.

Estha McNevin *(Missoula, MT) is a priestess and ceremonial oracle of Opus Aima Obscuræ, a nonprofit Pagan Temple Haus. She has served the Pagan community since 2003 as an Eastern Hellenistic officiate, lecturer, freelance author, artist, and poet. Estha studies and teaches courses on ancient and modern Pagan history. She offers classes on multicultural metaphysical theory, ritual technique, international cuisine, organic gardening, herbal craft, alchemy, and occult symbolism. In addition to hosting public rituals for the sabbats, Estha organizes annual philanthropic fundraisers, full moon spell-crafting ceremonies, and women's divination rituals for each dark moon. To learn more, please explore www.opusaimaobscurae .org and www.facebook.com/opusaimaobscurae.*

Foraging for Wild Berries: Why They Are So Good for You

✺ by Corina Sahlin ✺

The sound of children's laughter echoes in the forest and bounces off cedars that are thirty times as tall as the kids. Most of the children are between eight and thirteen years old, but the ringleader is my six-year-old daughter, Eva. She leads the group through a maze of moss-covered stumps, maidenhair ferns, and patches of kinnikinnick. My husband and I are leading a weekend wilderness and homesteading summer camp for kids, and as a part of it we are walking in the woods to forage for wild berries. Eva knows most of the local wild edible plants, and she now stops at her favorite: a huckleberry bush covered with the slightly sour, ruby-red treasures she loves so much.

She shows them to the group of city kids who stare skeptically, but as soon as Eva pops the tiny berries into her mouth, they hesitantly copy her. Some kids make faces and turn away, but others greedily pick the berries and shove them in their mouths. The excitement and novelty of picking food straight out of the wild takes over, and most of the kids eagerly move from one huckleberry bush to another, trying to spot the bright red berries from between all the greenery around them. When Eva tells them that some huckleberries are blue and then shows them evidence, they are ready to believe anything she says.

Most people are familiar with the more common berries like strawberries, raspberries, and blueberries, since they are widely grown and sold in supermarkets. Although these cultivated berries are wonderful and taste good (especially when it comes to sweetness), their wild and lesser known cousins are far superior nutritionally. These wild foods might not be as sweet and are, in fact, often more tart or sour than berries we buy at a store, but they contain many more phytonutrients, which are famous for reducing the risk of cancer, cardiovascular disease, diabetes, and dementia.

Little Eva and her older brothers know that our ancestors who foraged for wild foods were much less likely to die from degenerative diseases. We teach our children that eating wild foods is good for us. We tell them that the Greek physician Hippocrates is said to have proclaimed nearly 2,500 years ago, "Let food be thy medicine and medicine be thy food." Our kids are used to the taste of wild berries, and so they eagerly await their arrival each spring.

You don't have to live in the wilderness like us to forage for these berries and other wild foods. Let's go for a walk, and I'll show you our favorites. But before we start, let me emphasize something we teach to our kids and the kids who participate in our summer camps: Never pick berries you don't know! Always make sure you identify berries correctly and know they are edible before eating them. There are berries out there that are toxic and can hurt you, so only eat the ones you know. And please don't eat berries that might have been sprayed with chemicals (like on a roadside).

Salmonberry (*Rubus spectabilis*)

Hardy to USDA zones 5 through 9, salmonberries grow along the Pacific Coast from Alaska to California.

One of the earliest berries to emerge in our region is the salmonberry. They are reddish or yellow (we call them golden), thrive in wet places, and look a little bit like raspberries. Some people don't like their taste and call them "insipid," but many people (including kids) love them and birds devour them! Rufous hummingbirds are crazy about their pink flowers, and dense thickets of salmonberry bushes provide wonderful habitat for nesting birds and other small animals, who like to browse the leaves, twigs, and buds.

Eating 100 grams of salmonberries will provide 15 percent of the daily required amount of vitamin C, 10 percent of that of vitamin A, and minerals such as calcium, potassium, manganese, and iron. They are also a good source of dietary fiber. They are low in sodium, contain no fat, and are cholesterol free. How's that for a health food!

The time when salmonberries ripen in the Pacific Northwest is associated with the Swainson's thrush, also called "salmonberry bird." If you wonder why a berry is named after a fish, it comes from the fact that some Northwest Coast Native Americans mixed sweet and juicy young salmonberry sprouts with salmon meat or dried salmon spawn.

Red and Black Hucklebery
(*Vaccinium parvifolium* and *V. membranaceum*)

Hardy to zones 4 through 8, huckleberries grow throughout Idaho, western Montana, western Wyoming, Washington, Oregon, and British Columbia. Small outcrops occur in Utah, California, Arizona, and Michigan.

In our neck of the woods, these delicious berries grow in soils rich in decaying wood, on stumps or logs, and in coniferous forests or under canopy openings. These small, juicy, and flavorful berries taste quite sweet but can also be tart if not picked when they are fully ripe. The black (or blue) varieties resemble blueberries in taste and texture. Bears gorge themselves on these berries, and we often see their ample droppings colored with berries and seeds on the same paths we walk when we forage for the same berries.

Huckleberries are high in vitamins, are loaded with antioxidants, and contain large amounts of vitamin A, B, and C. They also are filled with potassium, calcium, and iron. Their taste can vary greatly depending on the location where they grow. So if you try the berries from one bush and don't like their taste, don't give up! Try huckleberries picked at another spot, and you may fall in love with them.

Huckleberries were used to treat diarrhea and soreness in the throat and mouth. Some Native Americans ate these berries fresh and dried or soaked in grease.

Thimbleberry (*Rubus parviflorus*)

Hardy to zones 3 through 9, thimbleberries grow in all states west of the Rocky Mountains, Alaska, Canada, and the Great Lakes states.

It's impossible to go for a walk with my family when thimbleberries are ripe. The children walk one step, pick thimbleberries for a minute, walk a few more steps, get distracted by yet more of the flashy red berries, let the berries tumble into their hands for another minute, take another few steps, and so on. When the berries are ripe, they literally tumble into your hand at the slightest touch. On a good day, we cover 100 yards in an hour.

It's worth it, though. These berries taste sweet to me, with a hint of apricot flavor. They are a little fuzzy and filled with seeds, and some people don't like this texture—but we love it!

Thimbleberries are low both in fat and calories and are a great source of vitamins A and C, with traces of potassium, calcium, and iron. Thimbleberry leaves are highly medicinal for treating blood deficiencies, and a thimbleberry leaf tea treats nausea, vomiting, and diarrhea and can increase appetite. If you are patient enough to collect a large amount of these delicate berries, you can make thimbleberry jam, which is sold at a high price as a delicacy in some parts of this country.

And in case you want to know what we do when we have to go to the bathroom in the forest: thimbleberry leaves make the best and softest toilet paper.

Trailing Blackberry (*Rubus ursinus*)

Trailing blackberry is also called wild mountain blackberry, Pacific blackberry, or Northwest dewberry. Hardy to zones 5 through 10, these berries are native to western North America and are found in British Columbia, Idaho, Montana, Oregon, Washington, and Baja California.

You probably know the common Himalayan blackberry (*Rubus armeniacus*), with its large, juicy berries growing from invasive, thorny bushes in many places, including abandoned lots. But there's a better, native blackberry called trailing blackberry. Growing low to the ground, this smaller berry is sweet and incredibly aromatic. Many gourmet bakers prefer this native berry to the more common Himalayan blackberry, claiming its flavor is superior, and it holds up much better in baking and jams.

Trailing blackberry is often found in woods that are fairly open to dense. It appears to thrive in clear-cuts, in fire scars, in logged areas, and under transmission lines.

The berries are high in antioxidants, vitamin C and K, fiber, phytoestrogens, and ellagic acid, and some even have anticancer properties. They are a good source of potassium, phosphorus, iron, and calcium, and the seeds contain omega-3 and omega-6 fatty acids. Blackberries have expectorant properties and make a wonderfully nutritious and tasty cough syrup. Blackberry vinegar is also a long-standing remedy for feverish colds.

Wild Strawberry (*Fragaria vesca*)

Wild strawbery is also called Alpine strawberry, woodland strawberry, or European strawberry. Hardy to zones 3 through 10, these berries grow throughout the northern United States.

Evidence from archaeological excavations shows that these berries have been consumed by humans since the Stone

Age. No wonder! Finding these perfumed fruits in a meadow is like finding treasure. My kids go crazy when we come upon a wild strawberry patch. The berries are much smaller than the more common strawberries sold in stores and much more intensely flavored.

Knowing that wild foods tend to pack even more nutrition than cultivated foods and considering that nutritionists have labeled strawberries a "superfood" filled with antioxidants, potassium, folate, fiber, and vitamins B, C, and E, you can only imagine how healthy these small berries are for us. They are considered a liver tonic and were used to treat gastritis and typhoid in the past.

Native peoples not only used them for nutrition, but they also applied mashed strawberries to treat burns, sores, and reddened eyes and used them as a toothpaste. (Mashed fruits were put onto teeth to remove tartar and relieve toothache.) I better not tell my kids about this, since they will want to "brush" their teeth with strawberries from now on!

Wild strawberries thrive in woodlands, forests, clearings, roadsides, hills, and even in gravel paths.

Blue and Black Elderberry
(*Sambucus cerulea* and *S. nigra*)

Hardy to zones 4 through 10, elderberries are native in the United States, Canada, and Europe.

Blue elderberry grows primarily along the West Coast, and black elderberry grows throughout the Midwest and the East. Both are amazing medicine with anti-inflammatory, antiviral, and anticancer superpowers. Besides lots of flavonoids and butt-kicking antioxidants, 136 grams of elderberries (about one cup) contain 87 percent of the daily value of vitamin C, and huge levels of vitamin A, potassium, iron, vitamin B_6, fiber, and beta-carotene. Elderberries contain more phosphorus and potassium than any other temperate fruit crop.

Some of this plant's uses are treating conjunctivitis, treating cold and flu symptoms, reducing congestion, relieving arthritis pain, soothing upset stomach, relieving gas, and detoxification.

Recent technology shows that the phytonutrient content of wild foods is many, many times higher than the fruits and vegetables displayed in our supermarkets.

Consuming Elderberries

Do not consume red elderberries, and do not eat blue or black elderberries raw. Their seeds, stems, leaves, and roots are poisonous to humans. They contain a cyanide-inducing glycoside, and you can get very sick from it. However, cooking the blue elderberries destroys the glycosides and makes them safe to eat.

The blue or purple berries are used to make delicious elderberry wine, jam, syrup, and pies. Some people dip the whole flower clusters in batter and fry them.

Our favorite way to consume elderberries is as elderberry syrup. Since blue elderberries grow more abundantly on the east side of the Cascade mountains, we drive over the mountain pass to gather elderberries there in late summer or fall.

My whole family works together to make syrup and uses it to prevent colds and the flu. Making the syrup ourselves saves us a substantial amount of money. Just go to a natural food store and compare the high price of a small bottle of elderberry syrup to the money you spend making your own. It's so worth it!

Here's how we make elderberry syrup. It's a bit of a job separating the tiny berries from the stems, but my kids help me, which makes the job faster and more fun. You just kind of rake the berries off the stems by holding them between your thumb and forefinger and pushing downward. Don't worry about smooshing the berries too much—it's okay. Also, don't worry about some of the stems staying on. You will strain everything through cheesecloth later, so you don't need to be too obsessive about this.

Last year, our harvesting frenzy amounted to eight cups of berries, which made two and a half quarts of finished syrup. That's ten cups of medicine!

Elderberry Syrup
> Blue or black elderberries (fresh or dried)
>
> Fresh ginger, grated (1 tablespoon per cup of berries) or dried (1 teaspoon per cup of berries)
>
> Ground cinnamon (1 teaspoon per cup of berries)
>
> Raw honey (½ cup per cup of berries)
>
> Water (1 cup of water to 1 cup of fresh berries, or 2 cups of water to 1 cup of dried berries).

Put the berries into a pot and add water. Grate fresh ginger or use dried ginger and add it to the pot of berries and water. Add ground cinnamon.

Now comes the part that makes me feel like a witch with a steaming kettle: boil this until it has reduced by half. It takes me an hour to get there. Make sure it's boiling nicely, not just simmering shyly. Don't put a lid on the affair because you want steam to escape.

After it has reduced by half, let it cool and then strain it through cheesecloth. Squeeze the heck out of it so you get every part of the liquid stuff.

Then add the honey. Do not put the honey in when you boil everything, since that kills of a lot of the good stuff in the honey. Also, obviously, don't feed this syrup to infants, since they shouldn't consume honey. Store the syrup in the refrigerator.

During cold and flu season, adults can take one tablespoon of elderberry syrup per day, and children can take one teaspoon per day. You could take this as a preventative by consuming the same amount above every single hour when you start feeling sick.

Resources

Nayyar, Namita. "Encyclopedia of Health Benefits of Berries." Women's Fitness. March 12, 2013. http://www.womenfitness.net/salmonberries.htm.

Pojar, Jim and Andy MacKinnon. *Plants of the Pacific Northwest Coast: Washington, Oregon, British Columbia & Alaska.* Vancouver: Lone Pine Publishing, 1994.

Robinson, Jo. "Breeding the Nutrition Out of Our Food." *New York Times*, May 25, 2013. http://www.nytimes.com/2013/05/26/opinion/sunday/breeding-the-nutrition-out-of-our-food.html.

Corina Sahlin *homesteads on five acres at the edge of the wilderness near the Cascade Mountains, where she grows a lot of organic food. Together with her husband, Steve, she raises goats, pigs, ducks, chickens, an adorable puppy, and a gaggle of three children, whom they homeschool. Corina was born and raised in Germany and is an artisan cheesemaker, writer, transformative life coach, obsessive-compulsive knitter, and teacher of homesteading skills. She teaches and inspires people to live healthier, simpler, more wholesome, and sustainable lives in her online courses as well as on her homestead. Together with her husband, she teaches wilderness and homesteading skills to children and adults. Visit http://www.marblemount homestead.com and http://www.marblemounthomestead.blogspot .com.*

A Calendar for Sowing Herb Seeds

⤞ by Kathy Martin ⤝

Many herbs can be planted from seed in our gardens—hundreds at least. If you're sowing a number of herbs, a calendar that organizes the optimum planting dates will save you time and effort.

Our herb gardens typically include the herbs used for flavoring foods—usually leafy herbs like parsley, oregano, and dill. These herbs can be annual, biennial, or perennial. While some perennial herbs like French tarragon don't produce seeds and can only be grown from rooted cuttings, the majority of perennial herbs can be grown from seed. For some perennial herbs, germination rates may be low and the plants may take some time to reach

full size, but they are great plants to grow from seed. Annual herbs are generally much easier to grow from seed, and biennial herbs such as parsley are also readily grown from seed.

Though there are many hundreds of herbs, most people don't set out to grow a hundred of them from seed in a single season. It does sound fun, if you've got the space and time. There are beautiful herb gardens at arboretums and public gardens with hundreds of herbs on display and their horticulturalists do raise large numbers of herbs from seed each spring.

Cilantro is one of the easiest herbs to grow. Grow it successively, sowing every two to three weeks for season-long harvesting. It tends to bolt in mid-summer and does best in cool weather. Pick a variety that is slow to bolt. The early spring and late fall crops will have more fragrant leaves. Let some cilantro go to seed in the fall garden to give you an easy early spring crop the next year.

But rather than hundreds, most gardeners start with more like ten or twenty types of herbs when first setting up an herb garden. They'll include perennials, biennials, and annuals. In my garden, about half my herb plants are perennials, half are annuals, and parsley is my representative biennial herb. I grow many of my herbs from seed. One reason for starting with seed is the cost: a packet of seeds is quite a bit less expensive than a potted plant. Starting from seed also gives you access to many more herb varieties. And it allows you to be more involved in growing the plant, even if it is a challenging perennial herb.

In any given year, I probably start about fifteen herbs from seed. My herb garden is relatively new—three years old—and I'm working on filling it out with seed-grown perennials like sages, thymes, and oreganos. I also grow many annual herbs from seed, like basils, borage, dill, and leaf fennel. Several annual herbs reach their harvest time quickly and need to be planted in succession (i.e., several times in a year) for a good supply. These include dill and cilantro. Some of my favorite annual herbs are ones that reseed themselves. Little borage, dill, and cilantro plants pop up in my garden in early spring where last year's plants went to seed. I love these happy-go-lucky plants! There's nothing like enjoying an early spring crop of fragrant cilantro without doing any work!

Optimum Sowing Times

Planting a number of herbs from seed in one season can be confusing. When do you sow each one? If you sow too early, the plants will outgrow their pots before they can be planted out. They'll need to be transplanted into bigger pots that take up more room on the planting shelves. If you sow too late, the plants will be too small to plant outside until later and may not reach harvest size by the end of the season or before hot weather comes. Each herb has an optimum time for sowing. Sowing times are generally listed on the backs of seed packets, so checking here is the first step. Often the packets don't list the sowing time, and you'll need to look it up time online. Recommended planting times are generally given as the number of days or weeks before your last spring frost. Sometimes they are given as the number of days or weeks before transplanting outside, and the date for transplanting outside is given as the number of days or weeks before or after your last frost. I used to do the research to find the recommended planting times, and then I'd write these times on the front of each seed packet.

To turn the recommended planting times into actual calendar dates, some counting backward is needed. And you'll need to predict the date of your last spring frost for the coming year.

Predict Your Last Spring Frost Date

Your last frost date can be predicted by averaging the frost dates in your garden over the last three to five years. It's interesting how frost dates are changing over the years; a date averaged from recent years is probably a more accurate predictor of the next year's frost than a date averaged over, say, the past ten years. And you need to realize that frost dates from one location to another can be quite different, even in nearby local areas. Microclimates are generated by buildings and concrete, as well as wind patterns and land formations. If you don't know recent frost dates for your area, it's best to ask a local gardener. As a last resort, look online. Many sites will tell you the date of the last spring frost in your general area using your USDA zone or postal zip code.

The last spring frost in my first garden was generally early April—about April 10. This urban garden just west of Boston, Massachusetts (USDA zone 6a), was protected by nearby houses and a lot of concrete surfaces. It warmed up early and cooled down late compared to other local sites. My second garden, a community plot less than a mile away from my first, is in an open field and at the base of a bowl-like land formation. The area catches the north wind and warms up late. Our last spring frost here is usually a month later than my urban site—about May 10. In addition to my community garden plot, I now have a new garden in the backyard of our new house. Just a little further west of Boston and also in USDA zone 6a, it's in an open space next to a small pond and protected to the north and east by tall trees. Over the past three years I'm finding that it has a last spring frost around May 5.

Of course, average last frost dates need to be taken as only estimates of when next year's frost will be. We've had years with heavy snow cover that doesn't melt from my garden until May, delaying the last frost date. We've also had warm years with almost no snow, and the soil will warm up fast. There are years when we think we've had our last frost already, and then we get a surprise late spring frost. So the actual time when you can set out plants will vary year to year with the weather, but knowing an average gives us our best guess at when to begin sowing.

Calculate the Date for Optimum Sowing

So, with the date of the last spring frost in hand, what's next? Well, those dates written on the front of each seed packet need to be counted backward from the frost date. For example, seeds with a sowing date of eight weeks in a region with a last frost of May 10 should be planted the week of March 15. That's eight weeks before the average last spring frost. I used to stack each packet with the same date in a pile, calculate the planting date for each of my piles, and write that date on a piece of scrap paper. Finally, I'd wrap each pile with a rubber band and line them up on an out-of-the-way table. When planting time came, I'd work my way through the lined up stacks of seeds as the weeks passed.

Organize Seed Packets

Over the years, with increasingly more seeds that I wanted to sow, it gradually became more difficult for me to make my stacks of seeds. In addition, by the end of the season I'd have an unorganized mess of seed packets. I'd start out organized— in January, before I started planting, I would organize all my seeds alphabetically in a box. I'd take them out of the box to make my rubber banded stacks and plant them. Inevitably as the season went on and I continued planting, I'd skip the step of putting seeds back in the box in any useful order. It's an easy step to skip, and it makes it very difficult to find any seeds you might want to add into your sowing schedule.

At a recent gardening class, I learned a wonderful way to organize seeds. At first it seems very simple, and I think the value of this method isn't necessarily clear until you try it. I have a box big enough to hold folders that open up to two inches wide. Most of my folders are brown, and a few are multicolored. They're made of a heavy paper, almost card-board, so they're pretty sturdy. I have about twenty of these folders, and I've labeled each with different types of plants. One folder holds my herb seeds, and others hold different types of vegetable and flower seeds.

This method allows me to just pull out a folder, get the seed packet I want, and then easily replace the packet and folder. No alphabetizing or other fancy organization is needed for packets or folders because it's easy to find one out of twenty folders and easy to find one seed packet out of the twenty or so packets in each. You can use fewer and smaller folders if you have fewer seeds or more if you have more seeds. I love this simple and effective method of orga-nizing seeds.

An Herb-Sowing Calendar

To continue to simplify my sowing, I next wanted to figure out how to organize my seed-planting times without making all those piles of seed packets. So I made a list of the planting times and then subtracted them all from my last frost date. The result is an herb-planting calendar for my garden. I can use this list to pick out the types of herbs I plan to grow that year and make myself a personalized herb-sowing calendar for them.

Here's my basic herb-sowing calendar for over thirty herbs. The times listed are those before or after a last spring frost. If you do the subtraction using your last spring frost, it will personalize the calendar for your garden. The calendar is appropriate for any area that experiences winter frost.

Time Relative to Last Frost	Herb
Late fall (in the garden)	Caraway (*Carum carvi*) Cilantro/coriander (*Coriandrum sativum*) Dill (*Anethum graveolens*)
11 weeks before (indoors)	Rosemary (*Rosmarinus officinalis*)
9 weeks before (indoors)	Lavender (*Lavandula officinalis*) Marjoram (*Origanum majorana*) Oregano (*Origanum vulgare*) Parsley (*Petroselinum crispum*) Thyme (*Thymus vulgaris*)
8 weeks before (indoors)	Chervil (*Anthriscus cerefolium*) Peppers and chiles (Genus: *Capsicum*)

Time Relative to Last Frost	Herb
7 weeks before (indoors)	Catnip (*Nepeta cataria*) Chives (*Allium schoenoprasum*) Mint (Family: Lamiaceae) Peppermint (*Mentha balsamea* Willd) Sage (*Salvia officinalis*) Stevia (*Stevia rebaudiana*) Summer savory (*Satureja hortensis*) Winter savory (*Satureja montana*)
7 weeks before (in the garden)	Cilantro / coriander Dill Lovage (*Levisticum officinale*)
6 weeks before (indoors)	Valerian (*Valeriana officinalis*)
5 weeks before (indoors)	Basil (*Ocimum basilicum*) Bee balm (*Monarda*) Bulb fennel (*Foeniculum vulgare* var. *azoricum*) Chamomile (*Matricaria recutita*) Hyssop (*Hyssopus officinalis*)
3 weeks before (in the garden)	Cilantro, resow Dill, resow Mustard seed (Genus: *Sinapis* or *Brassica*)
1 wk before (in the garden)	Borage (*Borago officinalis*) Leaf fennel (*Foeniculum vulgare*) Make second plantings of: cilantro and dill
2 wks after (in the garden)	Anise (*Pimpinella anisum*) Make additional plantings of: cilantro and dill
3 wks after (indoors)	Cumin (*Cuminum cyminum*)
6 wks after (in the garden)	Make additional plantings of: cilantro and dill

Calendar Notes

- The seeds of some of these herbs require special conditions for their germination. For example, seeds that need light should be planted on top of the soil. These include the perennial herbs catnip, chervil, lavender, marjoram, mint, oregano, rosemary, summer savory, and winter savory.

- Some annual herbs, including dill and cilantro/coriander, have a short time to harvest and should be planted successively so that they are always available.

- Some seeds overwinter well in the garden and grow well in cool spring temperatures. These can be planted in the late fall for an early spring crop. They include caraway, dill, and cilantro/coriander.

- Annual herbs here include basil, borage, caraway, cayenne, chervil, cilantro, dill, and mustard. Parsley is a biennial; chervil can be either a biennial or a short-lived perennial. The rest of the herbs in the calendar are perennials.

Personalized Herb-Sowing Calendars

Using your last spring frost date, you can adapt this calendar to your garden. Make piles of seeds that get planted at the same time, line them, and sow at the right time. Or you can use my folder approach and pull out the appropriate seed packets, sow them, and then replace them in their folder.

Still easier yet is an online calendar or a mobile device app. I've written an app that generates a personalized herb-planting calendar. It's called Skippy's Herb Planting Calendar. This app will calculate and display the optimum planting times for over thirty flowers and herbs in your garden. You can find Skippy's apps at http://skippysgarden.com/apps/.

You can type in your last spring frost date and select the herbs you want to plant. The app will then display when to plant each herb. It can tell you what you should plant in the current week, and it can send you reminders for when it's time to plant. Other apps for mobile devices for vegetables and herbs include Vegetable Tree—Gardening Guide and SOW—A Planting Companion.

Herb seed–planting calendars can simplify your planting. And whether you make your own calendar or purchase an app, it will last many years. Planting annual herbs becomes easier every year as you repeat the process and become familiar with the timing. Perennial herbs are more of a challenge, often having low germination rates, being slower growing, taking longer to reach harvest size, and requiring special conditions for germination. However, once you've grown a perennial herb, you can have it in your garden for many years. I enjoy knowing that I raised a challenging perennial herb plant from seed myself.

Whether you're planting a large herb garden with a hundred herbs or a modest one with five or six, a seed-planting calendar can help you simplify the process. Planting herbs from seed can be a lot of fun!

Kathy Martin *is a Master Gardener and longtime author of the blog Skippy's Vegetable Garden, a journal of her vegetable gardens. The blog has won awards including* Horticulture Magazine's *Best Gardening Blog. She manages the Belmont Victory Gardens, which, with 137 plots on two acres of land, is one of the largest and oldest community gardens in the Boston area. Kathy lives near Boston with her husband, son, and Portuguese water dogs. She strives to grow all of her family's vegetables and herbs herself using sustainable organic methods.*

Culinary
Herbs

Thai Basil: Tiny Leaves but a Whole World of Flavor

❧ by Anne Sala ❧

When I first set out to write about Thai basil, I intended to share recipes that showed how these licorice-sweet leaves could be substituted for Italian basil in certain recipes. But, with the recent passing of Thailand's long-reigning monarch, King Bhumibol Adulyadej, interest in the culture of this Southeast Asian country has been on the rise. I found myself intrigued by the stories told in the cookbooks I read and with the knowledge I gained from people who once lived in this country.

I quickly realized I did not want to waste space trying to shoehorn a unique herb into recipes that could be considered "old hat." Instead, I hope to open a new world of dishes so that readers can easily start using this resilient member of the basil family.

There are over 160 varieties of basil in the *Ocimum basilicum* species, which is part of the Lamiaceae family along with hyssop, oregano, mint, thyme, and many other familiar flowering herbs. Basil is thought to originate from India, where it has been cultivated for at least 5,000 years and is considered sacred to the god Vishnu.

With such an intense and unique scent, basil's popularity inevitably spread around the world. There are now native *Ocimum* species on every temperate continent. Thai basil's scientific name is *Ocimum basilicum* var. *thyrsiflora*. It is sometimes listed as 'Horapha Nanum', too.

The chemical compounds within basil have antibacterial and antifungal properties. It is used as a remedy for kidney and bladder conditions as well as aiding the function of the brain, heart, and lungs. It can also be taken to manage diabetes, and its scent is known as a stress reducer.

When one thinks of basil, the look and scent of Genovese basil might first come to mind. Thai basil does not look like that. Instead of large, domed, floppy leaves, Thai basil has small, spear-shaped leaves that become tinged with purple as they age. They grow on purple stems, which also produce purple flower spikes. The late-summer blossoms are mauve and white—making for a lovely mix of colors. Its flavor is also slightly different. The sweet "basil" taste carries a tint of licorice and is sometimes labeled as licorice basil or anise basil. Lastly, Thai basil's small leaves are sturdier than sweet basil's. Therefore, the leaves can withstand the heat of cooking better than its Western cousin.

There are actually two basils in Thailand that reign supreme: Thai basil and holy basil, also known as *Ocimum tenuiflorum* or tulsi. Holy basil has more of a camphor flavor and is used in specific recipes that normally cannot be made with other basils (well, of course they could, but the flavor wouldn't be right). Holy basil is also used extensively for its medicinal properties. The recipes that follow are all meant for Thai basil, and I only bring up holy basil in order for readers to know there is a distinction between them.

Thai basil is a popular and distinctive herb in the cuisines of Thailand's surrounding countries as well. Vietnam, Laos, and Cambodia all have recipes that specifically require Thai basil as a main ingredient. In this article, I hope to capture the essence of some of these recipes while maintaining my desire to offer simple instructions that will help incorporate this fun cuisine into your kitchen repertoire.

Afterward, if you want to look up more "authentic" versions of the recipes, please be my guest. I suggest tracking down *True Thai* by Victor Sodsook with Theresa Volpe Laursen and Byron Laursen and *Pok Pok* by Andy Ricker with JJ Goode.

Quick Green Curry

To start, if you don't already have a preference, just choose any green curry paste that is readily available. You could grind your own, but since this recipe calls for such a small amount, I think the list of ingredients required to make homemade paste is just not worth it—at least for the first time.

  1 tablespoon olive oil
  1 teaspoon green curry paste (you can increase this
    amount by a lot if you want)

- 1 pound skinless, boneless chicken breast, cut into bite-sized chunks
- 1 large onion, sliced thin
- 1 14-ounce can coconut milk
- 1 cup water or broth
- 1 cup peas or green beans, fresh or frozen
- 1 tablespoon fish sauce
- 1 lime, cut into quarters
- ¼ cup lightly packed Thai basil leaves

Heat the oil in a large pot or dutch oven over medium heat. Spoon in the curry paste and stir until fragrant. Add the chicken and onion and sauté until the chicken is no longer pink (it does not need to brown) and the onion begins to soften.

Pour in the coconut milk, broth, and fish sauce and simmer for another five minutes. Taste and adjust curry paste amount if you want more intense flavor.

Add the peas or green beans and simmer for about two minutes.

Spoon into bowls and garnish with a squeeze of lime and basil leaves. You could also spoon this over rice. Serves 4.

Weeknight Pho

Pho is a sacred meal for me. When I first had it, served to me in a café in the back of a pharmacy, this Vietnamese soup was a revelation of wonderful and heretofore unexplored flavors. I revere the process that goes into making the all-important broth (much like the ramen broth that supplies the backbone to that Japanese culinary touchstone). I eat pho on my birthday. I also eat it when I am sick with a cold. Or, more importantly, my whole family eats it if they are sick with a cold. And, while nothing will ever take the place of a fine simmered pot of pho from my favorite restaurant, sometimes a cold strikes when it is closed. So I adapted a recipe created by Lynne Rossetto Kasper, which has the right amount of shortcuts.

1 large onion, sliced thin

8 garlic cloves, crushed

3-inch piece fresh ginger, peeled and sliced thin

10 whole cloves

2 star anise

Freshly ground black pepper

8 cups chicken broth

4 tablespoons brown sugar

4 teaspoons fish sauce

16 ounces linguine-style rice noodles

16 ounces raw top round steak, sliced extremely thin

10 branches Thai basil

10 sprigs fresh cilantro

8–10 ounces bean sprouts

2 green chiles, sliced thin

1 large lime, cut into wedges

Hoisin sauce

Hot sauce, such as sriracha

Place an oven rack in the highest slot or about 6 inches from the oven ceiling. Turn on the broiler. Distribute the onion, garlic, ginger, cloves, anise, and about 5 grinds of pepper onto a rimmed sheet pan. Broil for 2 minutes, flip the pieces, and broil for 3 more minutes or until the onions start to toast along the edges.

Place the spices in a large pot set on high heat, and then add the broth, sugar, and fish sauce. Bring to a boil, cover with the lid, turn down the heat, and allow to simmer for about 20 minutes.

Prepare the rice noodles according to the package instructions, but soak them for a little less time than required so they keep a bit of their rigidity. Divide the noodles between 4 large soup bowls.

Meanwhile, place the Thai basil, cilantro, bean sprouts, chiles, lime wedges, hoisin sauce, and sriracha on the dinner table so guests can garnish the soups to their liking.

Just before serving, place the sliced beef in the bowls. When the broth is ready, quickly ladle it on top of the beef to cook it. Serve immediately. Serves 4.

Shortcut Banh Mi

Banh mi is a blanket term used for many different kinds of Vietnamese sandwiches. This version has ground pork in it, but I think a vegetarian version with a crusty baguette slathered with the sriracha mayo and the pickled vegetables is just as divine.

¾ cup shredded carrots

¾ cup thinly sliced cucumbers

½ cup shredded daikon radish

2 tablespoons unseasoned rice wine vinegar

2 tablespoons granulated sugar (for the vegetables)

¼ teaspoon kosher salt (for the vegetables)

½ cup mayonnaise

4 tablespoons finely chopped scallions

2–3 tablespoons sriracha or to taste

1 tablespoon vegetable oil

4 garlic cloves, chopped

1 pound ground pork

2 tablespoons fish sauce

½ teaspoon black pepper

½ teaspoon kosher salt (for the meat)

1 teaspoon granulated sugar (for the meat)

½ cup chopped Thai basil, plus more for serving

Finely grated zest of 1 lime

Juice of ½ lime

6 small hero rolls or 2 baguettes cut into thirds, split

Fresh jalapeño, thinly sliced and seeded, for serving

Mint sprigs, for serving

Cilantro sprigs, for serving

In a bowl, toss together the carrots, cucumbers, daikon, vinegar, sugar, and salt and let stand at room temperature for at least 30 minutes.

In a small bowl, stir together the mayonnaise, 1 tablespoon scallions, and the sriracha, to taste. Cover tightly and set aside.

Heat oil in a large skillet over medium-high heat. Add the remaining 3 tablespoons scallions and the garlic. Stir for 1 minute and then add the pork. Crumble it and cook for about 7 minutes until no longer pink. Stir in 1 tablespoon sriracha (if desired) and the fish sauce, pepper, salt, and sugar.

Remove from heat and stir in the basil, lime zest, and lime juice. Let cool 5 minutes.

Spread the mayonnaise mixture on the top and bottom pieces of the bread. Spoon the pork mixture onto the bread. Press the jalapeño, basil, mint, and cilantro sprigs into the pork. Spoon some of the pickled vegetables onto the sandwiches. Serve immediately. Serves 6.

Thai Rice Bowl

This recipe originally called for special red rice, and if you want to source some (there are varieties from Thailand, actually), go ahead. However, this recipe is also quite satisfying with brown rice—or any rice at all.

- 1 cup precooked rice of your choice, cooled
- 1 tablespoon olive oil
- 1 medium onion, diced
- 2 garlic cloves, minced
- 1 small red chile, seeded and minced (optional)
- ½-inch piece ginger root, peeled and minced
- ½ teaspoon ground coriander
- 1 carrot (Use a vegetable peeler to peel it into strips. Slice them into smaller pieces if desired.)
- 6 ounces green beans, trimmed and chopped
- ¼ cup coconut milk
- ⅛ cup soy sauce
- 2 large eggs, boiled, peeled, and sliced lengthwise (optional)
- 1 large lime, quartered
- ½ cup loosely packed fresh Thai basil
- ¼ cup toasted and chopped nuts, such as peanuts, cashews, or macadamia nuts (optional)

Place the precooked rice in a large heat-safe bowl. Set aside. Heat the oil in a wok or large pan over high heat. Add the onion, garlic, chile, ginger, coriander, carrot, and green beans. Stir-fry for about 3 minutes, until the vegetables are barely cooked.

Pour in the coconut milk and soy sauce and bring to a boil. If including the eggs, nestle them cut-side down into the broth. Allow the eggs to heat through before carefully tipping the pan's contents into the bowl of rice. Add the basil and nuts before gently tossing the rice mixture. Serve with a squeeze of lime. Serves 4.

Oranges with Thai Basil Syrup

Thai basil is a wonderfully adaptable herb. Not only can it tame fiery chiles, but it can play nicely in an elegant yet simple dessert.

6 oranges, peeled and segmented

2½ cups water

1 cup sugar

1 cup tightly packed Thai basil leaves, plus extra for garnish

Combine the water, sugar, and basil together in a small saucepan over medium heat. Bring the mixture to a simmer and stir occasionally to dissolve the sugar. Once all the sugar has dissolved, allow the contents to bubble for about 15 minutes, until it just becomes syrupy.

When it reaches the desired consistency, remove the pan from the heat. Allow to cool completely. Once cooled, pour the syrup through a fine-mesh sieve into a resealable container.

When ready to serve, arrange the oranges on a serving dish, drizzle with syrup, and sprinkle with reserved basil leaves. Serve immediately. Serves 6.

Basil Seed Pudding with Mango

Basil seeds are as amazing as they are small. When mixed with a liquid, they secrete a gel-like substance called mucilage, similar to the secretions of flax and chia seeds. Traditionally, in Thai cuisine, the seeds from the lemon basil plant are used for this dessert. However, I can sense no difference between the basil seed types, and if you have seeds from your Thai basil plants, they will work just fine.

Two mangos, the seed removed and flesh diced

3 tablespoons basil seeds

1 cup coconut milk

½ teaspoon vanilla extract

Zest of one lime

2 tablespoons granulated sugar

Divide the mango cubes between 4 bowls. Set aside.

Place the basil seeds in a large heat-proof bowl. Set aside.

In a medium saucepan over low heat, combine coconut milk, vanilla, lime zest, and sugar until it begins to bubble. Allow to simmer for about 3 minutes, then pour over the seeds. Stir, then allow to steep for about 5 minutes before stirring once more.

Spoon the congealed seed mixture over the mangos. Serve while still warm. Serves 4.

Anne Sala *is a freelance writer based in Minnesota. She recently moved into a new house, and even though it is autumn when she writes this, she has already started plotting out the gardens in her backyard.*

Green Gifts of Spring

⬗ by Susan Pesznecker ⬗

Springtime . . . Think of it and what "springs" to mind? You might picture gentle rains, soft-lit mornings, flowering trees, early flowers, adorable baby animals, and the color green filling the landscape with a variety of verdant shades and hues. After the long winter, the world is suddenly filled with spring's green gifts: not just flowers and trees but tasty goodies like fiddleheads, nettles, scapes, ramps, and morels, all waiting to be gathered and enjoyed. Get out your harvesting shears and grab a basket—let's collect dinner!

Fiddleheads

Fiddleheads are the immature furled fronds of young ferns—a phase that occurs only briefly after the ferns emerge and before the fronds begin to uncoil and fill out. Ferns grow throughout temperate climates across much of the United States, and fiddleheads appear from early to mid-spring, depending on location. The term "fiddlehead" comes from their resemblance to the scroll at the top of a violin, or fiddle.

Not all fiddleheads are edible, and eating the wrong kinds can make you sick. There are three varieties of edible fiddleheads: those from the ostrich fern (*Matteuccia struthiopteris*), lady fern (*Athyrium filix-femina*), and bracken fern (*Pteridium aquilinum*). They're fairly easy to tell apart, provided you have a good plant guide for your area; if you have any doubts, it's best to leave them alone. Only the fiddleheads themselves should be eaten—eating mature fern fronds can cause digestive problems.

Harvest fiddleheads when they're fully developed but before they begin to unfurl—usually during early to mid-spring. Use plant shears or a boline (a sickle-shaped blade used to harvest herbs), cutting the stems three to four inches below the fiddlehead.

To prepare, break off the tough lower stem in the same way you'd break an asparagus stem. Fiddleheads can be simmered in butter or salted water or can be steamed. Their taste falls somewhere between young spinach and asparagus, with fresh grassy undertones. They're excellent eaten by themselves as a fresh vegetable, and they also work beautifully in egg and pasta dishes.

Nettles

Nettles (*Urtica dioica*) are common perennials found in the wild throughout temperate North America. The plant's leaves and stems are covered with tiny hollow structures that hold a highly irritating substance; when touched, these structures act like hypodermic needles, injecting the irritants into the skin and causing a stinging, blistering rash.

But there's good news about nettles, too: they're delicious! When soaked in water or cooked, nettles lose their stinging nature and become a delicious vegetable. Tasting like a combination of spinach, greens, and sweet cucumber, cooked nettles are high in potassium, vitamins A and C, iron, calcium, and protein, making them extremely nutritious.

Harvest nettles any time following their spring emergence through mid-summer—and before they've flowered. After flowering, they lose flavor and become fibrous. Generally, the earlier they're harvested, the tastier they'll be. To avoid being nettle-stung, wear a long-sleeved shirt, long pants, and gloves. Clip the tender tops of the plant (i.e., the first few leaf sets). The lower part of the plant will be too fibrous for good eating, and by clipping over the top, you'll actually encourage the plant to become even bushier with new growth.

To prepare, steam the nettles or sauté in a bit of butter or olive oil. Some people enjoy them in pesto, where the pureeing with other substances is said to remove their sting.

Caution: don't serve nettles raw, like in a salad, as the raw plants retain the ability to sting while being chewed. (Ouch!)

Garlic Scapes

Garlic scapes are the uncooked buds of the hardback garlic plant (*Allium sativum*). They're rather outlandish looking, as if the garlic had put out a three-foot tentacle with a weird fig-shaped bud on the far end. But their taste makes the weirdness more than worth it. Garlic farmers remove the scapes in mid-spring to encourage the garlic buds to mature. If not harvested, the buds will eventually bloom with no harm to the plant, but farmers believe that pruning the scapes makes the garlic plants channel their energy into producing extra-large bulbs.

You won't find garlic scapes in the wild, but you will find them at your local greengrocers and farmer's markets, where they're a fleeting spring treat in a season lasting only a few short weeks. They're usually sold as tangled bunches of several scapes. They'll keep in the fridge for up to a week.

Garlic scapes have a flavor that's mildly garlicky and simultaneously spicy-sweet, like chives. They're delicious raw but even better when cut into manageable green bean-like segments and sautéed or stir-fried. The raw scapes can also replace basil in a favorite pesto recipe. Discard the fibrous distal ends before using.

Ramps

Beloved by chefs everywhere, ramps (*Allium tricoccum*) are a true darling of springtime. They belong to the wild onion family and are widespread throughout the United States, being especially common on the East Coast and at higher elevations. Their flavor is potent and blends the essence of onions and garlic.

When collecting ramps, gather both the aboveground leaves and the underground bulbs. Ideally, use a knife to loosen the soil around the ramp and then slice through the lower part of the bulb, leaving the roots and part of the bulb in the soil; this will encourage the ramp to regrow. And this is important, because over-harvesting of ramps has become a serious problem in some areas.

The entire plant, once harvested, resembles a short, rather plump scallion. Store the ramps in the refrigerator, uncleaned, for up to three days. Rinse and clean just before using. The best way to store ramps long-term is by freezing them whole or using them to create a compound butter and then freezing that. Drying ramps yields a poor result devoid of flavor.

To cook with ramps, use them in the same way you'd use onions, chives, or leeks. They're especially delicious with eggs, pasta, soups, or potato dishes.

A favorite culinary memory of mine is a dish of wild ramp and fiddlehead ravioli, served with brown butter and crispy fried sage leaves.

Wild Spinach

Wild spinach (*Chenopodium album*; also called lamb's quarters) is so common throughout most of North America as to be called a "weed" by most of us. Its leaves, young shoots, and aerial parts are best harvested in the early spring and used as a leafy vegetable. The flavor is much like spinach but less sweet and with a more earthy, mineral flavor. Wild spinach is high in vitamins A and C along with potassium, riboflavin, and calcium, making it significantly more nutritious than regular spinach.

To harvest, collect the leaves and leafy stem tips. Wild spinach can be used raw or cooked, much in the same way as regular spinach. Leaves harvested earlier in the spring have a milder flavor than those taken late.

Ramson

Ramson (*Allium ursinum*, "bear garlic") is a type of garlicky wild onion, also related to chives. Ramsons are native to Europe and Asia. The name "bear garlic" derives from the fact that the plant is an early spring favorite of bears, who often begin grubbing for the plant soon after waking from hibernation.

Ramson leaves and flowers can be collected and used raw (as in a salad) or cooked in any number of dishes. The strongly flavored plant is loaded with antioxidants and is known to have a number of health-supporting qualities.

Note that ramsons are often mistaken for several poisonous plants—including lily of the valley—and therefore should only be collected and used by those certain of their identification.

Morels

Morels (genus *Morchella*) aren't green, but they're definitely one of spring's gifts! This edible fungus (mushroom) has a tall, narrow cap and an unusual honeycombed appearance and can be found throughout the Northern Hemisphere. Morels are hunted and harvested early in the spring, and their unique appearance makes them an easy and relatively safe 'shroom to hunt. Even so, note that there are also toxic varieties of morels, so as with any mushroom hunting, be very certain of what you're gathering.

Morels should be stored without washing and washed minimally just before using. To use, sauté or simmer them as with any mushroom and either serve by themselves or add to a recipe. Morels can be frozen or dried for longer storage. To freeze, freeze individual mushrooms on baking sheets until solid, then store in plastic freezer bags.

Responsible Harvesting

It's important to harvest spring's gifts thoughtfully and with respect. Careless gathering can destroy the plant and, in extreme cases, can remove the plant from the local ecosystem. Consider the following:

1. Harvest only what you will be able to use and process.

2. Never harvest within 100 feet of a road or train track.

3. Follow the "one in twenty" rule: for every piece of plant material taken, nineteen others of equal or greater volume should be left in place.

4. Don't harvest more than one-third of any plant, and always leave the lower part of the plant and its roots intact so that it can continue to grow.

5. Harvest with clean cuts using a sharp pair of plant shears, a sharp knife, or a boline. Making sharp cuts—versus crushing the stems with your fingers—leaves the plant in the best shape to survive and regrow. Crushed, torn plants may easily fall prey to funguses, infestations, or other disorders.

6. Leave the largest "grandparent" plants behind: they are survivors and will continue to propagate sturdy offspring.

7. Don't harvest plants that look unhealthy, damaged, or are infested.

8. Never eat any plant unless you are absolutely certain it is safe. Some plants that are safe are almost identical to those that can be lethal. For example, Queen Anne's lace—also called wild carrot—is safe to eat. But it looks almost identical to poison hemlock, one of the deadliest

plants in the temperate forests: a small bite of poison hemlock can be lethal. Carry a good field guide, and if you have any doubts, leave the plant alone. Even better: learn good techniques from an expert teacher in a face-to-face learning situation. (This is a great example of a situation where online learning cannot come close to in-person instruction!)

9. Do your homework before you go. Some plants may be protected and should not be harvested at all. Be aware of regulations regarding gathering on private and public lands, state parks, and so forth.

Recommended Reading

Elias, Thomas, and Peter A. Dykeman. *Edible Wild Plants: A North American Field Guide to Over 200 Natural Foods*. New York: Sterling, 2009.

Kallas, John. *Edible Wild Plants: Wild Foods from Dirt to Plate: The Wild Food Adventure Series*. Bk. 1. Layton, UT: Gibbs Smith, 2010.

Pojar, Jim, and Andy MacKinnon. *Plants of the Pacific Northwest Coast*. Vancouver: Partners Publishing, 2004.

Susan Pesznecker *is a mom, writer, English teacher, nurse, and amateur herbalist living in Oregon. Sue holds an MS in professional writing and loves to forage in the woods for culinary and medicinal foods. She has authored* Yule: Rituals, Recipes, & Lore for the Winter Solstice *(Llewellyn, 2015),* The Magickal Retreat *(Llewellyn, 2012), and* Crafting Magick with Pen and Ink *(Llewellyn, 2009) and contributes to the Llewellyn annuals. Visit Sue on Facebook (https://www.facebook.com/SusanMoonwriterPesznecker).*

Dandelions

❧ by Suzanne Ress ❧

The first apartment my husband and I had together was in a building located in a narrow alley deep in the chaotic heart of Naples, Italy. Having come there from the farmed flatlands of central Ohio, I was shocked by the lack of surrounding plant life.

Early one spring morning as we walked down the alley past the Neopolitan low houses, a crone, dressed in black and leaning on a walking stick, called out to my husband from the doorway of her abode, "Giovanotto!"

"Eh?" said my husband, slowing down a bit.

"Could you pluck the leaves of that *tarassaco* for me?"

She lifted her walking stick and used it to point to a tiny chain-link-fenced square of overgrown grass and weeds.

I looked at this minute patch of weedy lawn in amazement, wondering why on earth it was fenced.

In the center of the eighteen-inch or so square grew a single yellow dandelion flower.

"I cannot reach it, but you are young and tall, and you can! Please, will you fetch it for me?" the crone pleaded. She spoke like a witch in a fairy tale, setting a task of daring for the young hero—he must steal this precious, protected flower for her.

Without hesitation my husband stepped to the fence, reached over, and plucked the entire dandelion plant from the ground. He handed it over to the crone.

"*Grazie*, young man, you are so kind!" she thanked him profusely as we hurried away to work.

Since then, we have moved to a more rural area in the far north of Italy, and I have become accustomed to seeing old couples or grandmotherly types lurking through fields and along roadsides with plastic bags in the spring. They are gathering the highly prized young dandelion leaves for their spring tonic salads.

The common name for this herb, dandelion, is a corruption of the French *dent-de-lion*, or "lion's tooth," because its jagged leaves resemble the sharp teeth along a lion's jaw.

Its botanical name, *Taraxacum*, comes from the Greek words *taraxo* and *akos* and means "remedy for disorders." Regular use of the plant was advised by the medieval Persian scientist Al-Razi, who called it *tarkhashqun*. Twelfth-century Italian translator Gerard of Cremona changed the spelling to *tarascon* in his translation from Arabic to Latin. From there it mutated to become the genus *Taraxacum*, which includes hundreds of known members. Dandelion is head of the family and an *officinale*, meaning it was one of the mainstays of the herbal pharmacy in the Middle Ages.

It is believed that the dandelion plant evolved about thirty million years ago in Eurasia. It has been widely used by humans as food and medicine for all of known history.

The dandelion's form has evolved to make maximum use of rain and soil nutrients, so it is able to survive and propagate in less than ideal conditions, including in very dry rocky soil, through cracks in cement, and at altitudes up to 6,500 feet.

Dandelions are not native to North America but were brought as pot herbs and salad greens by early European settlers.

Its flower opens wide to absorb the sun's light but closes at night and at the approach of rain to conserve its nectar. Its nectar is highly attractive to honeybees, bumblebees, butterflies, and other pollinating insects, which guarantees the fertility of its fast-traveling, wind-blown seeds.

The dandelion's leaves, in the shape of a low, tight rosette, pull in and direct rainwater to the plant's center, where it travels down into the very long taproot. The taproot, which can be as long as thirty inches, pulls up nutrients and moisture from deep within the soil, and even when the entire plant is plucked away, it can regenerate perennially from the root.

A single dandelion plant can produce as many as five generations of offspring in one season. The many tiny seeds from its fluff-ball stage can travel as far as five miles on the wind but can also use rainwater, human clothes and hair, and animal fur for transport.

In the spring the dandelion is one of the first flowers to bloom, providing an important pollen and nectar source for growing colonies of honeybees, which, at this critical building-up time of year, might otherwise starve.

The dandelion flower continues to bloom late into the fall, making it one of the last remaining flowers the bees have to visit before settling into their semihibernation stage for the winter, when they must depend on stores of honey and pollen inside the hive for survival. Dandelions are major pollen and nectar producers, and monofloral dandelion honey, if you are able to find it, is distinctively delicious, dark golden with a little bite to it.

A dandelion flower's stem, when broken, oozes white milky liquid. This is natural latex, the same substance found in the rubber tree. The long taproot and stems of dandelions have been studied and, in recent years, proposed as a valid major latex-producing plant. Dandelions have an advantage over the rubber tree, which only grows in tropical climates: the dandelion plant does well even in very northern climates.

Medicinal Uses

In some places the dandelion is called "piss-a-bed," which, vulgar as it sounds, is an accurate description of its diuretic property. Dandelions increase urinary output from the kidneys and are considered one of the best diuretics available, superior to synthetic concoctions. Diuretics are useful in cases of hypertension, water retention or bloating, rheumatism, gout, eczema, and joint stiffness.

Dandelion also increases bile production by the liver; thus, it can be used as an effective digestive tonic and appetite stimulant. It is also useful as a mild bowel stimulant in cases of constipation.

Dandelion is said to help regulate both male and female hormones and, all-in-all, is a great cleansing herb that removes waste from the body and replaces it with valuable vitamins and minerals.

One hundred grams of raw dandelion greens contain only forty-five calories and provide over 200 percent of a human's daily vitamin A requirement, over half the vitamin C requirement, 18 percent of the daily calcium need, 17 percent of iron, 11 percent of potassium, 9 percent of magnesium, and 14 percent of fiber, plus significant amounts of vitamin B_6, riboflavin, and manganese. It also provides huge amounts of the fat-soluble vitamin K (923 percent of an adult's daily requirement), which is necessary for blood coagulation and calcium absorption.

Culinary Use

All parts of the dandelion plant can be used in food and beverage preparation, from its root to its leaves and flowers. Not only is this plant good for you, it is delicious, too.

Here are some of my favorite dandelion recipes. Remember only to use dandelions you are sure have not been sprayed with insecticides or other dangerous chemicals.

Dandelion Croquettes

¼ pound freshly picked dandelion greens

1 medium potato, boiled and peeled

1 egg, beaten

3 tablespoons grated parmesan cheese

3 tablespoons finely grated breadcrumbs (plus more for coating)

Salt

Oil for frying

Thoroughly rinse the dandelion greens and cook them for about 15 minutes in a small amount of boiling water. Drain well and chop them up.

Mash the boiled potato and mix in the beaten egg. Blend in the cooked, chopped greens, the grated parmesan, and the breadcrumbs. Season to taste with salt.

Form this mixture into egg-shaped balls and flatten them slightly. Roll them in more breadcrumbs and fry in hot oil. Drain on paper towels and serve. Serves 2.

Dandelion Salad

½ pound freshly picked young spring dandelion greens

¼ pound bacon

1 clove garlic, crushed

1 thick slice bread, cut into cubes

4 tablespoon olive oil

1 tablespoon balsamic vinegar

Salt and pepper

Thoroughly rinse the greens and dry them well in a salad spinner. Tear bite-sized pieces into a large salad bowl.

Cut the bacon into ½-inch pieces and fry them, together with the crushed garlic clove and cubes of bread, until the bacon is crispy and the bread is toasty. Remove and discard the garlic, and pour the mixture over the dandelion greens in the salad bowl. Mix very well, then pour a vinaigrette dressing made from the olive oil, balsamic vinegar, salt, and pepper in the bowl, and toss again. Serve immediately. Serves 4.

Dandelion Tea

Steep 1 ounce fresh or dried dandelion leaves and flowers in 1 quart of boiled water for ten minutes. Sweeten with honey.

Dandelion Jam

    1 basketful dandelion flowers

    Sugar

    2 oranges

    2 lemons

    1 star anise

Gather a basketful of fresh, open dandelion flowers, and, using scissors, cut the green part of the calyx at the base of the flower away, letting the petals drop into a bowl. Quickly rinse the petals and place them in a large pot with water just to cover. Close the pot with a lid and simmer the petals for half an hour. Once cooked, run the petals with their liquid through a vegetable mill and pour back into the bowl.

Measure the amount of dandelion puree, and for every cupful, add ¾ cup of sugar. Put this mixture back into the cooking pot, grate in the rinds of the oranges and lemons, squeeze in their juice, and drop in the star anise.

Bring the mixture to a low boil, and continue cooking and stirring until it reaches the jelly stage.

Remove the star anise, and pour the hot jam into hot, sterile (from the dishwasher) jars. Cap the jars, and either refrigerate them for use within 2 weeks or process them for 10 minutes in a boiling water bath for long-term shelf storage.

Dandelion Coffee

Dig up an older (at least two years), established dandelion plant by the root. If the root is very deep, just take what you can manage and leave the rest to regenerate.

Cut the root from the rest of the plant (which can be set aside for some other use). Thoroughly wash the root, scrubbing away all the dirt with a small brush under running water.

Cut the clean root into ½-inch pieces. Spread the pieces on a baking sheet and roast them in an oven at 200°F for 1 hour.

Use a coffee mill to grind the roasted root. Simmer 2 teaspoons of ground root per cup of water for 3 to 5 minutes, then strain. Add honey or milk or both to taste.

Dandelion Wine

½ pound dandelion flowers, tops only

Water

1 cup orange juice

1 lemon

1 star anise

6 cups sugar

1 7-gram envelope brewing yeast (not bread yeast!)

Rinse flowers thoroughly and remove the green calyx, letting the petals fall into a large bowl. Soak them for 48 hours in a small amount of water at room temperature.

Place the petals in a large pot with 1 gallon of water, 1 cup orange juice, finely grated lemon rind, the juice of the lemon, star anise, and sugar. Stir well and bring to a boil. Boil for 1 hour.

Allow to cool slightly, and then strain through muslin into a large bowl.

When mixture is just warm to the touch, stir in the brewing yeast (available at beer- and wine-making supply shops and online). Cover and leave overnight at room temperature.

Using a funnel, pour the wine into bottles. Cover the tops of the bottles with uninflated balloons with two or three holes punched in, and leave in a cool, dark place for 1 month, until fermentation is complete. Cork the bottles and store at least 6 months before using.

Literature

Last but not least, dandelions have made a name for themselves in literature. Shakespeare wrote about them in his romantic comedy *Cymbeline*: "Golden lads and girls all must, / As chimney sweepers, come to dust." The dandelion's flowers are the golden lads and girls, while the fluffy seed heads, looking like chimney sweepers' brushes, are the flowers' end stage, or dust.

In 1957 Ray Bradbury published his semiautobiographical novel, *Dandelion Wine*. The title is symbolic of the story's essence, and it also refers to the qualities of dandelion wine (made by the main character's grandfather)—an inebriating concentration of summertime wildness and joy.

Suzanne Ress *runs a small farm in the Alpine foothills of Italy, where she lives with her husband. She has been a practicing Pagan* *for as long as she can remember and was recently featured in the ex-hibit "Worldwide Witches" at the Hexenmuseum of Switzerland. She is the author of* The Trial of Goody Gilbert.

Bread and Jam for Beginners

⤜ by Deborah Castellano ⤛

A few years ago, while in between jobs, I became fascinated by books that taught you to be more French. French women buy everything fresh and go to four or five stops on their bunny route! Since then, I've been trying to eat as many whole foods as possible without preservatives, ingredients I find questionable, or corn syrup. I figure "no preservatives" is about as close to a faux-French diet as I'm getting in New Jersey. The corn syrup isn't about any real political agenda on my part per se; I don't like the aftertaste of it and find it shows up in the weirdest places, like kielbasa and bread, so part of this quest has also entailed that I've started baking

bread . . . mostly in a bread machine, which to real bakers counts about as much as making a cake from a cake mix. Here's the thing: if I make it the "real" way and am solely dependent on that for my bread intake, I'm never eating bread again. I just don't have the time and energy to deal with a lot of aggravation, and I doubt you do either. So except for your "Miss Martha" perfect friends, everyone will be impressed that you made bread and jam by hand instead of buying from the store and won't question the methods involved. The jam we will be making is refrigerator jam, so it needs to be refrigerated and is good for about two weeks. We will also be using pectin, which is another sinful word in some circles, but for your first jams, it will make it so you aren't frustrated.

Thyme Clementine Jam

- 2 cups clementines, peeled
- 2 tablespoons fresh thyme
- 2 tablespoons lemon juice
- 2 cups sugar
- ¾ cup water
- 1 box low-sugar pectin

Put the clementines and thyme in a food processor and pulse a few times. Stir in lemon juice and sugar. Stir occasionally for about 10 minutes. Pour into a pot and heat on low until the sugar is dissolved. In a separate small saucepan, mix the water and the pectin on medium-high heat until dissolved, stirring constantly. Boil for 1 minute. Pour the pectin mixture in with the fruit mixture and stir. Pour into a mason jar that has been through the dishwasher. Cover and leave out overnight and then refrigerate.

Balsamic Strawberry Jam

  2 cups strawberries, hulled

  1 tablespoon dried woodruff

  1 tablespoon balsamic vinegar

  2 tablespoons lemon juice

  2 cups sugar

  ¾ cup water

  1 box low-sugar pectin

Put the strawberries, woodruff, and vinegar in a food processor and pulse a few times. Stir in lemon juice and sugar. Stir occasionally for about 10 minutes. Pour into a pot and heat on low until the sugar is dissolved. In a separate small saucepan, mix the water and the pectin on medium-high heat until dissolved, stirring constantly. Boil for 1 minute. Pour the pectin mixture in with the fruit mixture and stir. Pour into a mason jar that has been through the dishwasher. Cover and leave out overnight and then refrigerate.

Ginger Peach Jam

  2 cups sugar

  2 tablespoons low-sugar, light fruit pectin

  4 cups frozen sliced peaches, thawed

  1 teaspoon ground cloves

  1 tablespoon fresh ginger, grated

  ½ teaspoon ground nutmeg

  4 teaspoons lemon juice

If using a bread machine: Make sure your paddle is working correctly in your machine. Place ingredients into the bread pan in the following order: sugar, pectin, peaches, cloves, ginger, nutmeg, and lemon juice. Close the lid and select "jam." When it's done, unplug your machine and wait 30 minutes before opening. Open with oven mitts; it's very hot. Pour into a mason jar that has been through the dishwasher. Put the cover on and refrigerate.

If using a stove top: Mush the fruit a bit and put the fruit and the pectin in the pot on medium heat. Stir for about 10 minutes until it boils. Add the rest of the ingredients and stir until it boils again. Let it boil for about 1 minute. Put a metal spoon in it and let it cool. Take the spoon out and watch it for 30 seconds. Is the jam too drippy? It needs more time then. Is it thick enough? If not, add a little more pectin. If it's too thick, add a little water. Pour into a mason jar that has been through the dishwasher. Put the cover on and refrigerate.

Cranberry Preserves

    2 cups sugar

    2 tablespoons low-sugar, light fruit pectin

    1 16-ounce bag of fresh cranberries

    1 teaspoon cinnamon

    1 cup water

    4 teaspoons lemon juice

If using a bread machine: Make sure your paddle is working correctly in your machine. Place ingredients into the bread pan in the following order: sugar, pectin, cranberries, cinnamon, water, and lemon juice. Close the lid and select "jam." When it's done, unplug your machine and wait 30 minutes before opening. Open with oven mitts; it's very hot. Pour into a mason jar that has been through the dishwasher. Put the cover on and refrigerate.

If using a stove top: See instructions for ginger peach jam.

These cranberry preserves are perfect for a new spin on a vodka cranberry. Put 2 room-temperature spoonfuls of the preserves in a rocks glass. Pour 6 counts of vodka in the glass. Stir until mixed well. Add ice.

Cardamom Fig Jam

1½ cups sugar

2 tablespoons low-sugar, light fruit pectin

1 8-ounce package dried figs, sliced

3 cardamom pods, crushed

1 teaspoon rosewater

¾ cup water

2 teaspoons lemon juice

If using a bread machine: Make sure your paddle is working correctly in your machine. Place ingredients into the bread pan in the following order: sugar, pectin, figs, cardamom, rosewater, water, and lemon juice. Close the lid and select "jam." When it's done, unplug your machine and wait 30 minutes before opening. Open with oven mitts; it's very hot. Pour into a mason jar that has been through the dishwasher. Put the cover on and refrigerate.

If using a stove top: See instructions for ginger peach jam.

Chocolate Lavender Quick Bread

6 tablespoons 2% milk

⅓ cup low-fat sour cream

1 room-temperature egg

3 teaspoons honey

8 tablespoons sugar

1 cup white whole wheat flour

1 teaspoon dried lavender (culinary grade)

½ teaspoon baking powder

¼ teaspoon baking soda

½ teaspoon salt

½ teaspoon vanilla extract

½ cup chocolate chips

If using a bread machine: Add ingredients to your bread machine in the order they are listed here. Set your bread machine to the smallest loaf, quick bread setting, and lightest crust. As your bread machine is mixing, check to make sure the bread is mixing correctly. (Is it too sticky? Too dry? Add more flour or water as needed).

If using an oven: Preheat your oven to 350°F. Mix the ingredients together. Oil a loaf pan. Pour the ingredients in and bake for 25 minutes. Test with a toothpick to see if it's done.

Honey Whole Wheat Herbs de Provence Bread

1¼ cups hot water

3 tablespoons honey

1 tablespoon Herbs de Provence

1½ cups bread flour

1½ cups whole wheat flour

1 teaspoon salt

1 tablespoon olive oil

1½ teaspoons active dry yeast

If using a bread machine: See instructions for chocolate lavender quickbread, but use the whole wheat setting instead of the quickbread setting.

If using an oven: Preheat your oven to 350°F. Mix the ingredients together. Oil a loaf pan. Pour the ingredients in and bake for 40 minutes. Test with a toothpick to see if it's done.

Add ½ teaspoon of vital wheat gluten to make your bread more dense! Add 1 tablespoon of flax seed for more omega-3!

Rosemary Oatmeal Bread

- 1¼ cup hot water
- 3 tablespoons honey
- 1 tablespoon fresh rosemary
- 1½ cups bread flour
- 1½ cups whole wheat flour
- ¼ cup quick oats
- 1 teaspoon salt
- 1 tablespoon olive oil
- 1½ teaspoons active dry yeast

If using a bread machine: See instructions for chocolate lavender quickbread, but use the whole wheat setting instead of the quickbread setting

If using an oven: See instructions for honey whole wheat Herbs de Provence bread.

Irish Soda Bread

- 4 cups white wheat flour
- 3 tablespoons honey

1 teaspoon baking soda

1 tablespoon baking powder

½ teaspoon salt

1 cup milk

1 egg

¼ cup butter, melted

¼ cup plain Greek yogurt

¼ cup currants

1 tablespoon mint

If using a bread machine: See instructions for chocolate lavender quickbread, but use the whole wheat setting instead of the quickbread setting.

If using an oven: See instructions for honey whole wheat Herbs de Provence bread.

Strawberry Basil Quickbread

2 cups strawberry ice cream

1 tablespoon chopped basil

1½ cups bread flour

Let the ice cream soften for about 15 minutes on the counter. Mix the ingredients together in a bowl while preheating the oven to 350°F. Pour the mixture into a greased loaf pan. Bake for about 45 minutes and test with a toothpick.

Deborah Castellano *(www.deborahmcastellano.com) is a frequent contributor to the Llewellyn annual almanacs, PaganSquare, and* Witches & Pagans *magazine. She blogs at* Charmed, I'm Sure. *Deborah's book,* Glamour Magic: The Witchcraft Revolution to Get What You Want *was published with Llewellyn in the summer of 2017. She resides in New Jersey with her husband, Jow, and their cat.*

Herbal Candies

⁂ by Diana Rajchel ⁂

Candy making requires the following skills: the knowledge to make simple syrups, the patience to stir constantly, and the faith to trust a thermometer. A love of cream is a bonus. Keen observation, an apron, antifatigue mats, and oven mitts also come in handy. If you do not have the disposition, acts of will or an entertainment device nearby can help—binge watching *Supernatural* has brought more than one batch of caramel into being.

All candy making has syrup at its root. Learning how the different syrups and sugars meld together determines whether your sweet treats flop or fly. The better your understanding, the better your success.

This is also the place that determines whether you make a treat candy or an *herbal* candy.

Making Simple Syrups

Herbal simple syrups can take some finesse, depending on the plant. All simples start with tea—and for tea, you must choose an herb that can handle heat. Lavender buds, for instance, become bitter at too high a temperature, as do other leaf- and flower-based teas. Often stopping at just the right point with the tea can help, but if you're not willing to risk burning your tongue to test, lavender, elderflower, and similarly flavorful but delicate plants often come in prepackaged simple syrups.

For something you must DIY, this progression may help:

Flower	1–2 minutes, simmer only
Leaf	2–3 minutes, simmer only
Bud	2–3 minutes, simmer to boil
Stem	2–3 minutes, simmer to boil (hotter and longer if wood)
Bark	3–5 minutes, boil
Root	3–5 minutes, boil

Steep your desired herb in two cups of hot water—the stronger the flavor, the better the flavor surfaces above the sugars. Extract the best you can within the heat tolerance of the plant.

About Alternative Sugars and Syrups

Personally, I prefer to avoid refined sugar whenever possible. Artificial sugars such as sucralose and xylitol are a second choice to me as well. In the best scenarios, natural, unprocessed sugars, such as molasses and maple syrup, are my candy-making best friends. While most syrups caramelize at the same temperature as refined sugar, different altitudes will call for different temperatures during the baking process, so always check a temperature chart and check a corresponding altitude chart.

My base sweeteners in candy making are from the following materials:

- Maple syrup
- Molasses
- Coconut sugar[1]
- Honey
- Coconut nectar

While most of these syrups have flavors of their own, the right combination of herb with the right syrup makes it a complementary, delicious experience. For instance, maple pairs beautifully with allspice, while coconut, ginger, and vanilla seem to like each other.

*Herbal sugars are also a great way to get candy flavoring.
Take a jar, pour in a layer of sugar, and then add a layer of your
herb. Fill the jar, repeating this pattern. After a week,
the flavors will permeate the sugar.*

---

1. A note about coconut sugars: It is possible to make a simple syrup with them, but it takes more time, higher temperatures, and more stirring than it does with traditional refined-sugar recipes.

Creams and Milks

While I am an omnivore that takes pleasure in milks and cheeses, those with vegan inclinations are not excluded from the worlds of soft candies anymore. Each type of creamy substance can change the texture and flavor of a candy—for instance, heavy cream tends to bring out sweetness and smooth texture, while goat's milk enhances the richness of a flavor. The most common choices are these:

- Goat's milk
- Heavy cream
- Coconut cream
- Cashew cream
- Butter

Temperatures

Maple candy is a favorite go-to of mine for holidays. In Minnesota, I just needed to heat it up to the temperature *Joy of Cooking* said, and voilà! A grainy, melt-in-your-mouth candy in the shape of whatever silicon mold I poured it into. I found out the hard way that in San Francisco, especially in my near-the-ocean apartment, I have to go a good five degrees above the recommended 237 degrees Fahrenheit. So check your altitudes. Minneapolis is 830 feet above ocean level. San Francisco altitudes range from 0 to 52 feet—that's a significant difference. The lower the altitude, the more you need to adjust the temperature. There are several websites and cookbooks that offer sugar temperature charts. Aside from maple syrup, the other syrups here all transform at the same temperatures as refined white sugar.

Candy Molds and Pan Shapes

If you can, invest in some silicone molds and cookware. They hold up well at high temperatures and completely eliminate the need to grease a pan. For those concerned about the safety of silicone, admittedly the FDA has not done any research, but nothing in decent-quality silicone cookware registers as a health risk by environmental awareness groups. The presence of silicone products on the market is also the direct result of advocacy for people with disabilities and is recommended as safe based on research for people who are more vulnerable to chemicals.

Herbal Candy Recipes

Never mind all that technical stuff. Let's get cooking! The following recipes come from my own practice or from old pioneer herbal adaptations. You may want to swap out sugars and creams until you settle on your own favorite flavors and combinations.

Lavender Caramel

Lavender caramel is a foody, fun treat that I discovered during a foray into an ethnic grocery store. Curious about what wonders I might create with such exotica as rose and pomegranate syrup, I came upon lavender caramel as a favorite—with rose caramel coming in as a close second.

2¼ cups sugar or coconut sugar

6 tablespoons butter (salted or unsalted per preference)

½ teaspoon salt

1¼ cups lavender syrup

2 cups heavy cream

If using a metal baking pan, grease lightly with olive oil. Line the pan with parchment or wax paper. Lightly grease the paper. Combine the sugar, butter, salt, and lavender syrup in a saucepan and stir over medium to high heat until the caramel reaches 248°F or the equivalent temperature for your altitude. It is important to stir constantly, so having something to watch or listen to while you stir may help you with this process. As soon as the caramel hits the desired temperature (or a patch of it passes the "hard ball" test in water), remove from heat and stir in the cream. After stirring in the cream, return to the burner and reheat to 248°F. As soon as the mixture reaches that temperature, remove from heat altogether. Using oven mitts and moving very carefully (hot sugar burns like crazy!), pour the mixture into the pan. Allow to cool for 8 hours. After cooling, cut into smaller pieces. Wax paper makes wonderful caramel candy wrapping. Makes about 5 dozen chews.

Horehound Lozenges

People visiting old-timey candy stores may encounter horehound candies and lozenges, often in packages displaying a historic-looking font. While sold as a root beer–like flavored treat, horehound has a long tradition of treating minor respiratory ailments. Making it from scratch takes some finesse: you have to extract the plant before you add the sugars, so do this when you're thinking very clearly.

    1 cup fresh horehound leaves

    1 cup water

    2 cups honey or maple syrup

If using a metal pan, lightly grease it with olive or coconut oil. Simmer the horehound in a saucepan for 20 minutes. Allow to cool, then strain out the horehound, pressing on the leaves with a wooden spoon to get out as much fluid as possible. Add the syrup or honey to the saucepan, and, stirring constantly, boil to the hard crack phase, about 330°F. Add a small amount of cold water if the mixture crystallizes. Pour the candy into a pan and score the surface as soon as it is cool enough to touch safely. (Proceed very carefully!)

After completely cooled, cut apart the candies and store in old mint tins or cellophane bags. Makes about 3 dozen candies.

Licorice

Many people have a hate relationship with anise and licorice flavors. That's okay—it's like cilantro, where genetically you have a taste for it or you don't. For those that do love anise flavors, this is an old-school herbal treat.

8 tablespoons butter

1¾ cups molasses

½ cup goat's milk

⅛ tsp salt

¾ cup whole wheat flour

1½ tablespoons aniseed extract or
    ¼ teaspoon anise essential oil

Black food coloring (if desired)

If using metal or glass, line a baking dish with parchment or wax paper. In a large saucepan, bring the butter, molasses, milk, and salt to a boil. Heat to 265°F or your altitude equivalent. Remove from heat immediately and stir in flour, extract, and food coloring. Pour into baking dish. Allow to chill until firm, around 35 minutes.

Once cooled, cut into ¼-inch thick ropes and twist to shape if desired. (Candy squares are also okay.) Line up on baking sheets and allow to chill for another 30 minutes until set. Makes about 2 dozen 6-inch whips.

Herbal Truffles

There are a few choice ways you might want to add herbal flavor to this quick-mix truffle recipe. You can infuse an herbal flavor by letting the herb sit in oil for a set period of time, you can simply use premade flavoring extracts or minute doses of essential oils, or you can, if you like the flavor of an herb enough, simply stir about a tablespoon of the herb into the chocolate about an hour into its cooling phase. While often truffles involve making ganache icing and complicated operations, this just focuses on the simple pleasure of chocolate, not on intense artistry.

For this example, I am sharing a method for making orange peel–infused truffles. Keep paper towels or a dish towel handy for the rolling phase; it's a sticky business.

To make the orange peel infusion:

Collect discarded orange peels in a mason jar. Pour safflower or sunflower oil on the peels, filling to the top. Close the jar well. Allow to sit in the sun for no more than one week, shaking daily.

To make the chocolate:

  4 ounces baking chocolate

  2 tablespoons butter

  1–2 tablespoons orange peel–infused safflower oil

  2–3 tablespoons coconut sugar, run through a coffee
    grinder

Combine the ingredients in a microwave-safe bowl. Heat in 30 second intervals until melted. Stir well and place in refrigerator overnight. Roll out and dip in powdered sugar mixed with cinnamon or equivalent flavor. Makes about 3 dozen chocolates.

Marshmallows

Marshmallows are the grand finale of all candy making. They require patience, attention, and, usually, decent cooking equipment. The white puffs that float in your hot chocolate were actually named after the white stuff that used to appear when someone boiled the marshmallow plant. This recipe brings back the classic.

    1 cup water

    1 tablespoon powdered marshmallow root

    1 packet unflavored gelatin

    1 cup honey or coconut sugar

    Pinch of salt

Line a pan with wax or parchment paper. Oil both the pan and the paper.

In a saucepan, bring water to a boil. Add the marshmallow root and stir for 5–7 minutes. Refrigerate until cool. Strain the powder out of the solution and reserve half the water in a mixing bowl. Add gelatin and stir thoroughly. Place the other half of the water in a saucepan with the honey and salt. Heat to 240°F and remove from heat. Use a hand mixer or stand mixer and beat the marshmallow and gelatin mix on low. Slowly add the hot marshmallow and honey mix. Once fully combined, whip on high for 5–10 minutes.

Allow to cool overnight. You may wish to sprinkle lavender or lemon verbena over the top. After cooled, cut into squares and store in a cellophane bag or airtight container. Makes about 1 dozen smallish marshmallows.

The candy-making basics are all about temperature, stirring, cooling, and patience. Once you master basic herb extractions—or just skip straight to premade extracts—you are well on your way to your own herbal sweet treat creations. Now that new syrups and sweeteners are becoming available, there is a world of flavors waiting for your experiments.

Resources

Ehler, James T. "Silicone Cookware Safety." Foodreference .com. Accessed August 8, 2016. http://www.foodreference .com/html/silicone-cookware-safety-310.html.

Raquel. "Vegan Cashew Cream Caramels." *My California Roots* (blog). Accessed August 8, 2016. http://mycaliforniaroots .com/vegan-cashew-cream-caramels-recipe/.

Rombauer, Irma S., and Marion Rombauer Becker. *Joy of Cooking.* New York: Simon and Schuster, 1975.

Tiffany. "Coconut Simple Syrups." *Coconut Mama* (blog). Accessed August 8, 2016. http://thecoconutmama.com /coconut-simple-syrup/.

Diana Rajchel *is a witch, psychic reader, and practitioner of the dark arts of community building. She has practiced witchcraft for twenty years and cohosts the YouTube show* Psychic Witch Talk. *She is the author of* Divorcing a Real Witch *and a forthcoming title on urban magic. She lives in San Francisco, California. You can find out more on http://dianarajchel.com.*

Edible Flowers

by Charlie Rainbow Wolf

If you're at all interested in growing herbs, you'll already be familiar with how the leaves add aroma
and flavor to your cooking dishes.
Most growing guides will tell you
to pinch off the flower buds so that
the nutrients—and therefore the
taste—stay in the leaves. However,
you might want to think twice about
pinching back all the flower buds.
Some of those flowers are actually
gourmet delights in themselves.

Just like any fruit, vegetable, or
herb, the flower blossoms come in a
variety of colors, fragrances, and even
spices. You could think that this is a
cool idea for a garnish or a tea, but you
can go beyond that. Think of squash
blossoms stuffed with mushroom

pâté, decadent Turkish delight candies made from rose petals, and chive blossoms added to your savory bread dough recipes. Once you start thinking outside the box, you'll come up with some very creative—and delicious—ideas indeed!

A Word of Caution

While it's a fun and perhaps novel concept to eat flowers, there are some precautions that need to be taken, for not all blossoms are good for you. First, make sure that the flower is actually edible. If you have any doubt, leave it out! There are many good reference books on edible flowers, and if this is something that takes your fancy, then please consult them and make sure that you're acting not just with inventiveness but also with responsibility.

There can even be issues with flowers that you know are safe to eat. If you've purchased them from a garden center, they could be treated with herbicides or pesticides. If you are wild-gathering them, make sure you wash them thoroughly, as you never know what wild animal was near. It's also possible that the wildflowers along the roadside verges have been sprayed—they've certainly been exposed to car exhaust and other road fumes.

Make sure that you're only eating the part of the plant that is recommended. This is usually the petals, so you may have to "clean" the flower by picking the petals away from the rest of the receptacle or removing the reproductive parts. Some parts of the petals are bitter, too—roses and dandelions, for example.

A bit of care and attention during preparation can save you a lot of disappointment during consumption! It's also common sense to avoid any plant that you're allergic to, unless you're going to consume it as part of a doctor-monitored allergy desensitisation program.

Delectable Edibles

Borage

My friends all call it "star flower," but I know this plant as borage—*Borago officinalis*, to be exact. You may have had tomato juice or a Pimm's cup served with borage leaves, but the flowers are just as wonderful. Their cooling cucumber flavor makes a delightful diversion from the usual garnishes, especially when it comes to iced teas and lemonades.

It's possible to crystallize the flowers of the borage plant with sugar in much the same way as violet petals. The taste is very different, so experiment before covering a cake with them! Add the flowers to your designer herbal vinegars. They're captivating when mixed into a salad, and they make an absolutely divine jelly that is very sweet and unusual. People either love it or loathe it—there doesn't seem to be any sitting on the fence when it comes to borage jelly!

Dandelion

All parts of the plant are edible. A coffee-like drink is sometimes made from the roasted root, and those who have spent time in Great Britain might have seen the soda pop called dandelion and burdock. If you have any burdock root, it is possible—although not easy—to make it at home (our first attempt resembled sweet dishwater). The young leaves can be added to salads or even stews, and the brilliant yellow flowerhead has a number of uses.

When using the flowers, every bit of green needs to be removed—and it can be very tedious to separate all the yellow petals! This is imperative if you're going to avoid bitterness in your recipes, though. Dandelion wine is a very popular home brew. Adding dandelions and honey to your oatmeal cookie batter makes a quirky variation on this traditional recipe.

Hibiscus

If you're at all into herbal teas, you're probably already familiar with the rich floral essence of hibiscus flowers. *Hibiscus syriacus* is easy to grow and perennial in many places. The flowers don't bloom for long, but they're both beautiful and useful when it comes to kitchen creations.

Hibiscus is used in many regions for both sweet and savory dishes because it's flavor isn't unlike that of cranberry. This makes it ideal for that sweet-tart combination. Boiling hibiscus flowers and cinnamon with some sugar into a syrup makes a delightful cordial. Steamed and sautéed flowers make a unique substitute for meat in vegetarian recipes. Try hibiscus enchiladas or add some sweet potatoes and salad vegetables to make a different kind of wrap.

Lavender

You probably already know how valuable lavender is as a calming herb, and you might have gathered and dried lavender flower heads to add to sachets for dresser drawers and hope chests. Both the leaves and the flowers are also edible, with the flower's piquancy not being quite so bold. It's the English lavender (*Lavandula angustifolia*) that is the most suitable and popular for culinary uses.

Lavender may surprise you, for while it is definitely floral in both scent and taste when it's used in cooking, it also imparts a slightly citrus note. Like lilac, lavender added to your granulated sugar gives it a unique variation, it makes a tasty and colorful addition to salads and desserts, and it can be used to make Turkish delight candy and interesting jellies or sorbets.

The longer you dry lavender flowers, the stronger their influence will be in your recipes, so adjust the amount accordingly. Less is always more, because too much will turn your dish into cologne!

Lilac

Lilac wine might be the first thing that pops into your mind when you think about consuming these heady flowers, but it's not their only use. They are even more versitile than lavender. The best variety of lilac to use is the pale, lavender-colored old-fashioned lilac (*Syringa vulgaris*), but the deeper purple and the white varieties are just as useful. They may not have quite as strong a scent, though, so take that into consideration. It's time-consuming to remove the actual four-petaled blossom from the cluster of blooms, but it's worth it.

Lilacs are sweet, richly perfumed, and very pretty when used as decorations on cakes and other sweets. Add some fresh petals to your summertime lemonade for a fascinating contrast from the usual presentation. If you put some of the lilac blossoms into your sugar, it will impart a wonderfully sweet and provocative flavor to the stored granules—and that makes cakes and drinks very intriguing indeed! Finally, the blooms can be simmered down with sugar and pectin to make a delightful translucent mauve jelly that will add a touch of the exotic to any piece of toast or teacake.

Marigolds

Marigolds and calendulas (*Calendula officinalis*) can be used in much the same way as nasturtiums. They're very similar, being both tangy and peppery. The colors are similar, too, and add brightness for the eye as well as some zing for the tongue. They make a very warming addition to mushroom soup and to curries and stews.

Ground dried marigold petals to a powder and use them instead of saffron for coloring. They're colorful and warming in stews and stir-fries, too. Try them in a simple homemade mayonnaise to spice up a summer salad. Don't let the vibrant color put you off. You'll more than be rewarded by the warm taste and the interesting texture when you add marigolds to your favorite savory recipe.

Nasturtium

Nasturtiums add both flavor and visual appeal to a variety of recipes. They're also incredibly high in vitamins A, C, and D. The best types to grow for a kitchen garden are *Tropaeolum majus*, which trails, and *Tropaeolum minus*, which is more bushy. Nasturtiums are very easy to grow from seed, and they make a great garden companion to other plants, too.

Nasturtiums seem to brighten up any corner of the garden where they're growing, and they can do the same in cooking, too. All parts of the plant are edible. The flowers are somewhat nutty with more than a hint of pepper's heat, and they are useful with savory dishes. Add them to simple corn soup, use them to garnish a dessert, or pop them in your favorite chai for an extra hint of zest and warmth.

Rose

My favorite of all plants when it comes to floral consumption has got to be the old-fashioned rose, *Rosa rugosa*. The blossoms are beautiful to look at, their fragrance is sweet, and once the flowers are finished, the rose hips come with their own grace and flavor. The hips of the rugosa rose have an abundance of vitamins and minerals, including—but not limited to—vitamins C, A, and E and the B complex; minerals iron and selenium; and other organic compounds, such as pectin, lycopene, and beta-carotene, as well as antioxidants. Rose hip syrup, rose hip cordial, and rose hip jelly are among our autumn harvest staples.

Roses aren't limited to hips, though. The petals are sweet and fragrant, and as I mentioned previously, it's rose petal water that is used to make the traditional pink Turkish delight candy. Pinch off the white base of the petals before using them, as these can be very bitter. Rose petals can be used in sorbet, in jelly, and sugarcoated as a decoration on cakes and other sweet things. A decoction of the petals also makes a very good skin toner when dabbed on with a cotton ball!

Squash

The beautiful yellow and orange flowers of squash plants certainly brighten up the garden, and they do so for the table, too. Zucchini, summer squash, courgette, winter squash, pumpkin, and gourd are all members of the *Cucurbita* genus and are all edible. You'll find the fruits of these plants in most grocery stores, but what about eating the flowers?

One of the most divine ways to prepare the flower is to remove the reproductive organs, fill the bloom with a tasty pâté, and then close it and bake it or batter it and fry it. In fact, the blossoms are lovely battered and deep fried even without the filling! These versatile petals can be added to sauces, soups, stews, and salads. Somehow squash blossoms just seem to be a natural companion for cheese and nut butters. They make a great pizza topping and can be used in quesadillas, thrown in with an omelette or scrambled egg, and added to spinach and artichoke dip for a new twist on an old favorite.

It's usually the zucchini blossoms that are eaten, but the blossoms of pumpkin and other squashes will work in a similar way. Sometimes they're found in grocery stores or farmers' markets, but it's easy to grow your own. Just remember to pick the male flowers so that you get the fruit from the females, and don't get carried away picking the blooms—you want to leave some males there so that the rest of the plants get fertilized.

Violets

Wild violets are a member of the *Violaceae* family, which has over 500 species, including what we know as the sweet violet, the dog violet, and even pansies. Don't be tempted to grow the garden center pansies for your table, though! It's the sweet violet that grows in the wild—*Viola odorata*—that you'll want to find for your recipes.

Violets can be used much the same way as lilac and lavender—in fact, there's a candy in the United Kingdom called Parma Violets, little sweet violet-scented disks that come in a small cellophane tube. A syrup made from violets and sugar was a traditional cordial on Mothering Sunday. It's a wonderful base for a drink, and a few drops added to royal icing or fondant produce the most interesting color and taste.

Violet petals make an intriguing addition to salads as well as a colorful and delightful garnish to meat. The flowers dipped in beaten egg white and then in finely ground sugar are beautiful toppings for cupcakes and other sweets; they just need a bit of careful handling and attention paid to them while they're drying. It's worth the effort to see the finished result, though!

Conclusion

Whether you're looking to experiment with something new and different, trying to find a way to use the garden's over-abundance, or just fancy a change from your normal menu, cooking with flowers is an adventure. Be warned: it gets a bit addictive if you let it. Take it beyond a garnish, and titillate your taste buds by throwing in a different texture and flavor. From drinks to desserts, from junket to jellies, Mother Nature really does provide a bountiful harvest—once you know what to do with it!

Charlie Rainbow Wolf *is happiest when she is creating something, especially if it can be made from items that others have cast aside. Pottery, writing, knitting, astrology, and tarot are her deepest interests, but she happily confesses that she's easily distracted because life offers so many wonderful things to explore. She is an advocate of organic gardening and cooking and lives in the Midwest with her husband and special-needs Great Danes. Visit www.charlie rainbow.com.*

Herbs for
Health and
Beauty

Herbs for Eye Health

≫ by James Kambos ≪

At least 21 million Americans suffer some type of vision loss due to cataracts, glaucoma, and macular degeneration.

I am one of those people.

At a recent eye exam, my optometrist gave me the news that I have age-related macular degeneration. As an artist and a writer, that's not what I wanted to hear. My first thought was that some type of surgery would be recommended. Instead, the optometrist said the first course of treatment would be a vitamin/mineral/herbal supplement. He recommended one that I now take daily. It contains vitamins and minerals, but it also contains bilberry and grape seed extracts.

I began to feel a sense of hope knowing that herbs could help retain and perhaps even improve my damaged eyesight. It was also empowering to have a mainstream medical professional suggest herbs as part of my treatment. As I searched to find which herbs could help maintain healthy eyes, I began to feel I had some control over my treatment.

Let's take a look at the three major causes of vision loss I mentioned earlier. It should be noted that studies are beginning to indicate that these conditions can be helped to some degree by using herbal supplements.

Cataracts

Although rarely dangerous, cataracts can be found in over 90 percent of people by age sixty-five. A cataract is a clouding of the lens of the eye, caused by breakdown of proteins in the lens. Cataracts cause hazy vision. Herbs can't cure cataracts, but some herbs, which I'll discuss later, can slow their formation.

Glaucoma

This is a disease that damages the eye's optic nerve. It happens when fluid builds up in the front of the eye. The extra fluid increases pressure, which can damage the optic nerve. This can lead to the loss of peripheral vision. It can steal eyesight gradually. Though rare, it can be found in infants. It usually occurs in middle-aged to older adults. Early treatment can prevent blindness, and certain herbs can be a part of that treatment.

Macular Degeneration (MD)

Macular degeneration is also called age-related macular degeneration (AMD). AMD causes more vision loss than cataracts and glaucoma combined. It's caused by the deterioration of the central area of the retina (macula). It can rob a person of their central vision if left untreated.

There are two types, dry and wet. Dry AMD is more common and progresses slowly. Wet AMD is more serious and is characterized by the abnormal growth of blood vessels under the macula. They may leak blood and fluid, causing rapid vision loss. AMD usually occurs in people middle aged and older. There is no cure; progression of AMD is controlled with the use of doctor-recommended dietary supplements containing vitamins, minerals, and herbal extracts.

Lutein and Zeaxanthin

Before we get to specific herbs which help improve eye health, I want to mention lutein (LOO-teen) and zeaxanthin (zee-uh-ZAN-thin). These two carotenoids are antioxidants. Of the 600 carotenoids found in nature, only these two are found in the macula of the eye. They aid in filtering damaging wavelengths of light and maintain healthy cells. The body doesn't make them, so eating foods including herbs that contain them will help your eyes stay healthy.

Herbs That Aid Eye Health

Bilberry

This is an herb that grows in northern Europe. Its dark purple berry has been used as a medicinal herb since the sixteenth century. Today it's used to treat cataracts, glaucoma, and macular degeneration. It's not found in the United States, so we have to use bilberry extract. You may also find bilberry powder. The extract can be purchased in capsules alone or be included in a vitamin/mineral supplement.

*In recent years, American consumers have spent an incredible
$28 million annually on bilberry extract, making it one of
America's top-selling herbal supplements.*

Blueberries
Delicious blueberries are a fruit that is becoming recognized
as a "superfood." Blueberries are the American cousin to the
European bilberry just mentioned. They're full of nutrients
that aid eye health, especially fighting macular degeneration.
Eat them on your cereal, as a snack—heck, eat them anytime.

Eyebright
This small, flowering, annual herb, as the name suggests, has
been used to treat various eye ailments for years. However,
please take it internally only. Used as an eyewash, it can ir-
ritate the eye. The extract is sometimes found in vitamin/
mineral supplements for the eyes. It can also be taken as a tea.
In liquid form, a few drops may be added to water and taken
internally. It nourishes the eye, helps prevent cataracts, and
slows the progression of macular degeneration.

Gingko Biloba
The extract derived from this ancient tree is believed to control
glaucoma and macular degeneration. It can be taken in capsule form alone or as an ingredient in a vitamin/mineral supplement. In liquid form it may be taken with a small amount
of water.

Grape Seed Extract

This powerful antioxidant is quickly absorbed by the body. It can prevent or slow the formation of cataracts and macular degeneration. It's available in capsule form alone or as an ingredient in vitamin/mineral supplements.

Leafy Green Herbs

Many leafy green herbs are a good source of lutein and zeaxanthin, which I mentioned earlier. Fresh or dried are fine, but fresh is best. At the top of the list is basil, so all you pesto lovers, get busy. Others on this honor roll include parsley, thyme, oregano, and sage. Let's not forget lettuce, which is also considered an herb.

Raspberries

Eaten fresh or taken as a tea, raspberries can help our eyes process light and help us see in dim light. Extracts derived from the leaves are found in some herbal eye supplements.

Special Considerations

Before you begin taking any herbal supplement for eye health, talk to a medical professional. Let them know if you smoke or are pregnant. Some herbal supplements, such as bilberry, can thin the blood, so consult with your doctor if you're taking any anticoagulant medication such as Coumadin or Eliquis.

By bringing herbal treatments and science together, perhaps a cure for eye disease is in sight.

James Kambos *raises herbs and wildflowers in his garden. He also raises vegetables and enjoys cooking. He's an artist and a writer living in Ohio.*

Wild and Weedy First Aid

by Doreen Shababy

I'd like you to meet a few friends of mine, some of whom willingly travel over hill and dale wherever you want to go, while another needs just a little coaxing to get it to join in. These friends—plantain, chickweed, heal-all, yarrow, and cottonwood— are my five favorite weeds for first aid, and they are just the friends you want hanging out near the garden, along the hiking trail, or wherever else you might find yourself faced with bites, stings, scratches, or other common (but not serious) injuries. I will introduce you to each of these plants individually and explain how to make a simple oil extract using weeds, but first I will discuss the question that I know has been burning in your mind: What is a "weed"?

What Are Weeds?

Native (indigenous) wild plants are generally not "weeds." Weeds are usually introduced or naturalized plants, well-established but originating from another area of the country or another part of the world. To quote from *Rodale's All-New Encyclopedia of Organic Gardening*, "fast, tough, and common—that's all it takes to earn a plant the name *weed*."

As any gardener knows, weeds are opportunistic: they know how to take advantage of a situation. Weeds are often drought-tolerant, surviving and even thriving in very dry conditions (like mullein, *Verbascum thapsus*, which is another useful weed but not included in this article). In addition, weeds are very prolific, producing abundant seeds or easily rooting from broken pieces of stem (chickweed is a good example). Weeds such as knapweed, the wild cousin of the bachelor's button, can also send out vigorous root systems, sometimes to the detriment of neighboring plants.

Weeds are plants that greedy chemical corporate interests and county governments with no foresight have convinced people are "undesirable" and thus encourage the use of dangerous herbicides to remove them; do not be fooled by these tactics. They are not the methods you're looking for.

As far as I know, our weeds for first aid are not considered "noxious" weeds slated for slow death by the county spray schedule.

Weeds Are Useful

Weeds are indeed useful, and most are worthy of the status of "herb." They offer healing for the body, inside and out, and also the mind (consider St. John's wort). Weeds are food; they offer everything from soup to nuts. Bees create wildflower honey from weeds, including the above mentioned "noxious" knapweed. Weeds can produce cordage and other fibers; for instance, the trailing blackberry, which can grow into a dense tangle after excavation or logging, was once used to bind roof thatching. Some weeds are indicator species, helping determine soil type, sun exposure, deep or shallow levels of moisture and drainage, and so on. Weeds are also useful as erosion control, helping prevent damaging water run-off.

Weeds are companion plants and allies for garden veggies and hosts to beneficial insects. Their flowers encourage bees into the garden, of benefit to all neighboring plants, especially orchard trees.

And did I mention weeds can be used for first aid?

Where to Pick (and Where *Not* to Pick) Weeds
Do pick in backyard or garden areas, because this is where you are likely to find these weeds. Pick them anywhere you find the plants (within the parameters set forth below).

Do pick weeds or herbs where you have permission, from the landowner as well as the plants.

Do not pick weeds along railroad easements or roadsides, even if they look healthy. Some plants absorb heavy metals from fuel exhaust. Some trees, such as the ginkgo, are actually planted near freeways and interstates to absorb CO_2 and air pollution, as are silver maple and several types of pine. While these trees aren't on our weedy first-aid list, they show us that plants absorb what is in their surroundings, and no amount of washing on the outside can eliminate what has been absorbed on the inside.

Do not pick plants in wildlife refuges, state parks, or any protected, sensitive, or overburdened area. United States National

Forests may require you to obtain a permit if you intend to harvest more than a modest amount.

Do not pick in areas frequented or recently "visited" by animals. Keep an eye out.

Do not pick in areas sprayed by herbicide. How can you tell? You may detect a chemical odor. You will see certain plants abnormally shriveled for no obvious reason, wilting or turning brown before its normal growing season is over. It's a sickening feeling knowing that this method of weed control is so widespread and accepted. Please do what you can to encourage others to try alternative methods.

Weeds for First Aid

My five favorite weeds for first aid will help remedy ant bites or bee stings (unless you are allergic, in which case you already have your EpiPen handy); they also make a good mosquito bite remedy as well as repellant. These weeds can soothe minor scrapes and burns, can ease the pain of bruises and muscle aches, and can make for absorbent wound dressing.

Just a little note here about terminology: botanical names are based on a last-name-first, first-name-last system and are italicized when spelled out. In other words, my name would be written *Shababy doreen* in botany-speak. When I talk about a species, what I am actually referring to is its first name (species); certain plants share the same last name (genus), like a family.

This all helps a great deal with identification because you will know that as a "family" they share a certain characteristic, such as serrated leaves or air roots.

Let's meet our new friends!

Broadleaf and Lanceleaf Plantain
(*Plantago major* and *P. lanceolata*)

These plants, which can be used interchangeably for our purposes here, are native to Europe, and the broadleaf plantain is sometimes called "white man's footprint" in North America since it grew wherever the immigrants journeyed; use by Native American herbalists is widely recognized. Plantain leaf is a topical-relief analgesic that is anti-inflammatory. It contains mucilage, which soothes injured skin; tannins, which tighten and protect; and allantoin, a compound also found in comfrey (*Symphytum officinale*), which encourages the healing of wounds and rehydrates injured tissue.

Use plantain leaf for external skin irritations, stings and bites, and anything that itches. Simply squish and apply, which basically creates an herbal poultice; you can even chew it up into a pulp and slather it on your boo-boo. Plantain makes a good healing balm, either alone or with all the other plants on this list.

Chickweed (*Stellaria media*)

Sometimes called starwort ("wort" is an old-timey word for "herb," as in "wortcunning"), chickweed is native to Europe, although there are some species native to North America. We're talking common, weedy chickweed here. As a salad weed, the taste is mild and very agreeable, delicious when lush and green; do not eat in excessive quantities, as chickweed contains saponins, which could cause stomach upset.

For immediate first aid, this vigorous but dainty-looking weed makes an excellent cooling poultice for minor injuries, especially slivers, and is also useful for blisters. Analgesic, anti-inflammatory chickweed poultice can be placed on bruises and sprains. In addition, and since it usually grows in abundance, chickweed poultice or fresh juice could be applied to large areas as for sunburn, skin conditions such as eczema and psoriasis, nettles rash, or itching of any kind. It has a very soothing effect. Use the leaves and stems for these remedies.

Heal-All (*Prunella vulgaris*)

This plant is also called self-heal and is native to Eurasia; there is also a native North American species, *Prunella vulgaris* ssp. *lanceolata*, or lance-leaf self-heal, and either can be used. Heal-all makes a soothing poultice and eases the inflammation and pain of bites, scrapes, and bruises. Use the whole aboveground plant.

Prunella is also a cultivated garden flower, offering many color and foliage choices for the adventurous green thumb. It is an easy plant to grow.

This purple-flowered weed is a member of the mint family—it has square stems but little aroma—and contains betulinic acid, a triterpene that shows definite anti-inflammatory activity in addition to other properties; this compound is also found in the bark of white birch trees, *Betula alba* (for which the acid is named), and rosemary herb. You can even take a few stems of heal-all, twist them together a little bit to soften them, and lay them directly across the forehead and closed eyes for a while to experience a gentle cooling effect after a day of too much sun and fun.

Yarrow (*Achillea millefolium*)

Also called woundwort and carpenter's herb (clues to its usefulness), yarrow, originally native to Europe and Eurasia, is now circumboreal in distribution, meaning it grows in all regions of the Northern Hemisphere from the temperate zones to the Arctic Circle. All these northern cultures have a tradition of using yarrow for much more than first aid in their herbal materia medica, including remedies for fever and infection.

Yarrow flower and leaf contain aspirin-like compounds as well as the anti-inflammatory azulene and make for a useful pain-relieving poultice on bruises. The fuzzy fern-like leaf—*millefolium* means "thousand-leaf"—is astringent and can be used to halt the bleeding of minor injuries and nosebleeds. Yarrow leaf can be squished and applied to mosquito bites as well as rubbed on the hair and arms for a mosquito repellent.

Some people who are allergic to ragweed may also be allergic to yarrow, and others may experience contact dermatitis. (If this happens, you can treat it with chickweed or heal-all!)

Cottonwood (*Populus trichocarpa, P.* spp.)

This is our first-aid friend that needs a little encouragement to get her to share her healing properties. All poplars, including quaking aspen, contain salicin, from which our modern analgesic aspirin is developed. "Salicin" is related to the name of willow genus, *Salix*. (See what I mean about learning botany-speak? The relationship of words is very enlightening.)

The resinous, aromatic leaf buds, collected in late winter and early spring before the actual leaf emerges, make an incredibly fragrant oil extract, a truly sensual experience. Just walking outside on a spring morning, you can smell the fragrance in the air, balsam-like yet sweet and very intoxicating, at least for this herbalist. The oil can be made into a balm by adding natural beeswax to the oil extract of this or basically any plant. Some people call cottonwood resin the balm of Gilead. Cottonwood oil or balm can be rubbed into achy joints, sore muscles, or tired feet and can be used on any tender tissue, including burns and hemorrhoids, for a natural pain-reliever.

Making an Oil Extract with Weeds

This is a fun project and one with which the whole family can be involved, from picking the weeds to testing the final product.

First, have your equipment ready. I use a mini slow cooker, which is a fairly inexpensive investment, especially if you can pick one up at a yard sale, but you could use any small, nonreactive saucepan such as enamel or stainless steel. (The heating method will be slightly different than for the slow cooker.) You will also need a wooden spoon, a strainer or sieve, a funnel, and either a sharp knife and cutting board or scissors and a bowl. As for the ingredients, you will need:

2–3 cups of the discussed weeds, chopped or snipped

16 ounces (or more) of olive oil or coconut oil

2–3 ounces of grated beeswax

Place the plant material in your crock. Cover with oil. Do you want to boil your weeds in oil? No, you do not.

If using the slow cooker, place the weeds and the oil together in the crock, cover with the lid, turn to the lowest setting, and leave it until it starts to get warm. Then remove the lid and stir. Let this crock simmer away for a few hours—in the case of cottonwood buds, I let it go for a couple days, shutting it off overnight (covering with a cloth), and resuming the next morning.

If using a saucepan over the stovetop, you want to get just the barest of simmers going, and you may find you have to turn off the heat now and then to keep it from getting too hot. Heat is important, though, because it helps the moisture in the plant material evaporate; otherwise, you will end up with rotten leafy matter floating in oil—disgusting! Too much heat and you scorch the herbs. Making herbal oil extracts is a very organic, experiential process, but it is fun and not difficult.

You will know the oil is finished when it has turned dark green from the plants (and hopefully not brown from too much heat) and when the plants aren't so green anymore but rather pale in comparison to their earlier freshness. (The cottonwood bud oil will be deep red.) Let the oil cool for about an hour, then carefully strain into a very clean jar or bottle for later use.

If making a salve or balm (a hardened oil extract), strain the oil while still warm into a jar or bowl, wipe out the pan to remove any debris that might remain, and return the oil to the pan. Stir in some grated beeswax: 2–3 ounces for 1 pint of olive oil extract, or a little less for coconut oil. Test by putting a spoonful onto a saucer, placing in the fridge for a few minutes, and checking the hardness; add more beeswax if too runny or add a spoonful of oil if too hard. Test again. Carefully ladle into small dispensing containers for home use and gifting.

Take a Walk on the Wild and Weedy Side

I have chosen plantain, chickweed, heal-all, yarrow, and cottonwood as my five favorite weeds for first aid because they are so common. These plants can be found over most of North America, and they adapt to their surroundings. I discovered diminutive yarrows and velvety-leaved violets growing out on Smokey Bear Flats in California, which are over 9,000 feet in elevation and very dry. Plantain grows through the cracks of every sidewalk in the United States. Heal-all is a common sight in grassy meadows and at the edge of woodlands. Chickweed can actually become a pest in the garden bed, but when you find it growing out back near the water spigot, it's worthy of a cheese and grainy mustard sandwich.

And as for the popular *Populus*, the cottonwood tree will grow just about anywhere it can take root, which is why I call it a weed; it's common, opportunistic, and generous with its medicine.

Resources

Bradley, Fern Marshall, Barbara W. Ellis, eds. *Rodale's All-New Encyclopedia of Organic Gardening: The Indispensible Resource for Every Gardener*. Emmaus, PA: Rodale Press, 1993.

Hitchcock, Leo C. and Arthur Cronquist. *Flora of the Pacific Northwest*. Seattle: University of Washington Press, 1973.

De la Foret, Rosalee. "Cottonwood Benefits." Herbs with Rosalee. December 27, 2015. www.herbalremedies advice.org/cottonwood-benefits.html.

Kowalchik, Claire and William H. Hylton, eds. *Rodale's Illustrated Encyclopedia of Herbs*. Emmaus, PA: Rodale Press, 1987.

Lakshmi T, et al. "Yarrow (Achillea millefolium Linn.) A Herbal Medicinal Plant with Broad Therapeutic Use—A Review." *International Journal of Pharmaceutical Sciences Review and Research* 9, no. 2 (July–August 2011): 136–41. http://globalresearchonline.net/journalcontents/volume 9issue2/Article-022.pdf.

Moore, Michael. *Medicinal Plants of the Mountain West.* Santa Fe, NM: Museum of New Mexico Press, 1979.

———. *Medicinal Plants of the Pacific West.* Santa Fe, NM: Red Crane Books, 1995.

Shababy, Doreen. *The Wild & Weedy Apothecary.* Woodbury, MN: Llewellyn Publications, 2010.

Plants for a Future. "Stellaria media—(L.) Vill." Plants for a Future. Accessed on October 15, 2016. http://www.pfaf .org/User/plant.aspx?LatinName=Stellaria+media.

Weed, Susun S. *Healing Wise.* Woodstock, NY: Ash Tree Publishing, 1989.

Whelan, Richard. "Plantain." Richard Whelan: Medical Herbalist. Accessed October 15, 2016. http://www .rjwhelan.co.nz/herbs%20A-Z/plantain.html.

Doreen Shababy *is the author of* The Wild & Weedy Apothecary, *a book of herbal recipes and remedies. She has been using wild plants for food and medicine for decades, is an accomplished home cook, and has recently been making friends with food history and folklore. Doreen and her husband, Dave Veitch, run a herb business specializing in hand-crafted tinctures and salves. Visit them at www.wildnweedy.com. Visit Doreen at www.doreenshababy.com.*

Plant-Based Proteins and Meatless Meals: Not Just for Rabbits Anymore

⤳ by Mireille Blacke ⤳

I grew up heavily influenced by my Sicilian grandmother's cooking. As she stirred pots and created delicious meals, it was intriguing and amusing to hear her animated stories of her youth, many decades before the Internet. When I tell nutrition clients or students that humanity survived just fine before laptops, YouTube, Kindles, and smartphones, I glimpse now what my grandmother must have seen on my bemused face then. The difference is that my face was busy scarfing down eggplant-based dishes that would satisfy the most devoted carnivore.

Tradition and heritage remain a strong part of my professional life as well. As a registered dietitian (RD)

specializing in traditional and surgical weight loss, I've taught classes and educated my patients frequently in recent years on the role of culture in dietary choices. Every time I mention eggplant I remember my grandmother and wish that I could replicate that dish.

In discussing plant-based diets and protein sources, focusing on legumes, nuts, seeds, and whole grains, certain points are received better than others. While the notion of plant-based diets and healthier eating is appealing to many, the practice of it might be more challenging, especially when one is unfamiliar with plant-based protein foods and misinformation abounds in print and online.

Health Benefits of Plant-Based Foods

Numerous studies note that plant-based foods contain higher levels of important nutrients, such as vitamins, minerals, fiber, heart-healthy fats, and phytochemicals (health-promoting bioactive compounds found in plants), compared to animal food sources.[1] Further research into vegetarian eating patterns indicates that people who follow a plant-based diet tend toward lower incidences of obesity and reduced risk factors for cardiovascular disease, hypertension, type 2 diabetes, inflammation, immune dysfunction, and cancer (research on individual cancers is pending).[1] In addition, a plant-based eating style takes a lesser toll on the environment.[1] Just as every individual is a composite of overlapping and interacting biological, emotional, environmental, and cultural factors, the decision to follow a plant-based diet or switch to plant-based protein sources may be due to one or any number of these considerations.

Patients often ask me if plant-based diets provide adequate protein for their needs. Though individual protein needs vary based on age, gender, physical activity level, and health status, we all need protein to maintain muscle, bone mass, and a functioning immune system. While protein needs are adequately met by the "better protein package" of whole plant foods, some plant-based proteins are individually inadequate sources of one or more essential amino acids, the building blocks of protein that cannot be synthesized by the human body. In contrast, animal proteins provide a balance of all nine essential amino acids, such as lysine, which helps to synthesize protein in the body. But a well-balanced daily diet with a variety of whole plant foods, such as soyfoods (tofu, tempeh, and edamame), lentils, nut butters, and seitan, will ensure adequate amino acid intake and reduce risk for nutritional deficiencies.[2]

Aside from protein, nutrient deficiencies may develop by following a limited plant-based diet. Decreased or eliminated fish intake increases the risk of omega-3 fatty acid deficiency, and studies have shown those without a varied plant-based diet may have lower levels of vitamin B_{12}, calcium, and vitamin D_2. Maintaining adequate iron levels may be challenging; the heme form of iron from animal sources is absorbed more readily by humans than nonheme iron from plant sources. Increase your plant-based iron consumption by creating plates including tofu, leafy greens, legumes, and enriched cereals; select sprouted, soaked, or fermented beans, grains, and seeds when possible. In addition, you will enhance your iron absorption by pairing your iron-rich foods choices with sources of vitamin C, cooking with an iron skillet (really!), and avoiding calcium, tea, coffee, and cocoa for at least two hours after your ingestion of iron-containing foods.[2] As with meat-eaters, chronically inadequate intake of plant foods rich in vitamins B_{12} and D, iron, and calcium may require supplementation.

Going Global

Globally, plant-based foods remain the backbone of many traditional eating patterns in the forms of legumes, whole grains, nuts, seeds, herbs, spices, and regional fruits and vegetables. Most plant-based indigenous diets emphasized local, fresh, and seasonal ingredients and a minimum of processed foods.

Though Japanese eating patterns frequently incorporate fish, you will also find tofu, rice, green tea, and an assortment of pickled or steamed vegetables. In India, common dishes feature legumes such as lentils and peas, coupled with okra, potatoes, tomatoes, rice, my beloved eggplant, and copious herbs and spices. For example, bhindi masala is okra in onion-tomato curry. In West Africa, many of the ingredients mentioned are eaten daily, along with millet, corn, cassava, onions, peanuts, and chili peppers. Staples of the popular Mediterranean diet include beans, lentils, peas, nuts, heart-healthy olive oil, and a wide variety of vegetables, from artichokes to eggplant to zucchini.[3]

Meatless Meals and Plant-Based Snacks

There are easy, painless ways to integrate meat alternatives and plant-based proteins into your diet, even if you don't practice strict vegetarianism or veganism. Substituting plant-based proteins for your usual animal sources once or twice a week can offer dietary variety, lower intake of saturated fat and cholesterol, and provide health benefits. Meatless Monday programs encourage consumers to go meatless just one day per week for environmental and health benefits, and MyPlate (the modernized food pyramid) emphasizes loading up at least three-fourths of your plate with plant foods, based on the documented benefits from eating a plant-based diet.[3]

Plant-based diets and protein sources are increasingly popular, and with good reason. Simple substitutions of plant-based foods for animal sources as little as once or twice per week can lead to significant health benefits.

Legumes

Legumes include beans, peas, and lentils. Beans in particular are nutritious and economically efficient: dried beans cost about twenty-five cents per cup. Legume variety abounds with beans. Choose from black, red, navy, white, kidney, chickpea (garbanzo), lima, pinto, soybean (edamame), black-eyed pea, great northern, and fava. Your options multiply because beans are also available bagged, canned, frozen, and fresh. Choose beans with less sodium; if you select canned, rinse and drain the beans to remove up to 40 percent of the sodium.[4]

Try to eat at least three servings of legumes per day. Consider a hummus (made from chickpeas or red lentils) dip or wrap, scrambled tofu, peanut butter on whole wheat bread, bean burrito, veggie burger, lentil sloppy joes, pea risotto, and cereal with soymilk. Get creative with black bean brownies, tofu sriracha hummus, or roasted chickpeas. (See the online resources list for websites with recipe recommendations.)

Soyfoods

When it comes to plant-based eating, soyfoods (though classified as legumes) deserve their own section. Soy leads the pack of other plant-based foods for protein content.

Generally, when I have mentioned **tofu** (bean curd) over the years in nutrition counseling or classroom settings, I get "resistance face." It's not uncommon for people to have an aversion to tofu due to its white block appearance, soft, and cheese-like texture, and somewhat bland, neutral taste. But I contend that tofu can be a healthy, hidden ingredient in many dishes (e.g., replace sour cream in dips with silken tofu), and no one will be the wiser. I have made tofu sriracha hummus and a number of other tofu-based dishes with rave reviews from people who stated they couldn't stand tofu.

Tofu's versatility in cooking allows for inclusion in diverse dishes (from Thai curries to chocolate cream pie), due to its lack of competition with other flavors and its porous properties, which promote flavor absorption of foods prepared with it.[5] Tofu consistencies vary from extra firm, to firm, to soft, to silken. Softer tofu typically has lower fat content, and protein content varies as well. Use firm tofu in stir-fry dishes, in soups, or for grilling; choose soft tofu for blending or use in soups; and use silken tofu for pureed dishes and smoothies.[6] Tofu can also be used in recipes as a substitute for mayonnaise, eggs, sour cream, cream, cheese, and (obviously) meat.[5]

As tofu's lesser known cousin, **tempeh** is a versatile soybean cake that results from mixing soybeans with grains, followed by a fermentation process.[6] Tempeh's smoky, nutty flavor works well as an addition to soups, casseroles, pasta sauce, chilis, or on its own to be marinated, grilled, or eaten in sandwiches.[6]

In addition to tofu and tempeh, soyfoods include edamame, natto, okara, soymilk, soynuts (roasted soybeans), soy sprouts, and yuba. Whether fresh, frozen, in pods, shelled, or steamed, **edamame** can be used in soups, in stir-fries, in salads, and as an appetizer or snack.[6] Add roasted soybeans to salads or eat them as a snack. Use **soymilk** in smoothies and with cereal. Though **miso** and **soy sauces** (tamari, shoyu, and teriyaki) are also made from soy, they are typically low in protein, are extremely high in sodium, and should be used sparingly.[6]

An important note about soyfoods: Contradictory research into the link between soy and cancer risk has created controversy, has generated much misinformation over time, and has confused many a consumer and healthcare professional. Earlier studies conducted in rats do not hold up with current advanced clinical and epidemiological studies in humans, which consistently indicate that a moderate amount of soyfood consumption (two servings per day) does not increase a woman's risk of death or cancer recurrence. In addition, there is no evidence that the isoflavones in soy interfere with hormone-related treatment.[7] Ongoing research into soy consumption in humans has also clarified other common misconceptions: soyfoods are not linked to feminization in men, disrupted growth and reproductive development in infants, or inhibited thyroid function.[8]

Whole Grains

Whole grains are an important part of a balanced plant-based diet. Though it is technically a seed, **quinoa** surpasses many cereal grains in protein content (four grams per half cup) and can be used to create quinoa and black bean salad or substituted for bulgur to make quinoa and chickpea tabbouleh. Consider **oatmeal** for more than breakfast; try it as a thickener of soups and stews, added to meat loaf and meatballs in place of bread crumbs, or to top fruity desserts. Combining whole grains with beans will provide all essential amino acids (those not synthesized by the body), an adequate replacement to high-quality animal sources.[4]

As a meat analog made from wheat gluten, **seitan** has a neutral taste that is enhanced by the spices and flavors of other foods. As with most foods, it's advisable to read labels for sodium and fat content.

Nut and Seed Butters

As long as you are not allergic, your health may benefit from consumption of nut butters. Vary your nut butters for a range of nutritional impact: almond (vitamin E, calcium, potassium, phosphorus), pistachio (lutein, to lower LDL cholesterol), cashew (B vitamins), peanut (protein), and walnut (anti-inflammatory omega-3 fatty acids).[9] If butters aren't your thing, consider pureed nuts in dips and chilis, or nut oils for dipping, blending into dressing, or drizzling over food.[10]

Though nuts are a source of heart-healthy fat, eat them in moderation: a portion of walnuts is one ounce (fourteen halves). Consider sunflower butter (for protein, fiber, vitamin E, zinc, iron) or sesame seed tahini (for magnesium and iron) if you have a nut allergy.

Plant-Based Recipes

Tofu Sriracha Hummus
This recipe is adapted from House Foods Organic Tofu's recipe.

1 package extra firm tofu, drained and pressed

6 tablespoons lemon juice

1 15-ounce can garbanzo beans, drained

3 teaspoons garlic, minced

2 tablespoons sriracha sauce

½ cup olive oil

Salt and pepper to taste

Add tofu and lemon juice to bowl of food processor. Puree until smooth. Add remaining ingredients until blended. Season with salt and pepper to taste and serve.

Roasted Chickpeas

1 can chickpeas (garbanzo beans)

Dry seasoning of your choice (suggestions: cumin, garlic powder, black pepper, paprika, cayenne, cinnamon, Italian seasoning, cocoa, salt)

Nonstick cooking spray

Drain and rinse the chickpeas. Pat the chickpeas down with paper towels until they are as dry as possible. (Note: cooking time may increase significantly if chickpeas are not dry.) Spray shallow baking pan with nonstick cooking spray. Place dry chickpeas in shallow baking pan and cover with seasoning of your choice.

Bake at 350°F for an hour or until chickpeas are crisp. Chickpeas will become crunchier as they cool.

In a Nutshell

There are some misconceptions that a plant-based diet is boring, "rabbit food," bland, labor intensive, and expensive. It doesn't have to be, and the easiest way to maintain lifestyle changes is to keep them simple and basic. Maybe you don't want to give up the whole hog? Some people make adjustments to go-to dishes (beef tacos) and create new family favorites (bean burritos). Others follow a primarily plant-based diet but still allow for dairy products (milk and eggs). If you have a favorite ethnic cuisine or restaurant, use vegetarian dishes for inspiration, like Indian dal (simmered peas) or Greek barley biscuits (paximadia) with tomatoes and oregano.[3] Flavor your dishes with herbs and spices, and use fresh, local, and seasonal produce when possible. Substituting a meatless meal or two per week will still increase your health benefits (and decrease your grocery bill).

While Google and online recipes were nonexistent during my grandmother's lifetime, the importance of family heritage and traditions on meals continues, despite hectic schedules, increasing technology, and social media that results in decreased person-to-person communication. Though many people consider preparing meals together to be too time-consuming, it takes only minutes a day to rekindle an interest in foods linked with our heritage and create your own meal-time memories. (Rekindle as in the verb, not the reading device.) Luckily for me, my mother perfectly replicates my grandmother's treasured eggplant dish. Just don't get me started on her lasagna.

Online Resources

Search the dishes mentioned in this article and other plant-based recipes on the following websites:

- Physicians Committee vegetarian starter kit: www.pcrm .org/health/diets/vsk

- www.MealMakeoverMoms.com

- www.MeatlessMonday.com

- USDA and HHS protein and nutrient recommendations: https://health.gov/dietaryguidelines/dga2010/dietary guidelines2010.pdf

- Articles and recipes: www.RockGumbo.blogspot.com

- United Soybean Board: www.soyconnection.com

- US Dry Bean Council: www.usdrybeans.com

- Vegetarian Resource Group: www.vrg.org

- Vegetarian, vegan, traditional eating patterns: www.oldways pt.org, www.vegetariannutrition.net, www. vegankit.com

Notes

1. Palmer, Sharon. "Vegetarian Value." *Today's Dietitian* 15, no. 10 (2013): 24–28.

2. Palmer, Sharon. "Plant-Based Diets for the Whole Family." *Today's Dietitian* 17, no. 10 (2015): 28–34.

3. Palmer, Sharon. "Meatless Meals from Across the Globe. "*Today's Dietitian* 16, no. 2 (2014): 20–25.

4. Moore, Marisa. "Beans: Pantry Staples, Nutrition Stars. *Food & Nutrition* 2, no. 5 (2013): 16–19.

5. Messina, Virginia. "Tofu's Many Faces." *Today's Dietitian.* 17, no. 4 (2015): 22–26.

6. Webb, Densie. "Soyfoods Made Easy: A Soy Primer." *Today's Dietitian* 13, no. 9 (2011): 52–56.

7. Getz, Lindsey. "Soyfoods and Cancer." *Today's Dietitian* 15, no. 4 (2013): 30–33.

8. Thalheimer, Judith C. "The Top 5 Soy Myths." *Today's Dietitian* 16, no. 4 (2014): 52–53.

9. Dickinson, Grace. "Going Nuts—For Nut and Seed Butters, That Is." *Today's Dietitian* 15, no. 9 (2013): 64–68.

10. Antinoro, Linda. "Walnuts—They're Good for the Heart and Offer Other Health Benefits." *Today's Dietitian* 15, no. 10 (2013): 74–76.

Mireille Blacke, MA, *is a registered dietitian, certified dietitian-nutritionist, and addiction specialist residing in Connecticut. She is obsessed with the city of New Orleans, the various works of Joss Whedon, and her Bengal cats. Mireille worked in rock radio for two decades before shifting her career focus to psychology, nutrition, and addiction counseling. She has been published in* Llewellyn's Moon Sign Book *and* Magical Almanac, Today's Dietitian, *and* OKRA Magazine. *Mireille is also an adjunct professor at the University of Saint Joseph in West Hartford, CT, and works as a clinical dietitian at Bristol Hospital in Bristol, CT. Follow Mireille online at @Rock GumboRD, rockgumbo.blogspot.com, and radiowitch.com.*

Holistic Dentistry

by Stacy M. Porter

I really try to steer clear of hating anything. Hate can be such a drain on the emotions and a waste of energy. I meditate regularly, journal my feelings, and even try practicing laughing yoga to keep everything flowing nicely, never letting any emotion, whether happy or sad, get stagnant. But, with all that said, I can't help but hate the dentist.

I hate the smell of the office, the uncomfortable chairs, and even the music they play in the waiting room. I really hate how they always want to have a conversation with me when they have the little mirror and metal pick in my mouth. The things I hate about the dentist could fill this entire book, but I don't want to dwell on that.

Most of us only go to the dentist when we feel something is wrong. Maybe there is a sharp pain or a discoloration of a tooth. Maybe it suddenly hurts to eat ice cream. We go to the dentist wanting them to fix everything because we don't know how. I always tried to take good care of my teeth because I have had so many problems in the past. I was born extremely premature and was told I had a predisposition for cavities and the like. So, growing up, I did everything the dentist told me to do. I had a prebrushing mouthwash, this very specific dentist-approved toothpaste, floss, and postbrushing mouthwash. I did that twice a day every day and still, every year at my annual appointment, the dentist would inevitably find at least one cavity. After doing all of that and still needing a root canal, I decided that my dentist's prescriptions were not working for me. I'm sure they work for some people, but they were just obviously not working for me. I stopped hating the dentist when I realized that it was my fault for not taking the time to understand my teeth.

So I went on a journey to figure out what was best for my own well-being. Holistic dentistry became self-care, self-love, and self-empowerment. I still go to the dentist to get things checked out, but now I'm not afraid, because with consistent practice I have been able to ward off cavities, heal the trauma of my past dental experiences, and brighten my smile.

The first step, for me, was throwing out all of the ideas my dentist had given me. Sure, I still knew that brushing my teeth was a good thing, but I stopped believing that the only products that would work to keep my smile pretty were found in a store.

Growing up, herbalism had never been part of my life, so it took me some time to understand it. My mom has a black thumb, and even though my grandma always had a beautiful garden, it was mostly just flowers that were there to look pretty. I never gave herbs much thought until one day I ventured into a store that sold homemade soaps, balms, and other holistic goods. In the back, there was a cabinet full of things to cure headaches, allergies, and stomachaches. There was also this little bottle that claimed to ward off plaque and gum disease.

That sent me down the rabbit-hole, and I spent countless hours researching more natural ways to heal my teeth and my emotional well-being that had been traumatized one too many times from the dentist drill. I spent a long time researching plants and herbs. I spent even longer putting my new knowledge into action when I started my own garden. I learned that gardening is pretty much all trial and error. What works for some people doesn't work for others, depending a lot on environmental variables.

It's also important to know that what works for one person, in terms of the actual herbs used in recipes and holistic care, might not work for everyone. I'll use myself as an example. I think everyone hears, at one point or another, usually when their dentist is lecturing them about brushing their teeth more, that plague buildup is what leads to cavities. That is true, but in my research I found other reasons that lead to teeth problems. As I mentioned earlier, I was born very premature, and that set me up on my path before I even got to make the choice between milk, water, or grape Kool-Aid. So I have had to work extra hard to find what works for me and my teeth. Sometimes it doesn't matter if you brush your teeth ten times a day. Sometimes you need help in other areas of your life before your smile can really shine.

Herbs for Holistic Dentistry

Here is a list of herbs that I have found to be useful. I have included some basic care tips for each herb if you want to start your own garden (inside or outside) to cultivate your own holistic dentistry practice.

Lavender

The first herb I want to mention might not appear to do anything for your teeth, but, as I mentioned earlier, emotional well-being plays a key element in our overall health. I always recommend having some lavender in your life, whether it's hanging in your home to lend its beautiful aroma to your space or in a cup of tea.

Lavender plants love the sun and do best in well-drained areas (such as a pot with holes in the bottom or a raised bed if your garden is outside). You don't need to water them every day unless it's very hot. A good rule of thumb with lavender plants is to wait until their soil is dry before you give them any water.

Thyme

Thyme has disinfectant properties and can be used in mouthwash. I recommend using fresh thyme and adding it to warm water and some sea salt. You can also chew thyme to ward off tooth decay.

Just like lavender, thyme does best in full sun and requires good drainage because the roots are very sensitive to overwatering (so planting it in a pot with holes or in a raised bed is a great idea). To keep it lush and growing healthily, continue to pinch the tips of the plant.

Parsley

Parsley is often used as a garnish. I like to think of it as natural breath spray: chewing parsley gets rid of bad breath. In my experience, parsley can grow pretty much anywhere. It does really well in containers and in the garden but does best in full sun or partial shade. It's important to keep the roots cool and moist, so I recommend mulching around the plant.

To harvest the leaves, cut them from the base of the plant. They will grow back even bushier. Keep a close eye out for any flowers on the plant. If your parsley flowers, yank out the whole plant because that means those leaves will be bitter.

It's also important to note here that parsley is prime real estate for caterpillars. They won't kill the plants, but they will eat a lot of it. So, if your garden is outside, I would plant extra parsley so that you can enjoy the leaves, and you will also be giving the soon-to-be-butterflies food and a place to live.

I have never planted my own tea tree, but tea tree oil is extremely cleansing. I know many people who massage tea tree oil on their gums before brushing.

Oregano

I would be remiss if I did not mention oregano in this list. I like to add oregano to my coconut oil for oil pulling (explained in the recipe section). Oregano does best in a container where it can spill over the edges. It's also very sensitive to root rot and pests, so it needs really good drainage. It does best in full sun, with a touch of shade in the evening. Water oregano thoroughly, though only when the soil is dry to the touch.

I recommend waiting to harvest any of the leaves until the plant is at least half a foot tall. Also, I want to point out that this plant is stronger dried than fresh.

Peppermint

The last herb I want to mention is peppermint. This plant is so useful and not just for your teeth. Chewing peppermint gets rid of bad breath, soothes stomachaches, and clears congestion. It's like a super herb!

The most important thing about the peppermint plant is that it likes to spread, so keep that in mind wherever you have it. If it's outside, you might want to keep it blocked off in its own bed, so it doesn't take over your yard. Many people keep it planted in a container, whether inside or outside, to keep it under control. Once you understand that, peppermint is generally very easy to keep happy.

The key to having a healthy and vibrant peppermint plant is to harvest the leaves often and to make sure it's always moist. As for positioning the plant, the peppermint plant does like some shade, but putting it in full sun increases the plant's medicinal properties. If you do keep it in full sun, just make sure to give it extra water.

Stacy's Simple Toothpaste Recipe and Holistic Dentistry Routine

To make the toothpaste, you'll need sea salt, baking soda, and peppermint oil. You can make a whole bunch at once by pouring the salt, baking soda, and a few drops of the peppermint oil into a container, or you can make it one night at a time. To make a single serving, mix a teaspoon of sea salt, a teaspoon of baking soda, and two drops of peppermint oil together, and then apply it to your toothbrush.

If you only want to brush your teeth, that's totally up to you, but you'll get bonus points if you take a spoonful of coconut oil and swish it around your mouth, pulling it between your teeth, for ten to twenty minutes *before* you brush your teeth. This is called oil pulling, and it keeps your breath fresh, whitens your teeth, and cleans out any toxins in your mouth.

You can also gargle with warm water and salt water *after* you brush your teeth to add an extra punch. Sea salt is excellent for clearing out mucus and bacteria in the mouth, plus it reduces inflammation around the gums.

That whole process might seem like a bit much, but once you commit to the routine, it can become very healing to do. It can also save you time and money later, because this natural way to care for your teeth and gums can keep you from having to go to the dentist more often.

It takes time, but you're worth it. Think of the routine as self-care, and maybe perform it while listening to some of your favorite music to really make it fun! You are beautiful, and you deserve to have a beautiful smile—and one you can have without being uncomfortable in the dentist's chair!

Though, to be perfectly clear, none of this means you shouldn't go to the dentist. Even after everything I wrote about, I will point out here that I still go to the dentist for regular checkups. My holistic approach to dentistry is meant to help me keep my teeth healthy, but it's always a good idea to have things checked out by a professional.

Hopefully, with regular practice, the holistic habits will keep your mouth cavity-free and healthy, and your dentist will be asking you for tips instead of giving you their own (prescribing chemicals).

Stacy M. Porter *has studied politics in Africa, survived a Russian winter, touched a Michelangelo sculpture in Italy, and saved sea turtles in Nicaragua. She holds a degree in international studies with a minor in English from Juniata College, is a second-degree priestess in the Ravenmyst Circle Tradition, and is a certified yoga instructor through Bodhi Yoga Academy. Stacy is currently making magic in Orlando, Florida. You can follow her adventures on Instagram at www.instagram.com/stacymporteryoga and on Facebook at www .facebook.com/StacyMPorterAuthor.*

Herbal Remedies: What's Essential for Every Age and Stage of Life

⤞ by Sally Cragin ⤝

Walk into any natural foods store and you'll be overwhelmed by the array of supplements, vitamins, herbs, elixirs, and syrups. But where to start? Why is *this* bottle of tablets better than that one? How many times have you purchased a supplement and then seen that a "dosage" is three tablets or servings a day versus one?

It's easy to get into habits, and Madison Avenue relies on capturing our interest early so that we become lifelong consumers of a certain brand of corn flake or a particular kind of shampoo. However, our bodies may change as the years pass—and the diet of Red Bull and popcorn that served in our early 20s leaves us foggy and queasy a decade later. Here are some suggestions of herbs and plants that may be helpful to you during the ages and stages of your life.

Infants and Children

All babies are beautiful, but some can have skin conditions or colic that might prompt an anxious parent to explore herbal options. There are numerous recipes on the Internet, but here are some herbs to look for: chamomile, lemon balm, catnip, vervain, dill seed, and caraway seed. For diaper rash, try ointments with calendula, which promotes healing.

Children can be engaged in herb gathering, and this is a great way to open your child's eyes to the wonders of nature. **Dandelion** is a great herb to start with, and if you know you are gathering plants far from a roadside, have your child help you pull roots. An easy decoction to help loosen mucus is 1 cup of apple cider vinegar simmered with 4 tablespoons dandelion root for 10 to 20 minutes. Remove from heat and strain into a jar. Add ¼ cup honey while decotion is warm. Cover your jar and shake, store in a cool, dark place. Take as you would a syrup.

Fennel seeds can be a wonderful tummy soother—just nibble away! Every child is going to lose teeth, and if there is pain involved, a cold compress applied to the outside of the mouth, swishing and spitting a warm water and salt solution, and a minuscule dab of **clove oil** might relieve pain.

Teens through Early Twenties: College and Career Years

This is the period when you segue from growing up to being a "grownup." As glorious as it may be to have independence, there are unique challenges with this transition, particularly regarding education, career selection, partnerships, and child-bearing. Some people may find the pressure of being self-supporting a heavy burden to bear. Changing jobs may be a frequent occurrence, along with financial anxiety.

Helpful herbs include **echinacea.** The most common variety of echinacea is the purple coneflower, which some take for immune system support during cold season. If you have a cold or upper respiratory tract issue, you can take this in a variety of forms at 300 milligrams three times a day for no more than seven to ten days. The narrow-leaf coneflower variety of echinacea has been used to treat anxiety, and it's recommended that low dosages are best. If you are experiencing significant stress, try taking 20 milligrams up to four or five times a day. This is not recommended as an ongoing treatment.

If you're new at experimenting with herbs, **chamomile** is a wonderful flower to try, as it can be enjoyed throughout your life. For some, it may have sedative effects (as it did for poor Peter Rabbit after he escaped from Mr. MacGregor's garden). However, avoid this flower if you have sensitivities to ragweed or related plants. This stage is also the period when many adolescents leave home for good, which means diet and eating habits are up to them, not a caregiver. It's easy to get into horrific eating habits in college when you discover instant, cheap sugar-and-caffeine highs. Youth can substitute for good health habits for a while, but aim for meals that give you more fresh food than processed. Many people find their taste buds transition during those years, and vegetables and other foods they didn't care for as a child or teen may become more appealing. Give dark green and leafy veggies and the bright orange ones a chance (kale, spinach, carrots, and squash).

Boys can be subject to just as many mood swings as girls. Teen boys can show enormous empathy and selfishness, grow six inches in a year, yet continue to play happily with their Legos and Pokéman cards. Emotional turbulence can be connected with a lack of exercise and poor nutrition, so consider adding foods like Brazil nuts, tuna, halibut, and sardines. These are rich in selenium, which can be a mood lifter.

The teens and twenties are also when reproductive organs are fully operational and hormones can bring acne and other skin blemishes. For skin breakouts, oil of **lavender** or **tea tree** might help, along with keeping your skin clean and dry (acne is oil). Just a small dab of these oils (with a cotton swab) might make a difference. **Willow** root (or a crushed aspirin tablet, which I used when over-the-counter medications were beyond my budget) can also help absorb oil and bring healing, due to salicylic acid. If you want to address skin difficulties from the inside-out, consider adding dandelion root. **Dandelion** is one of the many helpful anti-inflammatory herbs and will also support digestion and kidney function.

Menstrual periods—heavy, light, frequent, rare—are the compass needle of the lives of many young women. A helpful herb for alleviating the pain of menstruation as well as premenstrual tension is **chaste tree** (*Vitex agnus-castus*). This ancient plant comes as a tincture and as capsules (which are usually less expensive). A standard dose is between 225 and 500 milligrams. You will want to research this particular plant, as recommended dosages vary, depending on whether you are taking it for initiating menstrual cycles (if you are experiencing amenorrhea), managing heavy periods, or helping with infertility issues. Chaste tree is sometimes marketed as "vitex" and is not recommended if you are taking fertility drugs. You may not see results from this herb for three to six months.

Child-Bearing Years for Women

These years can extend into one's forties, but the vast majority of women who become parents do so in their twenties and thirties. As mentioned, chaste tree is a helpful herb during this period. (It also helps your vaginal mucus achieve the "egg white" consistency more conducive to egg fertilization.) It can also help lengthen the luteal phase, lower prolactin, and increase the production of progesterone, all helpful to prepare the body for conception. I can personally vouch for vitex, which I began taking in my early forties, after having my first son at nearly forty-three. I continued to take this to help with menstrual cycles and became pregnant (delightfully and surprisingly) at nearly forty-eight.

Red **raspberry** leaf tea was known to midwives for centuries as a tonic for helping pregnant women deliver their babies. A study by the Australian College of Midwives found raspberry leaf tea "can be consumed by women during their pregnancy . . . to shorten labour with no identified side effects for the women or their babies." A follow-up study found a slight variation in results but indicated a benefit in shortening the second stage of labor. Research showed that one to three cups a day were recommended (one to two teaspoons leaf).

Raspberry leaf tea can be very expensive when purchased in teabags, so if you have a garden (or friends with one) and you know pesticides aren't used, save cuttings of the branches. Dry them on a screen or in bunches in a darkened room. A small handful can be soaked in two cups of nearly boiling water for ten to twenty minutes. Drink cold or warm.

Alfalfa tea also has a long history among midwives for helping with digestion and helping prevent blood loss. Recommended dosage is one tablespoon alfalfa per cup of water infused at least 10 minutes. However, if you wander off and return an hour later, the tea is still drinkable. (A little murky, however!)

Other herbs associated with fertility, pregnancy support during all three trimesters, labor, and postpartum include black haw, burdock, dandelion, German chamomile, ginger root, lady's mantle, motherwort, oatstraw, partridge berry, rose hips, and shepherd's purse.

Child-Rearing Years for Men

For men, fertility issues are getting increased attention, and if you are a man hoping for fatherhood, bear in mind that it takes sperm three months to develop. If you've been diagnosed with motility or potency issues and you are going on an herbal regimen, be patient. Recommended herbs and plants to address fertility include *Panax ginseng*, saw palmetto berry, *Ginkgo biloba*, *Rhodiola rosea*, maca root, *Tribulus terrestris*, and the charmingly named horny goat weed (which is said to improve blood flow). Exact dosages should be calculated with the help of an herbalist.

Late Twenties to Early Forties: The *go-go-GO!* Years

Whether or not you have a child (or more than one), chances are you may also be working outside the home, which means you may be rushing through meals or overdoing it on the caffeine. One sign that your body may be struggling to process caffeine is a headache if you skip the morning coffee. No, there is no equivalent for a big, rich, dark cup of steaming java straight from the caring hand of your neighborhood barista. However, if that headache becomes more frequent (or emerges during the late afternoon when the morning joe has worn off), you might consider some substitutes for your caffeine fix.

I speak as a reformed caffeine addict and can personally vouch for the following to wake you up in the morning: **mate** tea, **carrot** juice, and switchel (Yankee drink consisting of a scant teaspoon of apple cider vinegar in hot water with molasses, honey, or maple syrup to sweeten). And as sad as it may be to come to the conclusion that your body needs a caffeine break, tell yourself that you now get to enter the wonderful and healthy world of vegetable juices and herbal teas.

During these years, previous recommendations for herbs and supplements continue to hold, but do bear in mind that one person's activity level in their thirties might not be another's, given the wide range of years available for having children, completing an education, or achieving airborne status in a career. However, one common ailment to many in this age range could be fatigue, particularly if you are more sedentary or less careful about diet. During peak career years, men can easily get by on less sleep, high-fat diets, and lots of caffeine—for a while. If you are suffering from headaches, insomnia, or stress, consider adding magnesium to your diet as a supplement or increasing your intake of dark, leafy plants, nuts and beans, and whole grain cereals.

I have tried **ashwagandha**, probably the best-known Ayurvedic plant that is adaptogenic, meaning it can be taken for a wide variety of ailments. Stress reduction, immunity boosting, and brain-function improvement are all in this humble plant's wheelhouse. You'll find this as ashwagandha root extract, and like many herbs, it's recommended you take this with food. One method to explore usage is to take 300 to 500 milligrams a day. When you begin an herbal regimen, start with a low dosage and work your way up to full dosage in a month or two.

Late Forties through "Senior Discount" Years

Living more than half a century is a tribute to improved nutrition and a higher standard of living, and at our best moments we should be grateful every day for good health. However, if you are carrying extra weight (from poor diet and sedentary habits), now is the time to take action. No supplement or herb can take the place of intelligent choices in habit, lifestyle, and companions.

There is a wide range of herbs and plants to address aches and pains. Try aloe vera for gastric distress, mustard for respiratory disorders, and turmeric for inflammation.

The biggest issue I hear from friends and clients is feeling "overloaded," with resulting short-term memory loss ("Where did I put the keys?") and aches and pains. Plenty of herbs are cited as helpful for alleviating or arresting memory loss. These include *Gingko biloba*, gotu kola, periwinkle, and ginseng. It's also helpful to smell **rosemary**. Yes, smelling a rosemary plant is considered helpful for memory. ("Rosemary for remembrance," said the Elizabethans.)

This is the time when lifestyle and diet can be crucial for personal health (the other leg of the tripod being those mysterious genes). So maybe it's time to forgo the second glass of wine, the big piece of cake, or the high-calorie convenience food. Apply the sunscreen, but also get a hat.

As for herbs, vitamins, and health, talk to your doctor and use common sense. Doctors will tell you that your bones will start to become brittle unless you are mindful about ingesting about 1,200 milligrams of calcium and 600 international units of vitamin D, plus getting at least sixty minutes of exercise three times a week. It's a simple formula: eat well and move your body. You may be surprised to hear that an eight-ounce glass of milk (one cup), whether whole or skim, has the same amount of calcium as a cup of yogurt: approximately 300 milligrams.

Vitamin D is critical for bone health and will help with calcium absorption. The recommended dose is 600 international units per day, which you'll find in fatty fish (swordfish, salmon, and tunafish), milk, dairy products, and whole eggs. However, unless you're eating fish every day, it's difficult to get the recommended amount of vitamin D from food alone, according to National Institutes of Health, so supplements should be explored. And as much as we all look for the most current research, I was amused to find that there is one supplement that my grandmother—and probably her grandmother—agreed on: cod liver oil. One teaspoon contains almost exactly the recommended daily dosage of vitamin D!

Resources

"Ashwagandha." Examine.com. Accessed December 12, 2016. https://examine.com/supplements/ashwagandha/.

"Chasteberry." WholeHealth Chicago. Accessed December 8, 2016. http://wholehealthchicago.com/2009/05/11/chasteberry/.

"Echinacea." Natural Healthy Concepts. Accessed December 8, 2016. https://www.naturalhealthyconcepts.com/resources/articles/echinacea.

"Help with Teenage Mood Swings." WebMD. Last modified June 10, 2016. http://www.webmd.boots.com/children/features/teenage-mood-swings?page=2.

"Magnesium." WebMD. Accessed December 8, 2016. http://www.webmd.com/diet/supplement-guide-magnesium#1.

Office of Dietary Supplements. "Vitamin D." National Institutes of Health. Last modified February 11, 2016. https://ods.od.nih.gov/factsheets/VitaminD-HealthProfessional/.

Parsons, Myra, Michele Simpson, and Terri Ponton. "Raspberry Leaf and Its Effect on Labour: Safety and Efficacy." *Australian College of Midwives Incorporated Journal* 12, no. 3 (September 1999): 20–25.

Sarich, Christina. "6 Herbs to Help Boost Your Brain Power." Natural Society. December 2, 2014. http://naturalsociety.com/6-herbs-boost-brain-power-genius/.

Sally Cragin *is the author of* The Astrological Elements *and* Astrology on the Cusp. *Both books have been translated and sold overseas. She does astrological and tarot readings. Visit "Sally Cragin astrology" on Facebook or e-mail sallycragin@verizon.net.*

Beauty Begins in the Garden: Make Your Own Hair and Skin Treatments

⁂ by JD Hortwort ⁂

When we talk about using herbs from the garden, the first thought is often culinary uses. Who doesn't love the taste of fresh dill on fish or new leaves of basil for homemade pizzas?

Next, we think of health care—digging garlic for immune support or snipping sage for a brisk gargle to combat a sore throat.

It's about time we starting thinking of the herb garden for our beauty products. Many of the same herbs we treasure for cooking or medicine can add shine to dull hair, soothe dry skin, and help to hold Father Time at bay. Plus, you have the added benefit of knowing exactly what goes into your lotions, rinses, and balms.

These solutions are made with herbs commonly found in gardens in temperate areas in the United States. However, you can easily buy the herbs needed in most well-stocked natural foods markets if you don't have access to a garden.

One word of caution before we begin: the solutions for hair are meant for healthy, untreated hair. If you've used chemical dyes or recently permed your hair, it will be very hard to predict what will happen if you attempt to use these natural products.

Since before recorded history, men and women have been using every means at their disposal to make themselves more appealing—to themselves and to others. You don't have the treasures of Cleopatra to make your own beauty supplies. Just step out into the herb garden.

As for the facial rinses and body lotions, make sure you're not allergic to the herbs before you use the product. For example, those with ragweed or dandelion allergies should be careful around preparations that use chamomile. Chamomile is in the same family of plants and might trigger a reaction.

If you are unsure, take a teaspoon of the herb in question and soak it in a few tablespoons of hot water for up to five minutes. Squeeze out the water and put a dab of the wet herb on the inside of your forearm. Cover with a bandage for twenty-four hours. After that time, check for redness, a rash, or a blister. If you don't see a reaction, the herb is probably safe for you to use.

Hair

They used to say a woman's crowning glory is her hair. But who says ladies are the only ones concerned with glowing, flowing locks? Anyone can have dull hair. Dandruff can strike any gender. And we all like to tweak our natural color from time to time.

Brightening Colors

It's easy to do with simple teas or infusions. Bring out your blonde highlights with a **mullein** or **chamomile** tea. Redheads can brighten their locks with **alkanet** or **hibiscus** teas. Raven-haired beauties can use **elderberry** leaves (not the berries) or sage.

An infusion is made by allowing plant material to soak in boiling water. The plant material can be leaves, berries, roots, or bark. In the cases of the herbs listed above, we mean leaves. Use one ounce of crushed or shredded leaves per cup of boiling water. The longer your hair, the more water you will need. Pour the boiling water over the leaves in a heat-resistant glass, ceramic, or steel container, cover the container, and allow the mixture to come to room temperature. Strain away the herbs.

After washing your hair, use the tea as a rinse. Ideally, you should allow your hair to dry naturally in direct sunlight. The sun's heat opens up the hair cuticles for better penetration. But you can also blow dry your hair. It may take more than one application to achieve the results you desire.

Dealing with Gray

When time catches up to us, gray hair becomes a reality. Sadly, not all of us are blessed with snowy white or striking silver manes. My grandmother was a strong woman who resigned herself to having mousy brown hair. Coloring her hair at a salon was a luxury she could never justify. Besides, she would say, you can't fight Mother Nature.

Unfortunately, Mother Nature favored her in old age with a dreary yellow cast to her gray hair. Again, she shrugged and soldiered on. However, she could have made a tea from hollyhock leaves to help cover that yellow cast. For those wise women of a certain age with brown or black hair flecked with gray, the solution can be an **elderberry** or **sage** tea.

Actually dyeing your hair with natural products is a bit trickier. One approach is to begin as previously mentioned with one ounce of herb and one cup of water. Once the mixture has brewed, mix in enough kaolin clay to make a paste. Apply this to the hair and allow to dry. Rinse the clay out (do not shampoo). This should give more of a tint to the hair than simply using the tea as a rinse.

Black Walnut Hull Dye

For those with dark hair who want to go darker, a tea of **black walnut** hulls will certainly work. Be advised that black walnuts will stain not only your hair, but everything else they come in contact with. When trying this home solution, wear clothing you won't mind getting stained, wear latex gloves, use towels you might want to throw away afterward, and cover the kitchen cabinets and floors before beginning. Or pick a warm day and do your beauty treatment outdoors.

Gather a dozen or so black walnuts. Remove the green outer shell. Put the nuts in a large container and cover with water. Bring to a boil and monitor. You should get a rich brown stain within an hour. The longer the nuts boil, the darker the tea will become. When you get the shade you want, allow the mixture to cool, and then strain it.

Brave women use a large bowl or kettle so that they can dunk their entire head into the mixture for about five to ten minutes. The more timid of us use cotton balls to apply the mixture slowly. When applying with cotton balls, stop those trickles of walnut juice at the hair line with a line of petroleum jelly one to two inches wide all around your face and neck.

After allowing the dye to remain on your hair for the specified time, lean over a sink and thoroughly rinse with warm water. Once your hair is dry, you can tell whether you need to go back for another dunk.

Herbal Tea Rinses

Herbal teas can do more than modify the color of your hair. Use one tablespoon of **basil** in one cup of boiling water. When it cools, use it as a rinse to brighten dull hair.

Make a tea of one tablespoon each of dried **rosemary** and **peppermint**. Strain and use as a rinse to help combat dandruff. Rub it into the scalp and let it set for about five minutes before rinsing out.

Body

Natural toners and astringents for the face are also herbal tea infusions. You can make them as you need them, no artificial preservatives or coloring agents required.

One of my favorite recipes is for an astringent for oily skin. Way back in the 1980s, publishing companies would print little how-to booklets to display on the shelves above the candy bars and gum in the grocery checkout area. They were usually a dollar or less. I picked up every one I could find that even mentioned "herb" in the title. Some of the remedies in them worked; some didn't. (Oak bark tea as an appetite suppressant? What was I thinking?!)

Toners

I've long since misplaced the booklet I got this recipe from, but I've never forgotten it. Brew one tablespoon each of **sage** and **peppermint** in one cup of boiling water. When it cools, strain out the herbs. Add to the tea the juice of one freshly squeezed lemon. Top off the mixture with good-quality vodka to get two cups of fluid. I keep about one cup in a pretty glass bottle in the bathroom. I keep the rest in the refrigerator until needed. After cleansing my face, I dab this all over using a cotton ball. It's light, delicate, and refreshing.

Those with dry skin should avoid using alcohol as a base in a skin toner. For those individuals, I recommend a simple chamomile tea. One teaspoon of **chamomile** to a half cup of boiling water, brewed for three to five minutes, is all you need. When it cools, apply to your face before moisturizing.

For a pick-me-up for any skin type, make a **peppermint** tea using the same formula. As an added bonus, the presence of salicylic acid in peppermint makes this a useful tea for those who suffer from acne.

Because you should be making small amounts, there is really no need for preservatives in these facial teas. If you want to make several cups at a time, you can store the extra in the refrigerator until needed. I don't recommend making more than a quart at a time.

Moisturizing

There are plenty of recipes out there for skin lotions. Most start with a base oil and then add select herbs or essential oils.

I developed my own recipe to help combat the damage from many years working as a gardener and landscaper. I usually did a good job of keeping my head covered for protection from the sun's rays. I tried to keep sunscreen on my arms—for all the good it did.

Unless you have labored for eight to ten hours a day outdoors, you have no idea how hard it is to keep sunscreen on your arms. Bags of mulch dragged it off as I moved from shrub bed to flower bed. The dust from mowers and tractors settled all over me, and I just couldn't stand it. Before long, I would be at the garden hose, rinsing the dust and my sunscreen away. And, of course, there was the sweat.

Body Butters

Today, my face says age fifty-something, but my arms give away my true age unless I keep myself moisturized. This recipe starts with two cups of shea butter, gently melted over low heat. To that, I add one ounce each of **calendula** blossoms, **lavender** blossoms, **rosemary** leaves, and **rose geranium** leaves or flowers.

I steep these in a slow cooker on the lowest setting overnight. The next day, I strain out the herbs and add twelve tablespoons of jojoba oil, three tablespoons of vegetable glycerin, and one-quarter teaspoon of myrrh essential oil.

This is a very rich mixture, and you shouldn't use too much of it at a time. After some trial and error, I finally hit on a way to ensure proper use. I air whip the oil until it sets up as a light cream. To do this, put the oil and herb mixture in a bowl and then nest that bowl in a large bowl of ice water. Use an electric mixer to beat the oil. It takes about fifteen minutes to render a very light skin cream. I tried it once in a blender.

The resulting cream was good, but it was too hard to get the mixture out of the blender.

The light cream that results will hold up to room temperature. It should melt quickly in your hand from body temperature. It will not survive if set in sunlight or carried in a hot car. The cream won't go bad, but it won't have the airy texture. This is a very good lotion, but it is a bit heavy. I call it my winter body butter.

For those who want something a bit lighter, I make what I call a summer body butter. Start by reducing the shea butter to one cup. Add twelve tablespoons of grape seed oil in addition to the jojoba oil. As you whip the mixture, add fourteen to eighteen tablespoons of cold water, one at a time, until you get the right consistency. This mixture will be even lighter and will absorb even more quickly than the winter version.

The natural antibacterial properties of the myrrh will help keep these body treatments fresh. However, if you like, portion your body butters into small, two- to four-ounce decorative jars and keep the extras in the refrigerator until needed.

Better still, give them as gifts. Share the health and the beauty that can come from your own herb garden.

JD Hortwort *resides in North Carolina. She is an avid student of herbology and gardening. JD has written a weekly garden column since 1991. She is a professional, award-winning author, journalist, and magazine editor, as well as a frequent contributor to the Llewellyn annuals. JD has been active in the local Pagan community since 2002, and she is a founding member of the House of Akasha in Greensboro, North Carolina.*

Herb Crafts

The Power of Pomegranates: So Much More Than Seasonal Decor

☙ by Tess Whitehurst ☙

It's no secret that pomegranates are delicious and nutritious. But when it comes to physical beauty and sacred symbolism, they're unsurpassed.

In season from September to February, this botanical jewel does triple duty as a seasonal decoration, looking gorgeous in arrangements and centerpieces starting in late summer and continuing through fall and winter. Indeed, in Greece the pomegranate is a popular addition to many a home decor.

In the latter portion of this article, you'll find some simple, elegant ideas for each season to spark your creativity. But first, let's talk about the ancient symbolism you bring into your home when you decorate with this magical fruit, which runs the gamut from goddesses to gods, death to life to rebirth.

Divine Feminine Energy

Most of us have heard the myth of Persephone and how she cast her lot with Hades when she partook of a few pomegranate seeds in the underworld. But the pomegranate has also been known to be sacred to her mother, the harvest goddess Demeter, as well as her mother's mother, the primordial earth goddess Rhea. And Hera—who was an ancient sovereign in her own right before the Hellenic religion arrived on the scene and married her to Zeus—is also closely associated with the fruit. Even the Christian version of the Great Goddess, Mother Mary, is linked with pomegranates! There is a chapel in Greece dedicated to *Madonna del Granato*, "Our Lady of the Pomegranate."

Divine Masculine Energy

While less overt than the fruit's goddess associations, pomegranates are nonetheless unmistakably associated with gods. In fact, in ancient Greece they were said to have initially sprung from the blood of Adonis. And they've served as offerings to the creative, mysterious god of intoxication and fertility, Dionysus. In Judaism, Solomon's pillars and the high priest's gowns are said to have featured pomegranate imagery. In Christianity, the image of an open pomegranate has been employed as symbolism representing Jesus's suffering on the cross. As if all that weren't enough, pomegranates are also aligned with the Hindu god Ganesha, the beloved elephant-headed remover of obstacles. (Clearly, when ancient humans encountered pomegranates, they thought, "Divinity!")

Death and the Afterlife

Considering it's in season from September to February, the pomegranate is understandably aligned with autumn and winter, particularly in Greece. In myth, this is demonstrated by its alignment with the goddess Persephone and her yearly descent into the underworld at the fall equinox (a metaphor for the dark half of the year). The Eleusinian mysteries, which were based around this myth and which also incorporated the god Dionysus (likewise associated with the pomegranate), were said to comfort those who experienced them by emphasizing rebirth and curing them of the fear of death. Furthermore, as mentioned, the pomegranate was said to have sprung from the blood of Adonis, who features prominently in his own mysteries related to death and rebirth. In Christian iconography, the fruit has been featured in paintings to represent heaven and the afterlife. In Islamic art, it's also associated with paradise.

Aligned with beloved divinities throughout the ancient world, the pomegranate is one sacred fruit indeed. And its symbolic qualities are legendary! They include protection, rebirth, abundance, fertility, luck, love, the heavenly realm, and more.

Protection

Western herbal folk wisdom states that pomegranates and pomegranate branches protect from all forms of negativity. Similarly, according to POM Wonderful, in a painting from 467 CE, "Kujaku Myoo, one of the several 'Radiant Wisdom

Kings' worshipped in Japan, is depicted holding a pomegranate to repel evil spirits." Additionally, the author Judika Illes suggests that pomegranates can be magically employed to protect unborn children and ensure their health.

Abundance, Fertility, and Luck

With its bursting, jewel-like seeds, it's no small wonder that throughout many Eastern, Middle Eastern, and Mediterranean cultures, the pomegranate is prominently associated with abundance, fertility, and luck. That's why weddings and New Year celebrations may feature a blessing involving the breaking of a pomegranate on the ground or against a wall. In China, the pomegranate is employed as both a decoration and a charm for drawing fertility and wealth. The author Scott Cunningham writes, "The pomegranate is a lucky, magical fruit. Always make a wish before eating one and your wish may come true. A branch of pomegranate discovers concealed wealth, or will attract money to its possessor. The skin, dried, is added to wealth and money incenses."

Clearly, when you decorate with pomegranates, you're bringing in so much more than a lovely centerpiece! So without further ado . . .

Pomegranate Decor for Three Seasons

Summer: Scarlet Bouquet

This bouquet is a beautiful, unique way to surprise someone or just a gorgeous centerpiece for any late summer event. And it just might provide a boost of love and luck!

Wet floral foam to fit in pot

Faux moss pot (or other flower pot)

3 pomegranates

Floral wood picks

Red roses

Other flowers or greenery (as desired)

Floral moss

Strong scissors or garden shears

Place the foam in the pot. Pierce each pomegranate with a wood pick so that the navel is at the top. Stick them into the foam like flowers, and arrange the flowers (and any other greenery) around them. Arrange and tuck the floral moss around the base.

Fall: Harvest Bushel

This centerpiece is a delightful addition to any fall harvest celebration, from Mabon to Thanksgiving. But don't just decorate with it! Let it be a reminder of all that you have and how far you've come—because what we focus on expands, and gratitude always begets more of what we are grateful for.

3 pomegranates

Various mini pumpkins and gourds

Mini Indian corn

A pumpkin-shaped basket (or another fall-themed receptacle)

Simply arrange all the ingredients in the basket in an artful manner.

Winter: Yuletide Basket

This basket is a unique and elegant way to embellish your hearth or table throughout the month of December. Let it bring sweetness and joy to your winter months and magnetize the generous blessings of the season.

Winter garland of your choice

Basket

3–5 pomegranates (depending on preference and basket size)

Holly berries (faux or real)

Pinecones

Gather up the garland and place it in the basket. Nestle all other ingredients attractively throughout.

Resources

Cunningham, Scott. *Cunningham's Encyclopedia of Magical Herbs*. St. Paul, MN: Llewellyn, 1985.

Illes, Judika. *The Element Encyclopedia of 5,000 Spells: The Ultimate Reference Book for the Magical Arts*. London: HarperElement, 2004.

———. *Encyclopedia of Spirits: The Ultimate Guide to the Magic of Fairies, Genies, Demons, Ghosts, Gods & Goddesses*. New York: HarperOne, 2009.

Pedley, John. *Sanctuaries and the Sacred in the Ancient Greek World*. New York: Cambridge University Press, 2005.

"Rooted in History." POM Wonderful. Accessed December 9, 2016. www.pomwonderful.com/pomegranate-wellness/history/

Tess Whitehurst *is the author of* The Magic of Flowers Oracle *and a number of books, including* Magical Housekeeping, Holistic Energy Magic, *and* The Magic of Trees. *She's also the founder and facilitator of the Good Vibe Tribe, an online magical community and learning hub. Visit her at www.tesswhitehurst.com.*

Easy Miniature Greenhouses

❧ by Melanie Marquis ❧

Greenhouses have been utilized by gardeners for thousands of years. By enabling plants to grow further into the cold season, accelerating growth, and protecting from pests and poor weather, a greenhouse can benefit your plants in many ways. While a full-size greenhouse can be costly and take up a lot of space, you can utilize miniature greenhouses to reap many of the same benefits on a smaller scale.

Miniature greenhouses also offer the advantage of being transportable. If it gets too cold outside, you could bring an outdoor miniature greenhouse indoors, something that is definitely not an option with the full-size variety. There are infinite design

options to choose from, most of which can be made with very little cost, if any. In fact, many miniature greenhouses can be made with items you probably already own.

Whether you're starting seedlings, striving to protect your plants from the elements, or just hoping to grow your plants a little better or a little faster, there is a miniature greenhouse that's perfect for your needs. Here are a few basic ways to make your own miniature greenhouse. Let these ideas inspire you to craft a small-scale greenhouse that's just right for your space.

Mechanics of a Greenhouse

If you're planning to make your own greenhouse, it's helpful to understand what makes a greenhouse work. However large or small, greenhouses are designed to let in sunlight, keep in heat, and keep pests and harsh weather conditions out. Since a greenhouse is enclosed with the exception of a little ventilation to allow for airflow, the heat that builds up inside a greenhouse can't escape as quickly, so your plants get more heat than they would otherwise.

Greenhouses also make use of glass and clear plastics that can help capture, reflect, and magnify the sunlight so that your plants receive maximum benefit. When night falls, the heat that has been building up all day within the greenhouse is slowly released, keeping your plants warm throughout the colder, darker hours.

Another important function of a greenhouse is pest control. While pests will still find a way into your greenhouse if they're determined, they will definitely be deterred, and pest problems will be minimized. This allows gardeners to use pesticides in greater moderation or to forgo them altogether.

Elements of a Greenhouse

While your design options are virtually limitless, there are a few elements that are essential for any greenhouse, even a miniature one. First off, plants need light, so your design should be rendered with this fact in mind. It doesn't matter as much with a large greenhouse, as you can add artificial grow lights, but with a miniature greenhouse, it needs to be made of a transparent material such as glass or clear plastic.

Your greenhouse also requires ventilation. If there isn't enough airflow within the greenhouse, plants can't take in the carbon dioxide they need to photosynthesize. A stuffy environment can also lead to pests as well as mold. Be sure to add some ventilation to your design, not so much that it defeats the purpose of a greenhouse, but enough to allow for air to flow slowly in and out.

Depending on your design and the size of your greenhouse and how it's being utilized, you may be able to provide enough air circulation by simply opening the greenhouse for a few minutes each day. If you're using the greenhouse to start seeds, for example, you won't have a great need for ventilation until the seed sprouts become visible above the soil. You would still need to air it out daily, though, even before the seeds sprout, in order to prevent mold and mildew from growing.

Your greenhouse also needs to allow for drainage so that water won't pool up around your plant's roots. If your greenhouse doesn't have a bottom other than the ground beneath it, you won't need to worry about it. If your greenhouse does have a bottom, you will need to add a few small, equally spaced holes to the bottom floor of your design or add a layer of gravel beneath the soil.

Repurposed Furniture for Plants

If you want a greenhouse that's large enough to fit several plants inside, you can make one easily by repurposing an unneeded piece of furniture. Old shelves or dressers work very well. If you're using a shelf, simply cover the front with clear plastic sheeting (a clear shower curtain will also work) and attach it with tacks or staples on the top, the bottom, and one of the sides. Attach the other side with duct tape or adhesive Velcro strips to give yourself a way to access the plants once they're inside. If you're using a wire or wicker shelf that allows light to filter down through the top and on down to the lower shelves, just place the shelf normally and put potted plants on each shelf so that it's balanced and stable.

If it's instead a solid wooden shelf, you will want to lay the shelf on its back, so that the back of the shelf becomes the bottom of the greenhouse. If the shelf has a solid back to it, you will need to drill several holes in it for drainage. If the shelf doesn't have a back, you can simply lay it down on the ground and place your plants between the slots.

You can use an old dresser to make a greenhouse this same way. Just remove the drawers and it's now a shelf that can be converted as described above. Or, you could use the dresser drawers to make a whole set of miniature greenhouses. Simply drill holes in the bottom of each drawer and cover the top with plastic sheeting.

Greenhouse Glasses

If a much smaller greenhouse would suit your needs, you might consider crafting your designs out of glass. For starting seeds, you can use any wide-mouth, flat-bottomed drinking glass. Just fill with dirt, plant your seed, water it, and cover the top of the glass with plastic wrap. You can secure the plastic wrap with a rubber band around the glass so that it can be taken off or put back on easily. Poke a few holes in the plastic wrap for ventilation. This is a temporary, short-use greenhouse, so you won't need to worry about drainage as long as you don't overwater.

For a larger, more permanent design, make your miniature glass greenhouse from a large jar or even a fishbowl. Add a two-inch layer of gravel to the bottom of the container to help with drainage. Next, add the soil on top of the gravel layer so that it fills the container to about the halfway mark. For the top, you can use the lid from the jar from which you made your greenhouse, or if you made it from a fish bowl, you can cover the top with plastic wrap secured with a rubber band. Just remember to poke some holes in whatever top you use so that your plants will get enough fresh air. To make your glass greenhouse creations a little more creative and personal, try decorating them with window markers or paint, or attach stickers, beads, or ribbons to add some pizzazz.

Hanging Greenhouses

If your space is limited, a hanging miniature greenhouse may be just right for your purpose. You can make one using a clear plastic storage container or a clear plastic cup. You can get bins or cups with lids so you'll have a ready-made top; just be sure to poke some holes if needed for ventilation. Begin by poking a few holes in the bottom of the container or cup. Then, on opposite sides of the container or cup, about an inch below the top edge, poke a hole. Through these holes you can thread a length of sturdy cord or ribbon that will provide the hanging mechanism for your greenhouse. Start from the inside of the container and pull the cord almost all the way through, stopping short a couple of inches. Tie this couple of inches into a big knot. Secure the knot to the inside of the container with a piece of duct tape for additional reinforcement and to keep it from slipping. Bring the length of cord over to the other side of the container and pass the end through the hole, this time starting on the outside of the container and pushing the cord through the hole and into the inside of the container. Tie the loose end into a big, thick knot, and secure with tape as described above.

Try decorating an indoor miniature greenhouse with glow-in-the-dark star stickers for a night sky effect.

Now all that's left is to fill the greenhouse with soil and seeds, close it up, hang it up, and watch it grow. If you want to hang it indoors, though, you'll have to make a second bottom for it to catch the water drainage. Just use a second lid from a similar container and poke a hole on each side. Thread a length of cord through the holes as you did when you made the hanging mechanism for the main part of the greenhouse. Then connect this loop of cord to the cord on the greenhouse, looping them through each other so that they become intertwined or simply joining them together with tape or bits of string.

For a spherical hanging greenhouse, try a see-through hamster ball. These devices are designed to give pet rodents exercise outside of their cage. They have screw-on lids that lock in place and plenty of open slats for ventilation. To convert it into a greenhouse, all you need to do is to cover some of the open ventilation slats, placing pieces of duct tape over them on the inner side of the ball. Then attach a length of string through a couple of the slats near the top, and it's ready for use. This one is best hung outdoors as it's prone to leakage.

Miniature Greenhouse Maintenance

There are a few things you'll need to do to make sure your greenhouse remains a healthy environment for your plants. First off, don't neglect it. Check on your plants daily if possible and water when necessary. It's also a good idea to wipe down the inside of the greenhouse regularly to prevent moisture build-up that could lead to trouble. When you inspect your plants, check carefully for pests, poke around in the soil a bit, and look closely for any bugs or mold. If you find anything, try to remove it, picking pests off with a set of tweezers or scooping out any nasty bits of soil and replacing with fresh soil. If you find yourself with a pest or mold situation that's severe, you'll need to completely empty the greenhouse, wash it, wash the plant, and refill the greenhouse with completely new soil. The best way to combat major problems in your greenhouse is to stop them before they start or at least stop them before they get out of hand.

Many Mini Options

Miniature greenhouses give you a lot of new gardening possibilities. You could have an herb garden right in the kitchen. You could create a hanging greenhouse jungle in your bathroom. You can turn an empty window into a botanical showcase or add vegetation to a breakfast nook. You could even transform your car into a miniature greenhouse mobile on wheels. Miniature greenhouses also make fun and unique gifts. You might create a one-of-a-kind greenhouse for a friend, decorating it and adding details that highlight their personality and including seeds for flowers or herbs that make you think of them.

Miniature greenhouses are small in scale, but they're huge in possibility.

Melanie Marquis *is the creator of the Modern Spellcaster's Tarot (illustrated by Scott Murphy) and the author of* A Witch's World of Magick, The Witch's Bag of Tricks, Beltane, Lughnasadh, *and* Witchy Mama *(coauthored with Emily Francis). She is a local coordinator for the Denver Pagan Pride Project and is a frequent presenter at magical gatherings around the country.*

Seasonal Assemblage Art

❧ by Lupa ❧

I learned to watch the ground from a young age. I was quick to pick up coins on the sidewalk; in the 1980s a quarter was a pretty big sum of money for a six-year-old. But I also kept my eyes peeled for other treasures: rabbit skulls, bits of raw iron ore, pine cones, cicada shells. They all ended up in shoeboxes, safely tucked away for when I wanted to bring them back out and look at them.

My collecting tendencies continue today, only on a larger scale. My art room is full of animal bones, shed snakeskins, polished agates, and more. I bring back all sorts of knick-knacks from thrift stores, intending to "rehabilitate" them into artistic pieces.

And now that I have a garden and access to more wilderness areas, I'm able to collect a wider variety of plant materials, too.

These all become a part of my artwork; I've been creating with natural materials for almost two decades, and in the past few years I've become especially fond of assemblages. An assemblage is a sculpture in which you glue, nail, tie, or otherwise fasten items together in an aesthetically pleasing manner. If you ever glued leaves, seeds, and other natural items to a piece of paper, jar, or other background in school as a child, you were creating assemblage art!

Gathering supplies for assemblage art is a great way for everyone to have a fun scavenger hunt. Just be careful not to take too much of a particular thing, like all the flowers on a rose bush!

You can use just about anything you want in your assemblages, but here I'm going to talk about plant materials that you can easily get from your garden or yard. Assemblages can be temporary, like arrangements of sticks on the beach that will be taken away by the waves. This article is about permanent, wall-hanging assemblages that you can reuse year after year or give as gifts.

Why Create Seasonal Assemblages?

I know a lot of people who enjoy decorating their homes for the various holidays. While there are certainly plenty of commercial decorations out there, I think it's more fun—and eco-conscious—to create my own with things I find outside. And each year I can create something new; the assemblage I make for spring one year may be totally different from what I created the previous spring.

Collecting the plant materials for your assemblages can be a celebration in and of itself. Go outside, either alone or with friends and family, and see what sorts of leaves, sticks, seeds, and other items you can find at the equinoxes and solstices. You may be surprised at the variety in each season!

If you need to clean up your garden or yard, you can reuse some of what you're weeding or trimming in your art. Got pernicious weeds invading? Dig them up, roots and all, and preserve them whole (try flattening them in a big heavy book). Pruning a bush or tree? Save some of the branches and leaves. Got a bunch of dead annuals at the end of autumn? Put some aside before you compost the rest.

Collecting materials is a great way to connect to the land. When we drive around places, we don't spend a lot of time admiring the scenery, and we don't get a really detailed look at the flora, fauna, and fungi there. By walking around a place and looking for what plant materials are available, you may notice things you'd overlooked before—maybe certain plants you hadn't paid much attention to or what parts of the yard or garden get more sunlight than others. Your assemblages can be portraits of the land as it changes from season to season.

Finally, seasonal assemblages are a great way to create art with a minimum of human-created materials. It can be tough for some artists to let go of their paints, chalks, markers, and other tools and limit themselves to dried plants and some glue. But look at it as a challenge—you have talent, and now you're turning it to a different medium for a little while! That sort of variety can be really healthy for an artist.

What You'll Need

Backboards

This is the "canvas" on which you'll build your assemblage. For wall-hanging assemblages I frequently use old wooden and bamboo cutting boards, shallow wooden boxes, weathered cedar fence boards, and even very sturdy, thick cardboard. I recommend hitting up thrift stores for secondhand backboards, both to keep them out of the waste stream and to save yourself some money. Plus an old, scarred cutting board has a lot more personality than a new one!

Adhesives

For lightweight materials like leaves and grasses, white glue or school glue will work just fine, though some people prefer tacky glue. Once I start attaching heavier things like pine cones, I tend to switch over to more industrial-strength adhesives like E6000 or J-B Weld. However, be aware these industrial glues have a fair number of toxins in them, so you may wish to stick to white and tacky glues if you're concerned about chemicals, or at least keep the industrials to a minimum.

Old Paint Brushes or Cotton Swabs

These are great for applying adhesives to materials, especially small ones. You can also use them to nudge glue-covered materials into place if you don't want them sticking to your fingers.

Sandpaper

This is useful for sanding any rough edges on backboards that could splinter as well as for creating interesting textures on wood bark.

Picture Hangers and Wire

If your backboard doesn't already have a way to be hung up, you'll want to put a hanger or wire on the back before you start creating your assemblage.

Plant Materials

This, of course, is anything useful you find in your garden or yard. You can also collect from houseplants, and if you have friends or neighbors who are amenable, they may let you pick from their plants as well. Never take all members of a given plant species unless it's something invasive that needs to be removed, and take only part of a plant without killing it rather than removing the whole thing unnecessarily.

Preparing Materials

Pretty much anything you'll collect can be preserved by drying it. You'll first want to remove any dirt, spiderwebs, and other stuff. Some of it can be brushed off, but you can also give the materials a quick bath in warm water with a little mild soap. (Don't get delicate seeds like milkweed and dandelion wet, as it can be tough to get the fluffy bits to "fluff" again afterward, and they'll stick to *everything*.)

Once your washed materials have air-dried, you're going to want to dry preserve them. Leaves, flat husks like corn, grasses, and small mosses can be pressed between the pages of a big book. If you have very fleshy, wet plant materials you want to dry flat, you may wish to create a special plant press. This is done by take two flat pieces of wood, maybe eight inches square and a quarter-inch thick, and drilling holes through all four corners (make sure the holes line up when you lay the two boards on top of each other). Run bolts the same size as the holes through the holes on one board. Then layer absorbent paper (watercolor paper works if you have nothing else) and plant materials until the pile is a few inches thick. Place the other board on top with the bolts going through the corner holes. Place a wingnut on each bolt and tighten them all down to press the boards and paper together.

You can also press-dry plant materials with an iron. Place your plants between two thick, absorbent pieces of paper. Then iron this "sandwich" on low—make sure steam is turned off! Don't move the iron around; just keep it on for about ten seconds, then lift and check the plant material. Repeat until the plants are dry.

Be aware that flowers and other plant materials will lose their colors over time if dried. You can preserve a little more color by preserving plants with glycerin. It works best with flowers and leaves on thin, green stems rather than woody stems. After you've cut the plant material off, take it inside and clean it as needed. Then pour a three-inch layer of a mix made of one part glycerin and two parts water in the bottom of a mason jar. Take your plants and cut the ends off the stems while holding them under water; this helps keep the ends of the stems from drying shut. Immediately immerse the cut stems in the glycerin solution. Leave the plant materials in the glycerin until they're flexible all the way to the very ends. This may take only a few days or upward of a month.

You can also preserve flat materials like leaves and grasses. Pour a thin, maybe half- to one-inch layer of the glycerin solution in a shallow baking pan. Put the materials in the glycerin, making sure they're completely covered. Then press them down with another, similar-sized baking pan. Leave them until they feel flexible, usually for a few days.

Putting It All Together

It's time to put your assemblages together! I want to start out by saying there is no right way to create an assemblage. It doesn't have to look like a finely detailed picture or elaborate sculpture. Let your own creativity run free, and play with the colors, shapes, and textures of your materials. You may enjoy creating orderly rows of sticks bounded by a border of seeds, or mix together dried mosses, bark, and seed pods in a glorious disarray. (Or even some of both!) Here are some ideas for inspirational themes:

Celebrate the Season
Using materials just collected within the past couple of weeks, create an assemblage that celebrates the time of year you're in. Your spring assemblage could be full of new flowers, while autumn may be abundant with seeds and fruits.

I Love This Color
Play with a particular color that you really enjoy. Greens, browns, yellows, and the like will of course be easiest, but flowers and seeds can offer surprising hues. Or create a rainbow!

Trees of a Leaf
Try making an assemblage only of materials from one type of plant, like only trees or only grasses.

Make a Picture
Just as the title says, you can use the shapes of plant materials to create pictures. These can be of lifelike things like animals or your home, or they can be more abstract patterns and designs.

Playing with Textures

Nature is full of beautiful textures! You can try making as smooth an assemblage as possible, or throw together all sorts of unique rough edges, bumpy planes, and wispy fluff in one big mix.

Natural History

Make an assemblage that features one species. Treat it like an old natural history illustration, in which you might have a whole small plant in the center and then individual flower heads, seeds, and leaves on either side to showcase their individual structures.

Put your backboard on a level surface. If you wish to add anything to it, like paint, stain, or decoupage, now's the time. Make sure any additions are thoroughly dry before you start adding your plant materials, and be sure that you attach a hanger if one is needed before you go any further.

If you've never put an assemblage together before, you may wish to make a "dry" assemblage first. This simply means placing the materials on the backboard without gluing them into place. This will allow you to move them around and figure out where they look best. Pay attention to how many distinct layers your assemblage has.

Then start by gluing on the first layer. Let it dry thoroughly before adding the next. It's a lot easier to layer and overlap materials once the lower items are firmly in place. And let the entire assemblage dry thoroughly before you hang it up on display.

You don't need to do a lot to care for these assemblages. Keep them out of direct sunlight and away from heat sources like vents and fireplaces. Keep them away from pets that may try to chew on them, and take a look at them every now and then to be sure insects don't take up resident in them. (Allowing a spider to take up resident in the assemblage can help with bug proofing and adds a little more character!)

Lupa *is a Pagan author, hide and bone artist, naturalist, and eco-psychologist in the Pacific Northwest. She is the author of several books, including* Nature Spirituality From the Ground Up *(Llewellyn, 2016), and is the creator of the Tarot of Bones. You can find out more about her work at http://www.thegreenwolf.com.*

An Ornament for Every Season

❧ by Laurel Reufner ❧

You've got to love those amazing little plants we call herbs. They decorate and help out in our gardens, flavor our food and drink, beautify our skin, and can even keep us healthy. And they're also fun to craft with, helping scent and beautify our homes. In the following few pages, I'm going to give you some tips for making herbal ornaments. These can be tailored for just about any season, letting our herbal friends decorate our homes year round.

Wreaths of Thyme

This little project is based on one I discovered in Phyllis Shaudys's *Herbal Treasures*. I'd never thought of using the microwave to dry herbs or flowers, but for some things it works

quite well. The finished project is delicate looking, making it very different from my other projects here.

You'll need:

Fresh sprigs of thyme, about 8 inches in length

Thread

Paper towels

Little decorative bits, such as narrow ribbon, small flowers, etc.

For this project, you'll want thyme sprigs that are fairly young and thin in diameter. The thicker ones are likely to snap on you. It may take a little experimentation to figure out what works best for your needs and your microwave, but fortunately you can dry more than one sprig at a time.

Carefully coil your sprig into a wreath shape using thread tied here and there to help hold it in place. Zap it on a paper towel in the microwave for about 30 seconds and then check it. Continue drying the thyme in 10-second bursts, checking in between each. When the leaves start to feel dry and crisp, it's done. Remove from the microwave and set it aside to cool.

Personally, I think a small grouping of these hanging, undecorated, would be lovely. Or do them up with small bows of thin ribbon, with another ribbon for hanging. If you do decorate them further, make sure the decorations are small and light, in keeping with the delicateness of the thyme wreaths.

Seasoning Wreaths

Bouquet garni is a wonderful herbal mix for seasoning all sorts of soups, broths, and stews, and it's very easy to make. It only seemed natural to make several little bouquets and then attach them to a wreath. You can then hang it in your kitchen, snipping off your seasonings as you need. I've given two different approaches to making your seasoning wreath. Choose whichever works best for you.

For a fresh version, you'll need:

18 sprigs of parsley

12 sprigs of thyme

6 large bay leaves

Kitchen string or thread

6-inch vine wreath

Narrow ribbon in the color(s) of your choice

Begin your project by making small bunches of the herbs using the following proportions: 3 sprigs parsley, 2 sprigs thyme, and 1 bay leaf. You should have 6 bunches when finished. Trim the bottoms of the sprigs to about 5 inches in length. Tuck the bay leaf down against the area where you'll tie the bunch together, and wrap it all tightly with the string.

Once you have your bundles all tightly tied, pull out the wreath and arrange your bouquet garnis around it to your satisfaction. Tie them in place with the ribbons and hang to display. Over time your herbal bundles will dry out, but if used within 6 months or so, they'll do a good job of flavoring your food.

For a version using dried bundles, you'll need:

6 tablespoons dried parsley

6 teaspoons dried thyme

6 bay leaves

Clean muslin or cheesecloth

Kitchen twine or thread

Narrow ribbon

6-inch vine wreath

This variation on the seasoning wreath is very similar to the first version, only you'll be making small muslin bundles of the dried herbs instead of the fresh sprigs. You'll need to cut 4-inch circles out of your cloth. (I recommend pinking shears if you have them. They'll leave a nice decorative edge and help discourage fraying.)

In each circle, place 1 tablespoon parsley, 1 teaspoon thyme, and a crushed-up bay leaf. Gather up the edges of the cloth and tie it off tightly with the string. Leave a tail about 8 inches long, wrapping its length around your bundle. This tail will give you something with which to pull the bouquet garni out of your dinner.

Arrange the bundles around your wreath and, once again, tie them in place with your ribbon.

Sweet Posy Tussie-Mussies

This classic nature craft helped inspire the previous project. Make one to hang in a window, from a door knob, or anywhere else that could use a little brightening. Perhaps you'll want to give it to someone special. If you are making your tussie-mussie—Middle English for "cluster of posies"—to give as a gift, you might even want to consult a list of Victorian herb and flower meanings so you can make it personal.

You'll need:

Sprigs of dried herbs and flowers of your choice

Doily or decorative paper

Wire, about 12 inches

Floral tape

Ribbon

A quick web search will easily turn up dozens of sites offering information on flowers and their meanings, so it should be easy to figure out which ones send the message you want. Another option is to simply pick herbs and flowers that appeal to you. Either way, you'll want to choose the nicest-looking dried ones that you can. Arrange them in a small bouquet, something that will easily fit in your hand. Fold the wire into a U-shape and tuck it down in the bouquet as well. This will form a hanger. (If you don't want to be able to hang your sweet posie, then just leave the wire out.)

Wrap the stems with a rubber band to help keep them in place. Cut a simple X in the middle of the doily, with the cuts each being about 1 to 1½ inches long, and push the little bouquet through the middle. After you have your bouquet in place, you can start wrapping the protruding stems with the floral tape, followed by the ribbon.

Cinnamon Stars

I made these stars for our tree a few years ago using 3-inch cinnamon sticks, and they are so lovely. They would be very easy to adapt for other holidays and seasons by simply switching up the cinnamon sticks for twigs and altering the decorative bits. Also, use bigger sticks for bigger stars, which you can easily hang in a window or from a cabinet. Make them in two or three different sizes and create a graduated door hanging with the big one at the top and the smaller sizes hanging below it.

You'll need:

> Cinnamon sticks
>
> Hot glue gun
>
> Low-heat glue sticks
>
> Narrow ribbon or monofilament for hanging
>
> Small decorations such as small pine cones, bits of dried greenery, star anise, or whole spices

The directions for this one are pretty simple: just hot glue the cinnamon into a star shape and decorate. However, I've got a few tips for making it a bit easier. The biggest is to lay things out before you start gluing. I like to lay out the cinnamon sticks on top of each other to make sure I have a pleasing star shape, as well as make sure they touch where I'll need to put the glue. Do the same thing with your decorations so that you can make sure you like the way they look.

As for what to use for the decorations, it's really a matter of practicality and your imagination. I've used dried bits of greenery, whole star anise (one of my favorite things), little pine cones (such as Eastern hemlock), various other spices or herbal leaves (such as bay leaves), dried flowers, and even little charms or doodads. The bigger the star, the bigger the decorations you can use. My three-inch ornaments were a bit of a challenge when I first tried to figure out what would look best and not completely cover the star's cinnamon sticks. I've also found that I like to mainly orient them in the bottom right corner of the star, but play around and find out what pleases you.

You could also use some thin, decorative cording, ribbon, or embroidery floss to tie around the points, where the sticks are glued together, just to add to the decorative effect. Monofilament or more floss can be used to create a hanger.

Decorative Herbal Balls

These versatile beauties were inspired by the elegant kissing balls of Yule. Halfway through making the first one, all of these possible variations started to occur to me. You really can make these for pretty much any seasonal decor you want or need. And it all starts with some heavy craft glue, such as Aleene's, and a Styrofoam ball, plus any botanical decorations you choose. I used 3-inch Styrofoam balls purchased at our local dollar store (1½- and 2-inch balls would also work). They also sell a couple of varieties of moss, also found in the crafting section. I really liked it for the botanical base of my ornaments.

You'll need:

Heavy craft glue

Styrofoam ball

Dried moss

Small dried flowers and spices for decoration

Ribbon

Wooden skewer

Hot glue gun

Low-heat glue sticks

I like to pour some of the craft glue into a small container and then use an old paint brush to apply it. Working in small sections of roughly 1 inch, apply a good coat of the glue to the Styrofoam and then press on the dried moss. You may need to hold it in place for a moment in order for it to stick. Apply more dabs of glue as needed. In this fashion, cover the entire foam ball.

Allow your covered ball to dry for several hours. This is where the skewer can start to come in handy. Stick the pointed end into the ball and then prop it in a tall glass, jar, or bottle. This will let the air circulate all around the ball.

Once your ball is nice and dry, it's time for the really fun part—decorating. I found it easiest to either hold the skewer or rest the ball on top of a glass or vase, so I could easily turn it to see where more decorative bits need to go. Then it's just a matter of hot gluing on various bits and pieces wherever you want them. I started my first decorated herbal ball by wrapping a ribbon around it from the top to the bottom, fastening the ends down at the top with a dollop of hot glue. I added a sprinkling of dried wild violet flowers, little bits of cinnamon sticks (about ½-inch long), and Eastern hemlock cones. I snipped the bottoms off the cones with a pair of scissors and then glued the flattened bottom against the ball. Another loop of ribbon went on top for a hanger.

That finished ornament is rather subtle, but the second one I did was covered in dried lavender flowers and then decorated with chunks of dried statice and sprigs of baby's breath. A dragonfly found at the dollar store and a monofilament hanger finished it off. The hanger was held in place with a double-pronged pin found at the craft store. This one has more dimension and pop than the first, but they're both lovely.

The real beauty of this project is its versatility, starting with the decoration options. I personally like the moss base if I'm going to be adding other decorative bits, but I've also covered them in lavender buds and dried rose petals. I think whole spices would also look lovely.

There are endless possibilities for decorating these herbal balls. When testing out this project, I limited myself to what I had on hand, and it gave me some great ways to use up those small amounts of herbs and flowers that I'd accumulated—just in case—over time. The purple statice and baby's breath, I'll confess, were bought at a grocery store. Queen Anne's lace, dried strawflowers, or zinnias would all look wonderful, as would the blooms of any number of herbs. And don't rule out the beautiful foliage of some herbs or the seed pods and bark of some spices, such as star anise.

The versatility continues with your display options. You can hang them with ribbons, monofilament, or even chain. Display several in a pretty bowl or tuck one here and there for a little extra something. Or leave them topped on their skewer and tuck some in a vase with other dried or silk flowers for something a little different.

Remember to check your local dollar store for basic craft supplies. That's where I get my glue sticks, small grapevine wreaths, Styrofoam, cinnamon sticks, and little decorative bits.

Really, for these projects I had more ideas than I did time (or funds) to try, but maybe my suggestions will give you some incentive to set your own creative streak free. Write in and share them with me—I'm always looking for new, fun things to try.

Laurel Reufner *loves writing about all sorts of topics. Craft projects of all types and techniques entice her, so she loved the challenge of writing this particular article. Laurel lives in beautiful southeastern Ohio with her husband and two rapidly growing semiadult teenage daughters, who both continue her wild child legacy. Drop in and visit her on Facebook.*

Create a Butterfly Garden with Your Kids

❧ by Thea Fiore-Bloom ❧

Butterflies enchant us, but their populations are dwindling due to herbicides and overdevelopment. So how about helping out these endangered beauties by planting a welcoming environment for them to flutter through?

"That would be swell," you might say, "but don't I need a rambling English meadow to attract butterflies?" Nope.

"Well, a lawn then?" Nope.

"Oh, come on, at the very least I'm going to have to have some of those raised beds of dirt built on top of the deck!" No, not even.

"You can help our struggling butterfly populations by planting something as simple as a window box," said horticulturalist Barbara Smith, Cooperative Extension agent with South Carolina's Clemson University, in a 2016 interview with me. "If you live in an apartment, even in an urban area, and you've got a patio or balcony, you have what you need to begin to help butterflies."

It's not just pollinators like hummingbirds, bees, and butterflies that benefit. You benefit, too. "Mentally, gardening is extremely beneficial, especially for city dwellers. You've probably heard of the studies that have shown that patients whose hospital rooms faced green spaces heal faster than patients whose hospital rooms faced brick walls," said Smith.

Benefits for Kids

Kids, too, benefit from butterflies. Planting a mini butterfly garden is a perfect project to do with children for the following reasons.

Kids Need Dirt

"As we become *more* of an urban society, our children are becoming *less* connected to the land," said Smith. "All children need to get their hands in dirt—in actual soil." Butterfly gardening can make nature real for city kids. And approximately 77 percent of American kids are now city kids.

Butterflies Breed Conservationists

Making a butterfly garden is a great way to introduce kids to conservation. It will encourage them to support and learn about other forms of endangered wildlife. Butterflies coax young and old alike into becoming responsible stewards of the earth.

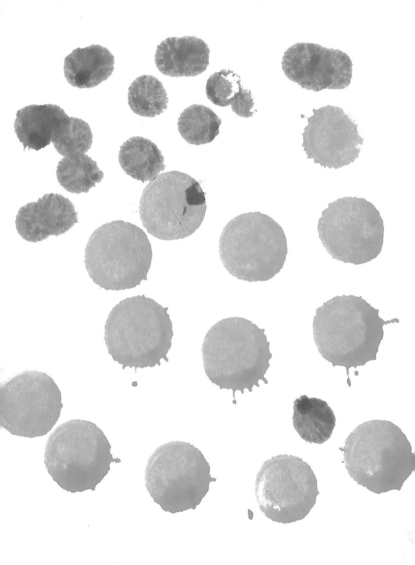

Gardening Teaches Accountability

The study of these gorgeous insects also encourages a second form of responsibility: personal responsibility. As Smith puts it, "You can't let a new puppy suffer if your children forget to feed it, but you can let a plant die if your children don't water it." When kids see a dead plant, they are absorbing a gentle lesson about consequences.

Butterflies Get Kids Excited about Science

Butterflies mesmerize kids. When kids are enthralled, they learn rapidly. Smith remembers how exhilarated and proud her then-eight-year-old son was when he could shout out, "Oh, look, Mom! It's a silver-spotted skipper!" When you help children learn basic butterfly biology, you're helping them get excited about science and gain self-confidence.

How to Make Your Mini Garden

So let's learn how to bring butterflies to balconies. "You can plant a butterfly box anytime during the warm months after the fear of frost has passed. Planting in the spring will give the plants time to mature and provide the butterflies with food and nectar sources," said Smith.

Step 1: Meet The Locals

The first part of the mission is to find out what particular butterfly species are flitting about your neck of the woods. Ask your tablet-obsessed kids, "How about we look up which butterflies are in our area?" Or visit gardenswithwings.com, punch in your zip code, and presto—you have an illustrated list of your area's butterflies. Now choose one of the most common species in your locale so that you'll have a good chance of luring them to your balcony.

Luckily I had my boyfriend's smart young niece as my gardening buddy for this project in Southern California. We decided to try to help out local anise swallowtails (*Papilio zelicaon*).

Step 2: Plan Your Larva Lounge

"Butterflies go through four stages of development or metamorphosis: egg to larva (caterpillar) to pupa (chrysalis) to adult," said Smith. Your second step is to find out the plants your butterfly's larva will devour.

There are several herbs that many larva species love. "Parsley and dills are excellent larva foods. Coriander, oregano, fennel, various kinds of sage (*Salvia*), and lavender are other options," said Smith. Butterflywebsite.com has a good, simple list of who eats what. It also has fun butterfly-themed learning games for kids. Anise swallowtail caterpillars, for example, are partial to dill, sweet fennel (*Foeniculum vulgare*), and parsley, so these herbs headed up our shopping list.

Step 3: Nectar Needs

After the adult butterfly emerges from its chrysalis, it needs to take in nectar to nourish itself. "Nectar is a sugary fluid that flowers secrete to attract pollinators like butterflies," said Smith. Butterflies are drawn to profusions of brightly colored flowers. They are especially fond of red, orange, yellow, and pink blooms. But these beautiful insects won't just go for any bright blossom. Shape is also a key factor.

Butterflies are perchers by nature. Hummingbirds prefer trumpet or tube-shaped blossoms. Butterflies favor single flat flowers or groups of blossoms that form fairly level clusters so that they can rest their feet on a stable surface while drinking nectar.

General crowd pleasers nectar-wise are hyssop (*Hyssopus officinalis*, also known as hummingbird mint), dwarf butterfly bush (*Buddleia*), and marigolds (*Tagetes*). Smith notes, "Purple mistflower (*Ageratum*) would work well. Globe amaranth (*Gomphrena globosa*) is good. Your pentas (*Pentas lanceolata*), sages (*Salvia*), zinnias (*Zinnia elegans*), and wildflowers are all sound container options for butterflies." Anise swallowtails are fond of nectar from colorful zinnias, asters, and butterfly bush. I jotted these down on our shopping list.

Expert agents at your local county's cooperative extension office are there for you, no matter where you live in the United States. Each extension provides no-cost gardening and agricultural advice to its own residents. Find your extension agent by clicking on your state and county at pickyourown.org/countyextensionagentoffices.htm.

Choose native species of plants over exotic species if you can. Native plants support local ecology and often are more drought-tolerant than exotic species. On top of that, most native plants need less maintenance and less pesticides and tend to attract more area wildlife than those imports do.

Step 4: Shopping Time! Or Maybe Not . . .

Now it's time to hit the nursery for plants (seeds are fine, too, if you have more than a day to devote to the project). A couple of herbs and a couple of flowers per pot will be great. You don't have to go nuts buying many different kinds of plants, but do get enough of each.

"Plant a lot and expect it to get devoured," said Smith. "For example, the larvae of the swallowtail butterflies that we have here in South Carolina eat parsley and dill. If you get swallowtail larva on your parsley, for instance, it will totally defoliate it in some cases—but then you get swallowtail butterflies." When it comes to butterfly gardens, defoliation equals a job well done.

If you are the thrifty, creative kind, you may avoid the nursery altogether by asking a gardening relative or neighbor to share or trade cuttings with you. And you needn't buy a fifty-dollar majolica pot to put your plants in. You can opt out of buying any pot for that matter. Killer vintage containers are often left discarded in alleyways. There also are respectable pots to be had for under five dollars at neighborhood garage sales. Keep your eyes peeled but always inspect the base of the pot.

Step 5: Avoid Blocking Drainage

"The biggest mistake people make," said Smith "is buying a really pretty pot with no drainage holes in the bottom. The water gathers. It's got nowhere to go. The plants rot. The person thinks they're a bad gardener. Then they give up gardening. Just because they didn't use common sense when it comes to proper drainage holes."

Plastic containers work. Just remember to carefully punch open the sealed holes at the bottom. Even a railing planter or hanging basket with sound drainage will make a good home for a mini butterfly garden.

Step 6: Planting

Now for the fun part—planting. As far as soil goes, you want a good plain ol' potting mix (not planting mix). "If you're using a wooden box that has some height to it and is, say, six inches wide, you can do two or three layers. You know, taller things behind—short stuff in the middle—and trailing plants or vines in front. Keep spacing in mind. Read the label for info," said Smith.

Step 7: Watering—It's Not Rocket Science

"You can't give people a watering recommendation across the board because needs will vary with container type, sun, wind, and other factors," said Smith. "Here's the best way you or your children can measure the water needs of your butterfly box. Stick two fingers in the dirt every few days. If the soil is no longer moist, add water. If it's still a bit damp—leave it alone."

Step 8: Find Your Place in the Sun

Place your box garden in an area with at least six hours of sunlight per day. Butterflies love a place in the sun, but not too much sun. Smith recommends ideally placing pots in a place that has a full spectrum of high shade to full sun daily.

Step 9: Don't Be So Serious

You might think the best gardeners are meticulous perfectionists. And you'd be wrong. "'Experimentation' and 'play' are the watchwords of good gardening," said Smith, who has a master's degree in ornamental horticulture and landscape design. "Try and try again. See what lives and what dies. Find out what you love and what you don't. Let your inner artist out." Allow yourself to create your own version of beautiful.

Step 10: Expect Surprises

It had been a month since I expectantly parked our pocket-sized garden on my narrow patio. Not a butterfly in sight. No anise swallowtails, no nothing. I was crestfallen. My boyfriend's niece, being more mature than I am, had taken it in stride.

The day after I had given up, I was having my usual early coffee on the patio when a mourning cloak (*Nymphalis antiopa*) glided by. My jaw dropped open. Mourning cloaks are not unheard of in Southern California, but they typically seek out oak and willow tree–rich gardens. And there this one was, dipping about my urban balcony in all her exotic, velvety, maroon, sky-blue spotted wonderfulness.

Since that morning, other species have followed. So I say be patient. Stay open. Nature has a few sublime surprises in store for you.

Thea Fiore-Bloom, *PhD, is a California gardener, writer, artist, and literacy volunteer. She welcomes mail at her website www.thea fiorebloom.com.*

Creating the Minimal Garden

❧ by Emyme ❧

Several years ago I wrote about the naturalization of my property. I allowed a fallen tree to remain as a playground for chipmunks and squirrels. I did not cut back the perimeter grasses and plants. I allowed the lawn to grow higher. There were numerous bird feeders. It may sound as though caring for that yard required less maintenance. The truth is it was just as much work, and when I decided on a less natural style, it was quite the chore to clean it all out. Over the past few years I have found it difficult to bend or kneel as easily as I did in the past. It got me wondering, what can be done when we can no longer care for a yard or garden as in the past?

Over ten years ago when we acquired this home, the curb appeal was—to be blunt—ugly. Rocks and trees and shrubs were moved or removed, and young, fresh plantings were brought in. For some time I looked forward to three-season gardening. After recent years of benign neglect due to my escalating lack of mobility, it was determined the lovingly designed flower beds needed a major overhaul. Everything was right back to ugly.

The first challenge was finding a landscaper. This turned out to be surprisingly difficult. Eventually, the correct fit came along via word of mouth, and it was certainly a learning process in patience. While planning, obtain a few estimates. The quotes received for the work covered in this essay were all in the price range of fifteen hundred dollars.

However, this entire project could have very well been done without a landscaper. Younger, more able homeowners can easily do the research and get tips from books, the Internet, and home and garden stores. Know that what is saved in money will be spent in time. My project was no weekend makeover, but a homeowner determined to say "I did this" could, indeed, do every part.

Minimizing: Tidying and Replacing

After all that natural look, a less busy and less time-intensive style was needed. Four bushes planted for privacy in front of the master bedroom windows had become too tall (higher than the gutters), and during the winter, one had bent permanently during a heavy snowfall. Three smaller bushes planted for contrast had become leggy and sparse. Sadly, I cannot recall the names of all that shrubbery. Miscellaneous flowers, a few spiky **gladiolas**, and a lot of **vinca** had to go. All of it had been surrounded by a low-profile wooden retaining wall, which over the years had faded and splintered.

Between that bed and the front door stood a huge **butterfly bush**. I had planted it to provide some shade to the southern-facing front porch, for color and (obviously) for the attraction of butterflies and bees. However, over the years it had become quite a monster. Many summers the new growth would tower over eight feet. Several times it was cut back almost to the ground by chain saw, which only served to strengthen the root system. I was not present when the bush was removed, but the landscaper informed me it was rather a chore, and I think he was being kind in his assessment. There was a trade-off in taking down that bush: our front door can get very hot to the touch. A less cluttered look was more important to me than the shade.

As with most home projects, the tedious part is the prep work. Once all the old plantings were gone, it was short work to put in three lovely **boxwoods**, which served as a backdrop for two **golden thread** bushes. The bed is rounded out from the house in a perfect half circle and mounded slightly up. There is no paver wall; it eases into the lawn. Fresh black mulch creates an elegant look. Master bedroom windows, long hidden, are now in full view, and the front of the house looks bigger. Simple and sleek, an appreciable difference.

Along the garage side of the house is one long wall, uninterrupted by windows or a door. Between that wall and the walkway to the backyard lies a long, narrow bed. When this spot was cleared years ago, we planted four **dwarf Burford holly** bushes. In the middle was a large **yucca** plant, one of those plants that look like a huge pineapple and whose spiky leaves can be very hard on a casual gardener without the proper gloves or clothing. Over time we donated the yucca plant to a neighbor (shoots still occasionally arise) and replaced it with a **dwarf Alberta spruce**. It had been our hope it would grow at least to cover all but the dish of the satellite. Alas, it never got taller than two feet—merely cute, definitely dwarf. I was never really able to properly keep up with the weeds in this bed. It had become overgrown and sloppy.

Regarding holly bushes or trees, it is most important to plant both male and female. Although it is possible (bees can travel far), do not depend on bees to locate a male holly for pollination.

Landscaping: Consider Sun and Timing

The cute little spruce was found to have mites—completely dead and brown once you got past the first few inches of green. Large irregular-shaped rocks that served as the border were removed. The bed was ruthlessly weeded and the top layer of old mulch and dirt shoveled off. Lovely rectangle pavers hold in new black mulch. My landscape artist even mitered the corners of the paver bricks—amazing. (Those four well-groomed holly bushes share space with a television satellite "tree.") Two low-to-the-ground **popcorn rose** bushes in creamy white, pale yellow, and a hint of pinky peach complete the look.

In the past I enjoyed seeing my gardens full of flowers. This new design allows for space between the plants. If you do not wish to see as much of the bed or mulch and prefer a softer, cozier garden, here are a few suggestions:

First determine how much sun the bed receives and if you want **perennials** (grows for years) or **annuals** (one season only). The golden threads chosen by the landscaper for the front garden are full-sun perennial plants. Our hot southern New Jersey summer got the best of them, even with consistent watering. They were replaced with yellow and white **chrysanthemums**, which love full sun. Usually deemed an annual, mums may come back year after year; it is a wait-and-see situation. **Black-eyed Susans** are taller perennials usually added to the rear of a garden as background color. Another option is bulbs, planted in the fall (**daffodils**, **tulips**, **crocus**) or spring (**calla lily**, **gladiola**).

Had this transformation taken place in the spring, I may have considered annuals. Marigolds, ageratum, and begonias take full sun and are very popular in zone 7. **Marigolds** come in a variety of sizes and shades of gold, orange, and yellow. Their scent is a natural insect repellant. **Ageratum** is low to the ground with purple flowers and can make good ground cover. **Begonias**, too, come in many colors, both flowers and leaves. A mix of orange marigolds, purple ageratum, and red or white begonias makes for a delightful summer flower bed. Might I point out all of these plants are what I call "messy" plants and require trimming of dead flowers and leaves. Take that work into consideration when planting. **Grasses** are another decorative plant that works well in the sun and requires little maintenance. One plant I wanted to definitely avoid was **impatiens**: they thrive only in a shade garden.

Our Minimal Garden

Some homeowners maintain their property for the joy of spending leisure time outdoors. Our family is one that prefers to look at a well-maintained yard rather than spend a lot of time there. Being forced to do less than I wish, these minimal gardens are just the thing: lovely to look at and easy to care for. It is a joy to see the clean lines of this transformation.

Just as fashions go through fads and trends, so do homes and gardens. Years back, the trend was flowers and plants in precise rows. A few seasons ago, it was the cluttered, natural English garden or woodsy look. Currently, it is minimal and less work, a few shrubs and planters holding the colorful flowers. In the near future, the trend will likely be ecologically inclined, with a kitchen garden, a compost heap, and a rain catcher in every yard. One of the joys of gardening and yard care is changing your mind and changing your style. I have greatly enjoyed this process of minimizing, and I hope it has given you a few ideas about your own landscaping projects.

Emyme, *an eclectic solitary, resides in a multi-generation, multi-cat household in southern New Jersey and concentrates on candle spells, garden spells, and kitchen witchery. In addition to writing poetry and prose about strong women of mythology and fairy tales, Emyme is creating a series of articles on bed and breakfasts from the point of view of the over-fifty-five single female Wiccan traveler. Please send questions or comments to catsmeow24@verizon.net.*

Herb History,
Myth, and Lore

The Marshmallow Plant:
A Long, Sweet History

⤞ by Sandra Kynes ⤝

For most people, the word "marshmallow" brings to mind the warm, gooey center of that campfire favorite called s'mores. Although the marshmallow plant (*Althaea officinalis*) was the inspiration for the puffy, white sweet, it is no lightweight and has been used for a wide range of medicinal purposes.

The word "mallow" was derived from the Greek *malakos*, meaning "soft," in reference to the plant's velvety leaves. Also from Greek, marshmallow's genus name comes from *althaia*, meaning "to heal," emphasizing its primary use. The plant's common name refers to its preference for wet locations.

Like many herbs, marshmallow has a plethora of folk names. In reference to its hollyhock cousins, it has been called hock herb and wild mallow. Another name, "mortification root," comes from its reputed ability to prevent infection. It shares the folk name "cheeses" with the common mallow (*Malva sylvestris*) because their seed heads look like little wheels of cheese. Last but not least, the name "sweet weed" comes from the sweet taste of its roots.

Use of this plant dates way back—millennia. According to archeological evidence, marshmallow was one of several plants that appeared to have been intentionally placed in a Neanderthal burial. In historical times, marshmallow was introduced into ancient Egypt from Syria, where the root was boiled and combined with honey as a remedy for sore throat. Nuts were sometimes added to this syrup and enjoyed as a treat. Along with poppies and saffron, marshmallow flowers were woven into Egyptian mortuary garlands to symbolically comfort the deceased in the afterlife.

Greek physician Hippocrates (468–377 BCE), who became known as the father of medicine, recommended a decoction of the root to treat bruises, wounds, and sores. The leaves were also used for this purpose. Considered the father of botany, Greek naturalist Theophrastus (c. 372–287 BCE) noted that the roots steeped in sweet wine served as an effective remedy for chest ailments. Both the Greeks and Romans ate the flowers to soothe tickly coughs.

Traveling throughout the Roman Empire, Greek physician and botanist Pedanius Dioscorides (c. 40–90 CE) prescribed a poultice of marshmallow to ease insect bites and an infusion to relieve toothache. He also noted that the plant could be employed as an antidote to poisoning.

Roman author and naturalist Pliny the Elder (c. 23–79 CE) considered marshmallow a cure-all and recommended the daily use of it as a type of apple-a-day food to stay healthy. The Romans considered marshmallow leaves a delicacy that they cooked as a vegetable. In fact, they enjoyed it so much that they took marshmallow with them as the empire expanded and introduced the plant into the British Isles.

Practitioners of Ayurvedic medicine in ancient India used marshmallow flowers in cough remedies and the seeds specifically for dry coughs. In the Middle East, physician Avicenna (980–1037 CE) prescribed marshmallow to counteract tumors. In addition, the root was used for treating internal and external inflammation.

Impressed with its healing properties, Emperor Charlemagne (742–814 CE), who ruled most of Western Europe, promoted its use by decreeing that marshmallow be planted throughout his realm. A few centuries later, German abbess, mystic, and healer Hildegard of Bingen (1098–1179 CE) recommended steeping marshmallow in vinegar and then drinking the concoction to break a fever.

During the Middle Ages, folk healers in Europe employed marshmallow to ease a range of ailments from toothache to urinary problems. Decoctions of the root were often made with milk or wine. Looking like a thin, yellow carrot and containing mucilage, the raw root served as a teether for babies. During this time, when trial by fire was a form of determining guilt, the crushed plant was rubbed on the hands and other parts of the body for protection from burns.

Although the Romans ate the young shoots as a vegetable, in other areas around the Mediterranean marshmallow was regarded as food for the poor. However, in medieval Europe the roots—boiled and then sautéed with onions—served as a dietary staple when cultivated crops failed. In addition, the shoots were used to make a syrupy drink. Raw seed capsules were also eaten and frequently added to flavor cheese. Not letting anything go to waste, people used the fibrous stems as a source for blue dye.

A golden age of herbalism was sparked in the Elizabethan era by the expanding use of the printing press. Both famous herbalists Nicholas Culpeper (1616–1654 CE) and John Gerard (1545–1612 CE) included marshmallow in their books and advocated its use for a wide range of applications. Gerard mentioned that it was especially good for digestive issues and relieving pain. Culpeper noted that it was medicinally more effective than other mallows.

In the nineteenth century, the delicate color of the mallow flower became all the rage in Europe after the British royals took a liking to it. Clothing, house furnishings, even writing paper was produced in the color called mauve, from the French for "mallow."

Marshmallow was one of the important apothecary plants that English settlers brought to North America, unwilling to leave it behind. It now grows wild in parts of the eastern United States and Canada.

Before the invention of gelatin, marshmallow (*guimauve* in French) provided just the right consistency to give certain dishes a fluffy texture. One such confection was *pâté de guimauve*, which became extremely popular. Bearing its English name, the overly sweet descendant of this treat no longer contains anything from the marshmallow plant. However, while the plant's culinary uses may have diminished, its healing legacy has not been forgotten. Marshmallow continues to hold its own in a wide range of herbal remedies.

Bibliography

Chevallier, Andrew. *The Encyclopedia of Medicinal Plants*. New York: Dorling Kindersley Publishing, 1996.

Curtis, Susan, and Louise Green. *Home Herbal*. New York: Dorling Kindersley Publishing, 2011.

Dobelis, Inge N., ed. *Magic and Medicine of Plants*. Pleasantville, NY: The Reader's Digest Association, Inc., 1986.

Grieve, Margaret. *A Modern Herbal*, vol. 2. Mineola, NY: Dover Publications, 1971.

Kear, Katherine. *Flower Wisdom*. London: Thorsons, 2000.

Kowalchik, Claire, and William H. Hylton, eds. *Rodale's Illustrated Encyclopedia of Herbs*. Emmaus, PA: Rodale Press, 1998.

Martin, Laura C. *Wildflower Folklore*. New York: East Woods Press, 1984.

Storl, Wolf D. *A Curious History of Vegetables*. Berkeley, CA: North Atlantic Books, 2016.

Sandra Kynes *is an explorer of history, myth, and magic and a member of the Order of Bards, Ovates and Druids. Her inquisitiveness has led her to investigate the roots of her beliefs and to integrate her spiritual path with everyday life. Sandra likes developing creative* *ways to explore the world, which serves as the basis for her books. She has lived in New York City, Europe, England, and now coastal New England. Her work has been featured in various Llewellyn publications and* Utne Reader, SageWoman, The Portal, *and* Circle *magazines. She enjoys connecting with the natural world through gardening, hiking, bird watching, and ocean kayaking. Visit her website at www.kynes.net.*

Native American Plant Lore of the Great Lakes Region

⁂ by Calantirniel ⁂

O riginally, as a trained herbalist, my intentions were to share with you, dear readers, the herbal medicinal uses for plants considered native in North America by those who are indeed indigenous to the land and were here hundreds, perhaps thousands, of years prior to European arrival (which is somewhat in dispute due to archeological evidence findings of late, but no matter).

After receiving a recommendation from a friend to access material closest to the source of this intention, I eagerly set out to read *Plants Have So Much to Give Us, All We Have to Do Is Ask* by Mary Siisip Geniusz. What I delightfully discovered is that the most-discussed herbal remedies have counterpart species in the Old World (Europe and Asia). Not so surprisingly, the uses of these herbal remedies are uncannily similar to Western uses. In other words, yarrow (*Achillea millefolium*) is used the same way for physical (and often spiritual) healing qualities for virtually identical illness and disease symptoms.

So why did I find this book such a delight, you ask? The stories that are told in this book are a beautiful lens inside a worldview quite different from ours, despite arriving at the same place in relation to a nature-based, vitalistic approach to health. It is akin to traveling to a place via a chosen route and meeting someone at the destination who describes his or her own route with similarities to and differences from yours; your mind then flickers back and forth comparing your experience to that of the other traveler, while feeling through this process that you yourself have traveled both paths. I hope to provide the essence of the stories while simultaneously recognizing I cannot do justice in my retelling efforts and for this, reading authentic sources by Native authors is highly recommended.

Anishinaabe Cosmology

Anishinaabeg hold absolute reverence in every way for the wonderful-smelling *Thuja occidentalis*, or "Grandmother Cedar," as they always addressed her. The Anishinaabe stories reflect four levels of creation. The first is that of the sky, waters, rocks, and fire. Earth herself and stories happen to belong here, allowing us to observe that in this viewpoint, stories existed before, not after, each level of creation came into existence. The second level is that of the plant kingdom. Trees in particular are seen as wise ancient ones, and Grandmother Cedar has the top place, likened but not identically to the world tree Ygdrassil in the Nordic tradition, an ash tree. The third level is that of the animal kingdom, with special note to those who flew in the air, those who were four-legged on land, and those who swam; finally, the two-legged (humans) came to be.

While orthodox Western cultures' mindsets, shown through such things as biblical writings, may have viewed humans being at the top of creation, the Anishinaabe view places humankind at the bottom. From this perspective, we can then deeply respect nature on all levels and avoid the desire to control or change it into a short-sighted benefit at a cost of upsetting the natural balance. This is frowned upon rather than encouraged.

Grandmother Cedar

Grandmother Cedar came into being when it was decided that there was a need for communication between the different levels of creation that were called holes: spirit, sky, touching land, and under the ground. There were trees that already existed, but the qualities for certain food, shelter, and medicine needs were not quite right. So prayers were answered, and up sprang the magnificent tree who grew straight, had healing oils, and had a light wood that was also strong and would not rot, which solved a great many problems. She was an exact reflection above the ground as below the ground: birds nested in the upper part, and the mirrored counterpart underground sheltered the ground critters.

Bearberry (*Arctostaphylos uva-ursi*), through a much longer tale, was created through Bear at the same time, so these two plants became the necessary ingredients in the incense/smudge that was intended as an offering when praying (communicating) to the Great Spirit. This mix, called *asemaa* or *kinnikinnick,* can also include other plants, depending on availability and intention. A kinnikinnick recipe may include yarrow (*Achillea millefolium*) to remove negativity and sweetgrass (*Hierochloe odorata*) to bring loving, positive energy (these are often used in tandem), as well as mullein (*Verbascum thapsus*), sweet clover (*Melilotus* spp.), and a wide variety of other plants, especially if they make pleasant smoke.

Bearberry had another use among the Anishinaabeg: infertile couples used it to conceive! The flowers were dried and then smoked by the man with the family pipe, and he would breathe the smoke all around his wife from head to toe every night at bedtime for a month.

Along with Grandmother Cedar, is the important Grandfather Birch (*Betula papyrifera*), as referenced in an origin story shared with children called "Traditional Anishinaabe Advice to Youth" and intended for survival as well as to provide a feeling of safety despite your surroundings: If you ever find yourself lost or alone, "Climb to a high place. . . . If you can see the white gleam of Nimishoomis-wiigwaas, Grandfather Birch, and the tall spires of Nookomis-giizhik, Grandmother Cedar, relax! You are safe! You are with your relatives! Between them Grandmother and Grandfather will provide everything you need for life, and they will get you home again in this life or the next."

That is a mighty big claim, but let's look deeper. A child would learn the skills necessary for survival and thriving. Grandmother Cedar can be offered as kinnikinnick to pray for anything that is needed, and there is faith that what is asked for will come. Water and food are high on the survival list, and Grandmother Cedar has a great need for water, so her roots go deep into it. The inner bark of cedar and the milder, sweeter birch can provide starch as a survival food and can stave off hunger to find better food. Birch, especially when tapped in the spring thaw, can make a mild syrup similar to maple (*Acer saccharum*), which is sweeter.

Cedar can provide cordage of various thicknesses, especially if the raw material is from a fallen tree—the outer bark peels easily without tools. It can be used for fishing line strong enough for smaller fish, as a rabbit snare, and even as a decent bow string (with a yew bow) to possibly hunt a deer. Cedar is excellent for building a fire, even in wet weather, and some lit cedar cordage stored in fungi can be carried to more easily start the next fire. The deer skin is used for clothing, the meat is for eating, and sinew from the deer is gathered for future hunting needs.

You can make a tasty tea with the foliage of both cedar and birch. Cedar has a high vitamin C content, which can help fight colds and is also good to settle the stomach and clear gas. It helps after a fish supper to smell fresh, and it has its own medicinal value where cleaning is needed; the oils are considered great for the skin and can clear warts.

Once you have food, water, and medicine, shelter is next. Cedar is an excellent building material that can change colors depending on changing situations, and as it is mold-retardant, it provides great food storage. Along with the shelter itself, mats can be woven and used for flooring or overhead protection. To go further, birch bark can make a canoe, which can be tied with cedar cordage. Drums, boxes, and bowls can also come from cedar.

While it is not specifically mentioned in this story, other smaller plant life and animal life would be nearby these trees and would all have a use in survival. One in particular that comes to mind and is mentioned in the book elsewhere is an amazing medicinal, nourishing, blood-cleansing tonic, the birch fungi that is called chaga or shaga (*Inonotus obliquus*).

Learning from Story

There is an interesting difference in plant identification between Great Lakes Native American herbalism and Western herbalism. Western herbalism speaks of something called the doctrine of signatures, wherein a plant's appearance reflects its application. For instance, if a plant has seeds shaped like a person's kidneys, it is said to be beneficial kidney-related medicine. Geniusz stresses that this idea does not parallel anything in the indigenous herbalism that she was taught and is entirely a Europe-based phenomenon.

Rather, Geniusz discusses at least twenty other plants (herbal medicines) in her book and offers memorable accompanying stories to demonstrate their lore and application. Honestly, story is the best way to learn herbalism. It's best when the healing story is from the storyteller's own experience, but is also wonderful to retell from one's teachers. Even old legends and myth have much to teach. When you remember how to identify and how to use the plants, do it, and actually witness healing, the feeling is indescribable the first time it happens.

The author also has plenty of stories of her own as well as those of her herbal elder and teacher. Here is a brief summary of a story that really shows stewardship and accountability, "The Year the Roses Died":

Many animals depended on the rose (*Rosa virginiana*) for food and medicine, and one year the roses didn't bloom at all. The animals then got together to discuss who was to blame, each passing the blame to another. Despite all of them eating the roses, they punished the rabbit by stretching his ears and breaking his tail off. The spirit who watches over the place told them their actions would not bring the roses back. Though all of the animals noticed the dwindling rose supply, they took portions anyway. There was no honor in this, and they did not maintain the balance that was there since the beginning. The spirit then decided to bring the roses back but added protection. To this day, the ears and tail of rabbit and the rose's thorns remind us of this story and our need to be mindful of not overfeeding or overharvesting.

So the next time you are sipping a cup of freshly harvested yarrow tea for menstrual cramps, harvesting dandelions for urinary tract relief, or even smelling the roses while harvesting medicine that cools your sunburn, don't just reference the disconnected, sterile herb facts. Instead, recall the stories you have learned, as well as your own healing experiences, which then become stories you tell so that others learn herbal medicine. Whether the stories are ours or another's, they have deep meaning and significance. Thus, they are memorable, accessible, and easy to put into practice.

In the Obijwe words of the author, *"Mii iw, Miigwech,* That's it, thank you."

Resource

Geniusz, Mary Siisip. *Plants Have So Much to Give Us, All We Have to Do Is Ask: Anishinaabe Botanical Teachings.* Minneapolis: University of Minnesota Press, 2015.

Calantirniel *(San Diego, California) has been published in nearly two dozen Llewellyn annuals since 2007 and also in three anthologies published by John Hunt Publishing's Moon Books in the United Kingdom. She has practiced many forms of natural spirituality for over two decades. She is a professional timing expert as well as an astrologer, herbalist, tarot card reader, dowser, energy healer, ULC reverend, and flower essence creator/practitioner. She is also a co-founder of Tië eldaliéva, meaning the Elven Path, a spiritual practice based upon the Elves' viewpoint in J. R. R. Tolkien's Middle-earth stories, particularly* The Silmarillion. *Please visit ElvenSpirituality.com and IntuitiveTiming.com.*

Deep in the Wooded Glens: An Armchair Herbalist's Tour of Circe's House and Garden

⤳ by Linda Raedisch ⤳

As the Aegean spring slides languidly into summer, we find ourselves in the kitchen garden of one of the most powerful witches of the ancient world. No, not the witch from "Rapunzel" but Circe, daughter of the sun god Helios, sister of the terrible Medea, and soon-to-be-seductress of Odysseus. It's about 1250 BCE, the Age of Heroes, and this is the island of Aeaea. Where exactly is Aeaea? There are thousands of islands in the Aegean, so take your pick.

The Greek historian Diodorus, writing around 30 BCE, made Circe out to have been just another Bronze Age queen, albeit an especially nasty one. Like her sister Medea, Circe was a wizardess in the stillroom, testing her potions on anyone who was foolish enough to sit down with her for a meal. According to Diodorus, Circe was not native to these parts; she hailed from Colchis on the eastern shores of the Black Sea. After she poisoned her husband, a king of the Scythians, she was exiled to Aeaea with only a handful of her loyal serving women—"nymphs," as Homer calls them in his *Odyssey*.[1]

The Greek verb pharmakeuein *means "to practice witchcraft" and gives us the English word "pharmaceutical." Keep that in mind the next time you consult your pharmacist.*

The name "Circe" may indicate that she is indeed a Circassian, a native of the Caucasus Mountain region between the Black and Caspian Seas, a region that, in Roman times, will be famed for its golden-haired slave women. The poet Homer seems unsure what to make of her. He never calls her a witch but vacillates among "the nymph with lovely braids," "the lustrous goddess," and simply "woman." We, the readers of the twenty-first century, take one look at Circe with her magic wand, herbal potions, and penchant for turning men into beasts and come to the immediate conclusion that she is a witch, but Homer had no such precedents from which to work. His Circe *became* the precedent, the blueprint for every Greek witch or *pharmakeutria*, women who were defined by their skill at brewing deadly potions, who came after her.

1. All quotes from Homer's *Odyssey* are from Fagles's translation.

The Garden Tour

In case you haven't noticed, we are not alone here in the garden. A wolf sits watching us from under an olive tree, and here, strolling between the vegetable beds, comes a dark-maned lion. Wild animals seem quite at home here. They appear to have no desire to bound over the walls and into the untidy tangle of trees creeping down toward the sea. Outside these walls, the woods are composed of holly-like holm oaks, true oaks, beeches in pale leaf, and dogwoods in full pink flower. These will provide the acorns, mast, and cornel fruits that Circe will feed to Odysseus's men after she has turned them into swine. There's almost as much growing among the roots of the trees as in the garden, for where the sun peaks through the branches, wild lilies, orchids, and asphodels thrive.

Circe makes good use of all the plants that grow on her island, slicing and dicing the roots to throw into her cauldron and distilling sweet perfumes from the petals. Inside the garden's walls grow the fussier herbs: coriander, rosemary, silphium, sage, and thyme. Here's wild rue (not yet blooming) madder, woad, weld, and elecampane, all for dying wool. There are even a few saffron crocuses, though only enough to color the tiniest handkerchief. And here are vegetables for the table: onions, garlic, chicory, asparagus (finished now), and cucumbers just turning from flowers into fruits. There's even rampion, *Campanula rapunculus*. Wouldn't Rapunzel's mother be delighted?

Môlu

Somewhere among these neatly planted beds must be the mysterious *môlu*, the herb which the god Hermes will sneak to Odysseus to make him immune to the spell that turns men into swine. Homer tells us that môlu has black roots and milk-white flowers and that it is dangerous for mortals to pull it from the ground. It cannot, therefore, be the rampion, whose white roots taste like radishes. So what is môlu? No one really knows, though there are already enough theories to fill an ancient Greek herbal.

A favorite candidate is the mandrake, whose shriek is death not just to the one who uproots it but to all within earshot. The black hellebore or "Christmas rose" with its black roots and iridescent white flowers also conforms nicely to Homer's description, a little less so the "Pentecost rose," or peony, whose blossoms are white as often as pink and whose shiny black seeds were used in antiquity to keep night demons away. The Germans' fallback magical prophylactic, the leek, has also been put forward, despite the fact that it's distinctly white at the root. Others would identify môlu as *Inula helenium*, the elecampane we saw towering over the other plants in the dye garden, but that is really Helen's flower, not Circe's. If you don't like any of these for môlu, consider the snowdrop, which exudes a milky poison and whose white flowers, when closed, remind some of a shrouded corpse—a preview of what will happen to you if you eat it. The snowdrop sounds like a northern flower, but it's actually native to southern Europe all the way east to Circe's native Colchis.

The Old French name for mullein, *molegn*, sounds a little like "môlu." Molegn comes from an older Celtic root meaning "yellow," but there are also white-flowered varieties native to the Mediterranean. The Greek word for mullein is *nekua*, the "plant of death," an appropriate herb for a necromancer's garden. And there it is, standing tall and proud among the lesser herbs, waiting for Hermes to come and tear it from the earth or for Circe to simmer the flowers in a pot with some wood ash and apply it to her "lovely braids." But if môlu is mullein, then one has to wonder what part of the plant Hermes gave to Odysseus—the soft leaves or the flowers? Odysseus could hardly have toted a full-blown mullein stalk into the magic halls of Circe unobserved.

More important than the question of *what* môlu is, is the question of *why* its identity was lost. Môlu's etymology and even its linguistic origins are unknown. It may have sprung from an Indo-European word akin to the Sanskrit *mulam,* which means simply "root." If môlu was derived from an older version of Circe's story, a relic surviving in name only, then Homer himself may not have known which plant it was. Variations on the tale told in book 10 of the *Odyssey* can be found throughout the Middle East, in India, and even in sixth-century Ceylon, but Homer's is the only one to mention môlu.

Barley

Barley is another herb that recurs in all forms of the story. It is a mixture of barley, cheese, honey, and the strong, dark Pramnian wine that Circe feeds to Odysseus's men to turn them into swine. In another version, written down in Sanskrit, the role of Odysseus is played by the Indian hero Bhimaparakrama. Finding himself the guest of a witch, Bhimaparakrama sleeps with one eye open. In the middle of the night, he observes the witch scattering barley grains over the floor to the accompaniment of a whispered incantation. It must be an earthen floor, for the grains sprout, take root and grow up toward the ceiling, the ears ripening quickly enough that the witch is able to harvest the grain and grind it before morning. She deposits this magic meal in a brass pot, but when she steps out to fetch water, Bhimaparakrama swaps it for ordinary meal from the bin, keeping the bewitched portion aside. Long story short, the witch ends up serving herself the enchanted breakfast porridge and is immediately transformed into a goat.

We know that at some point the *Odyssey* crossed paths with the *Epic of Gilgamesh* and that Circe took on certain aspects of the Mesopotamian goddess Inanna, if they were not hers already. Like Inanna, Circe expects to have her way with Odysseus, and like Gilgamesh, Odysseus is not all that impressed. Both heroes are painfully aware of what happens to the goddess's lovers once she has tired of them: she discards them. In Circe's case, she turns them into beasts. Circe also resembles the *Epic*'s character of Siduri, proprietress of the alehouse at the end of the world, whose patrons would have enjoyed warm bowls of thick barley beer sipped through reed straws. When Gilgamesh walks into her establishment, Siduri tries to turn him from his quest, encouraging him to eat, drink and be merry much as Circe does when she plies Odysseus and his men with Pramnian wine. (Gilgamesh, like us, was also searching for a magical herb, one that would grant him immortality, but that is a story for another day.)

Circe's Home

From the garden, Odysseus and his men would have entered the *dromos*, or vestibule, proceeding thence into the *megaron*, or throne room. The megaron is more like an enclosed court-yard than a room, the supporting pillars reminding one of the trees in the woods outside, or perhaps of the more imposing forests of Colchis. But Circe's palace is not all courtyards and grand reception halls. There are also smaller rooms tucked away in corners and up hidden flights of stairs. The most important is the stillroom, for that is where the magic happens. As Circe *polupharmakê,* "Circe of the many drugs," she probably would have spared no expense in decorating this hallowed space, luring any number of itinerant fresco artists to the island to adorn the walls.

What would such a room look like? I imagine the *dado,* or bottom half of the wall, painted scarlet, while above it a painstakingly brushed field of opium poppies nods in the wind. Above our heads, a specimen of each herb we saw growing in the garden has been tied into a bundle and suspended from the beams of the ceiling. Flower petals lie drying on wide wicker trays, and there is a brazier for heating water to distill their sweetness. At the workbench we find a golden knife, the split-apart seed heads of poppies, and a bowl of some sticky black substance. Could it be that all that Odysseus is to experience in books 10 and 11—the transformation of his men into swine and back again, the torrid nights spent in Circe's bed, and his journey to the underworld, where he will converse with the shades of the dead—was nothing more than a long, fitful opium dream?

There is another hidden room, veiled in cobwebs, that leads to Persephone's grove, a mournful garden of twisted black poplars and shriveled willows just outside Hades. We'll leave that one alone for now.

We won't wait to meet the formidable lady of the house, even if she is giving out free perfume samples. I am tempted to ask her to point out the môlu and settle the question once and for all, but what's the hurry? The enchanted isle of Aeaea isn't going anywhere, and neither is the notorious pharmakeutria. We'll stop by another day.

In the meantime, we ought to consider the opinion of the fourth-century Greek Theophrastus, who identified môlu as that humble kitchen herb, garlic. We know that the Greeks looked to the elder civilization of the Nile for advice in all matters magical, and the Egyptians considered garlic a cure-all, so why should it not also have been an antidote to Circe's spell? Garlic was a staple of the ancient Egyptian diet. There are, as far as I know, no stories of Egyptian herb-witches attempting to transform men into beasts, perhaps because such a spell could never work in a country where everyone was munching garlic cloves for breakfast, lunch, and dinner.

Of course, Odysseus knows exactly what herb it was he took from Hermes' hand, so if we really want to know, all we have to do is seek out his shade on the dry riverbanks of Persephone's grove. And I fully intend to do so: I'll be fetching up in that dusty place soon enough, as we all do. In the meantime, I'm content to let the mystery of môlu remain just that: a mystery.

Resources

Edmonds, I. G. *The Mysteries of Homer's Greeks*. New York: Elsevier/Nelson Books, 1981.

Garland, Robert. *Ancient Greece: Everyday Life in the Birthplace of Western Civilization*. New York: Sterling Publishing, 2008.

Homer. *The Odyssey*. Translated by Robert Fagles. New York: Viking, 1996.

Hughes, Bettany. *Helen of Troy: Goddess, Princess, Whore*. New York: Knopf, 2005.

Ogden, Daniel. *Magic, Witchcraft, and Ghosts in the Greek and Roman Worlds*. 2nd ed. New York: Oxford University Press, 2009.

Page, Denys. *Folktales in Homer's Odyssey*. Cambridge, Massachusetts: Harvard University Press, 1973.

Linda Raedisch *is a paper artist, housecleaner, and author with two books and numerous articles to her credit. She is also a lover of words who admits she spends more time strolling the grounds of her local arboretum than working in her own garden. She writes, "I'll never have the skill to keep a Welsh poppy or night-blooming cereus alive in my garden, but even if I can't grow a wide variety of plants, I can tell their stories."*

The History and Healing of Tulips

≈ by Tiffany Lazic ≈

The flowers of spring awaken our hearts with the first color and fragrance of the warming months. Daffodils, hyacinths, crocuses, and snowdrops all dazzle, but none have the history, mystery, and intrigue of the simple yet stunning tulip!

Turkey's Exotic Gift

Practically synonymous with the Netherlands (Holland), it is hard to imagine that this somewhat demure flower has its deep roots in the exotic warmth of Turkey. The *lale*, as it is known in Turkish, was long loved by Turkish sultans and first arrived in Europe in 1554, a gift from Sultan Suleiman the Magnificent to the Holy Roman Emperor, Ferdinand I.

The move from east to west seems to have also created a shift in name from lale to "tulip," most likely a reference to Turkish turbans. There is certainly the sense that the tulip shape itself somewhat resembles a turban, and this may account for the name. More likely, "tulip" is derived from the Turkish word *tulbend,* which is the name for the muslin with which a turban is made. The very first tulip festival, which occurred in Turkey over four hundred years ago, was said to have been held under a full moon to amplify the tulip's mysterious beauty.

In 1573, the man who was to change the horticultural world arrived in Vienna to set up the imperial medicinal garden. Carolus Clusius, who can be considered a father of botany, was interested in experimenting with his garden creation, incorporating some unknown and exotic flowers such as the tulip. After sixteen years of careful cultivation for Maximilian II, Clusius saw it razed by order of the new Holy Roman Emperor, Rudolf II, who had decided to move the imperial garden to Prague. Relieved of his position in Vienna, Clusius eventually took a position as professor of botany at the University of Leiden in the Netherlands, setting up a new garden at the age of sixty-seven. So it was that the tulip arrived in Holland, setting the stage for what was to become a defining point in Dutch history. As curator of the university gardens, Clusius was the first to have written about it in his books and guarded his bulbs so proprietarily that interest was, of course, piqued. If these bulbs were that special, they were worth stealing and, perhaps foreshadowing the intrigue to follow in just a few short years, steal them people did.

The tulip arrived in Holland at a particularly opportune time. Trade in goods from the Far East was creating significant wealth in the merchant class, and the preferred manner to display that wealth was in establishing large country estates with spectacular gardens. This relative newcomer to the flower world, the tulip, took the Dutch merchants by storm. It was by far the most coveted flower for one's showcase garden. By the 1630s, the market for tulips was tremendous, and what happened in 1637 is the stuff of legend.

A Craze for Tulips

In a pattern that has become sadly recognizable, the tulip appears to be the first example of an extraordinary market bubble leading to a devastating economic crash. Though there have been some revisions in theory over the past number of decades, for almost two hundred years the events in Holland between 1634–1637 have been referred to as "tulipomania."

With the natural flow of supply and demand, the price for tulip bulbs had been steadily on the rise from the time of introduction. Because of the nature of purchasing bulbs that will be blooming in the future, the tulip trade was, in essence, a speculative one. As such, the Dutch created a form of early "futures market" that allowed merchants to draft contracts to purchase bulbs at the end of the season that would come due for the next growing season. Tulips flower in April and May. Between September and November is the perfect time to transport and transplant for the following year's crop. Futures contracts depended upon continued price growth, with much of the activity occurring on paper (rather than goods changing hands) and taking place in taverns (to the joy of the tavern owners). At the agreement of a contract, the buyer had to pay a minimal fee up front, which was referred to as "wine money." The balance of the contract would be due when the actual bulb changed hands. Contracts that were finalized in February would come due sometime in the fall.

Though part of the exotic draw of the tulip was its singularity of bold color, the most sought-after bulbs were actually those that resulted from a virus that created beautiful streaks and feathered patterns on the petals. As the passion for certain extremely rare bulbs caught hold, it was not unusual for bulbs to be sold and resold many times over, with the buyer agreeing to pay higher and higher prices. If there was not enough actual money to be had, contracts could be cobbled together from several commodity sources, including butter, grains, cheese, livestock, and household items. The most expensive bulb ever sold was the 'Semper Augustus', a gorgeous white tulip with stunning deep red "flames." It fetched 5,500 guilders—truly phenomenal when one considers that the annual wage for a skilled laborer at that time was 150 guilders! Imagine paying thirty-seven times a salary for a single tulip bulb, and that gives a sense of the mania that caught hold of seventeenth-century Europe.

At the height of tulipomania, legend holds that one merchant was horrified when he came across one of his ship's sailors "eating a breakfast whose cost might have regaled a whole ship's crew for a twelvemonth," having mistaken the bulb for an onion. Almost 300 years later, during WWII, the starving, desperate people of occupied Holland ate the widely available but bitter bulbs, which required careful preparation to remove the poisonous center.

The crash came fast and hard in March 1637, in part as a result of the plague. When buyers refused to show up at auction in Haarlem in February due to a plague outbreak, the tulip traders did not have the audience required to sell their bulbs at the inflated prices. Recognizing the potentially dire situation, the Dutch government responded by allowing an "opt out" clause on futures contracts. Buyers could void contracts for a 10 percent fee, leaving the traders literally holding the bag—of tulip bulbs. Some accounts of these events hold that massive fortunes were lost, leading to the destabilizing of European economy. Other more conservative accounts suggest that, since little actual money exchanged hands, it was more the "potential for fortune" that was lost. Regardless, those few years in Dutch history remain legendary and certainly cemented the tulip as the national flower of the Netherlands.

Healing Body and Soul

Historically, in no small part given the price for bulbs, the tulip was appreciated more for its decorative beauty than its healing properties. Though the bulb is held to have high nutritional value, one would be loath to snack on something equivalent to several year's salary. Petals can also be eaten, having a slightly sweet flavor. As with other edible flowers, they add gorgeous color to a salad or as a garnish to an appetizer dish. For the ease of itch and pain with rashes and bee stings, tulip petals can be crushed into a poultice and applied topically.

In the language of flowers, the tulip is exquisitely eloquent. Perhaps best known as a flower of love and passion, it offers a variety of nuanced messages depending on its color.

Red says you are deeply in love. Cream adds the message "I will love you forever." Yellow offers a bright, sunny message perfect to give to a friend who needs a boost. Orange lets someone know that you feel a special connection with them. Pink sends a message of joy and caring, perfect for a celebration or "just because" gift. White is the conciliatory color to offer in humility, gratitude, or apology. Purple, the color of royalty, gives the message of deepest respect and admiration. But, of course, with variegated tulips such as those that caused such a storm in seventeenth-century Holland, a single tulip can present a wonderfully complex message. Perhaps you want to say, "Cheer up, honey. I love you so much." Choose a yellow-red tulip. Choose purple-white for the message "I am so sorry. I really do have such a deep respect for you." There is almost nothing that cannot be conveyed with the perfect tulip choice.

A Bloom of Gratitude

Along with Turkey and the Netherlands, the tulip holds a special place in Canada's heart. Offering refuge to the Dutch Royal Family after the Nazi invasion of the Netherlands in 1940, Canada housed Princess Juliana and her daughters in what is now the official residence of the Leader of the Opposition. In 1943, when the princess gave birth to another daughter, Canada temporarily declared the maternity ward of the hospital extraterritorial so that the newly born Princess Margriet would hold exclusively Dutch nationality. In the midst of the dark times of war, this birth was seen by the Netherlands as a symbol of hope. In gratitude, Princess Juliana, who became queen in 1948, gifted Canada with 100,000 tulip bulbs and continued to gift thousands of bulbs to Canada every year during her long reign. In anticipation of Canada's 150th anniversary in 2017, the Kingdom of the Netherlands and Canada's "official gardener," the National Capital Commission, developed a very special tulip known as the Canada 150 or the Maple Leaf Tulip. This white tulip with red "flames" is reminiscent of another white and red tulip that caught a nation's fancy and caused such an enormous stir almost 300 years ago.

Resources

Colombo, Jesse. "The Dutch 'Tulip Mania' Bubble (aka 'Tulipomania')." The Bubble Bubble. June 15, 2012. http://www.thebubblebubble.com/tulip-mania/.

Dash, Mike. *Tulipomania: The Story of the World's Most Coveted Flower & the Extraordinary Passions It Aroused*. New York: Crown, 1999.

Mackay, Charles. *Extraordinary Popular Delusions: And the Madness of Crowds*. New York: Noonday, 1974.

McLeod, Judyth A. *In a Unicorn's Garden: Recreating the Magic and Mystery of Medieval Gardens*. Millers Point, New South Wales: Murdoch, 2008.

"The Tulip Legacy Story." Canadian Tulip Festival. Accessed December 15, 2016. http://tulipfestival.ca/about/tulip-legacy/.

Tiffany Lazic *is a registered psychotherapist and spiritual director with a private practice in individual, couples, and group therapy. As the owner of the Hive and Grove Centre for Holistic Wellness, she created two self-development programs focused on teaching inner alchemy and intuitive tools from around the world and is a staff facilitator in the Transformational Arts College of Spiritual and Holistic*

Training's Spiritual Directorship and Esoteric Studies Programs.
She is an international presenter and retreat facilitator, the founder
of Kitchener's Red Tent Temple, and serves on the Council of the
Sisterhood of Avalon. Tiffany is the author of The Great Work:
Self-Knowledge and Healing Through the Wheel of the Year.
Visit Tiffany at www.hiveandgrove.ca.

Why Grow Yarrow?

⁊⁊ by Ember Grant ⁊⁊

Yarrow is one of those herbs that's unfortunately overlooked since it's not well-known for its use in the kitchen. However, the plant is rich in folklore and praised as one of the most valuable medicinal herbs. And the best part is it's easy to grow. If you're an herb gardener, you need yarrow.

Yarrow is classified in the Asteraceae/Compositae family—the same group that includes asters, sunflowers, and daisies—yet the appearance of yarrow is quite different from these flowers. If you've never seen yarrow, imagine very tiny bouquets of miniature daisies packed tightly in a cluster—these are called umbels. There are dozens of umbels on tall stalks; the leaves are soft and feathery. In fact, many names that have been used for yarrow throughout history allude to the plants' feathery leaves. The Ojibwe call it *adjidamowano*, "squirrel tail." In the Southwest it's often known as *plumajillo*, "little feather" in Spanish.

History and Folklore

Speaking of names, the Latin name for yarrow is *Achillea millefolium*. As you may recognize, this name has origins in the story of Achilles. Legends say that Achilles used this herb during the Trojan War to ensure the health of his warriors. In one story, the centaur Chiron is the one who taught Achilles how to use the herb. A more popular version says that King Priam's son-in-law Telephus tripped over a vine, causing Achilles to wound him by accident. Achilles scraped some rust from his spear, and the plant grew from where the scrapings fell to the ground. He then used the plant to heal the wound.

Legends and myths are accurate on one account for certain—yarrow's use in medicine. In medieval England it was called "woundwort." Some say the name yarrow came from the Anglo-Saxon word *gearwe*, which may have meant "to repair." According to *The Secrets of Wildflowers*, in 1649 Nicholas Culpeper wrote that "an ointment of the leaves cures wounds, and is good for inflammations, ulcers, fistulas, and all such runnings as abound with moisture."

Because the plant actually contains iron, calcium, potassium, and other trace minerals, it's no wonder it has such a long history of being used as medicine. It is reputed to lower blood pressure, reduce fevers, and relieve diarrhea, indigestion, and flatulence. Applied to the skin, it can be used as an astringent and to cleanse minor cuts and irritations. In fact, it has been scientifically proven to be anti-inflammatory and to curb bleeding. Other uses include relieving rheumatism, toothaches, sore gums, and fevers and stimulating the appetite. Throughout history, yarrow has also earned a reputation as a sedative. It contains thujone, a chemical that is also found in absinthe (obtained from the wormwood plant, *Artemisia absinthium*, a plant in the same family as yarrow). Some of the other names yarrow has been called include knight's milfoil, bloodwort, thousand leaf, dog daisy, and field hop—the Swedes once used it to make beer.

While some believe yarrow was brought to America by European settlers, many botanists believe it was growing wild here already. However, of the many varieties, only one has been proven native: Siberian yarrow, found in the northernmost parts of North America. Traces of yarrow were found in a burial site dated 60,000 years old, revealing that it was used by Neanderthal people. While we can't know for certain why the plant was there, it's a testament to how long people have been using this plant.

In addition to being used medicinally throughout history, yarrow has a firm place in magical folklore. Its use in spells and charms has earned it the name "devil's nettle" because it was said to be used for evil magic, yet it was also hung in churches and homes for protection and above cradles to protect babies—the church associated yarrow with St. John.

In China, the flower stems were cast in a form of divination, and the English used the herb for love—maidens would sleep with it under their pillows to learn the identity of their future husbands.

If someone dreamed of picking yarrow, good news was forthcoming. At weddings, people would eat yarrow leaves; placed in the bridal bouquet they would ensure that love would last for at least seven years. Yarrow was also said to ease broken hearts. One very specific folk remedy, used especially for fevers, says to pull a yarrow leaf from the plant with your left hand while saying the name of the sick person. Eat the leaf, and the fever will be relieved. Metaphysically, yarrow has feminine qualities; is associated with Venus and the element of water; promotes courage, love, friendship, and psychic powers; and can be used to ward off negative energy and malevolent spirits.

Growing and Using Yarrow

There are still more reasons why yarrow is an exceptional garden plant. For one thing, it's extremely easy to grow, either from seed or by purchasing from a nursery. Yarrow is perennial in zones 2 through 8 and requires full sun. It even thrives in poor soil. Since the stalks can reach three feet tall, staking is often required.

In the wild the flowers are typically white, but the most common garden cultivar is yellow. I grow the bright yellow variety called 'Moonshine' and a pink variety as well. The flowers bloom throughout the summer; you'll get more blooms if you cut them from time to time. And you'll want to cut them—yarrow is a beautiful addition to flower arrangements. Since it holds it shape and color so well, it's an excellent dried flower for bouquets and wreaths.

Yarrow is actually unappealing to most insects, making it a good plant to repel pests like Japanese beetles. Its odor actually protects it from predators, giving the plant an extra edge for survival. However, it's still attractive to bees and butterflies. It also helps prevent erosion due to its complex root system, which has incidentally led some people to call it a weed—it's persistent.

Yarrow flowers work equally well in the herb garden or flower bed. In a flower bed against a wall or fence (which actually provides nice support), be sure to put them in the back since they're so tall; in a round or square bed, they would be a good choice for the center. Later in the season, after the peak bloom time, you may want to tidy up your plants by removing the spent stalks and some of the basal leaves—the bottom of the plant can become messy in appearance.

My favorite way to use yarrow is for decorating. Simply cut several stems and dry them by hanging upside down away from humidity. Place them in arrangements or cut the flower heads and use hot glue to attach them to a wreath or other project. An early summer arrangement of red roses and yarrow adds a burst of dramatic color to any room; the yellow flowers also pair well with purple. In my experience, the pink yarrow flowers don't hold their shape as well as the yellow 'Moonshine' variety.

The fresh, young leaves can be used in salad, and yarrow can be steeped to create infusions, either for topical application or to drink. It can even be used to make a yellow dye. To take advantage of yarrow's medicinal properties, try this cold remedy:

1 teaspoon dried yarrow leaves and flowers

1 teaspoon dried elderflower

½ teaspoon dried peppermint

Pour boiling water over the herbs, cover, and steep for ten minutes. Strain. You can even add a pinch of cayenne pepper, if you wish. Add a bit of honey, too. Drink it while it's hot—but be careful not to burn your tongue!

As with any herb, use caution, consult a physician, and avoid using if pregnant. The remedies listed here are not intended to replace medical attention. Do some research and experiment with a variety of these wonderful plants. When you grow yarrow in your garden, you join a long and colorful history.

Selected Resources

Cunningham, Scott. *Cunningham's Encyclopedia of Magical Herbs*. St. Paul, MN: Llewellyn Worldwide, 1985.

Drew, A. J. *A Wiccan Formulary and Herbal*. New Jersey: New Page Books, 2005.

Picton, Margaret. *The Book of Magical Herbs*. New York: Barron's Educational Series, 2000.

Sanders, Jack. *The Secrets of Wildflowers*. Guilford, CT: The Globe Pequot Press, 2003.

Swerdlow, Joel L. *Nature's Medicine: Plants that Heal*. Washington, D.C.: National Geographic Society, 2000.

Webb, Marcus A. and Richard Craze. *The Herb and Spice Companion*. London: Quantum Publishing, 2000.

Ember Grant *has been writing for the Llewellyn annuals since 2003 and is the author of three books and more than fifty articles. Her most recent book is* The Second Book of Crystal Spells. *She also sells handmade crafts and enjoys nature photography. Visit her online at EmberGrant.com.*

Moon Signs,
Phases, and
Tables

The Quarters and Signs
of the Moon

Everyone has seen the moon wax and wane through a period of approximately 29½ days. This circuit from new moon to full moon and back again is called the lunation cycle. The cycle is divided into parts called quarters or phases. There are several methods by which this can be done, and the system used in the *Herbal Almanac* may not correspond to those used in other almanacs.

The Quarters

First Quarter

The first quarter begins at the new moon, when the sun and moon are in the same place, or conjunct. (This means the sun and moon are in the same degree of the same sign.) The moon is not visible at first, since it rises at the same time as the sun. The new moon is the time of new beginnings of projects that favor growth, externalization of activities, and the growth of ideas. The first quarter is the time of germination, emergence, beginnings, and outwardly directed activity.

Second Quarter

The second quarter begins halfway between the new moon and the full moon, when the sun and moon are at a right angle, or a 90° square, to each other. This half moon rises around noon and sets around midnight, so it can be seen in the western sky during the first half of the night. The second quarter is the time of growth and articulation of things that already exist.

Third Quarter

The third quarter begins at the full moon, when the sun and moon are opposite one another and the full light of the sun can shine on the full sphere of the moon. The round moon can be seen rising in the east at sunset, then rising a little later each evening. The full moon stands for illumination, fulfillment, culmination, completion, drawing inward, unrest, emotional expressions, and hasty actions leading to failure. The third quarter is a time of maturity, fruition, and the assumption of the full form of expression.

Fourth Quarter

The fourth quarter begins about halfway between the full moon and the new moon, when the sun and moon are again at a right angle, or a 90° square, to each other. This decreasing moon rises at midnight and can be seen in the east during the last half of the night, reaching the overhead position just about as the sun rises. The fourth quarter is a time of disintegration and drawing back for reorganization and reflection.

The Signs

Moon in Aries

Moon in Aries is good for starting things and initiating change, but actions may lack staying power. Activities requiring assertiveness and courage are favored. Things occur rapidly but also quickly pass.

Moon in Taurus

Things begun when the moon is in Taurus last the longest and tend to increase in value. This is a good time for any activity that requires patience, practicality, and perseverance. Things begun now also tend to become habitual and hard to alter.

Moon in Gemini

Moon in Gemini is a good time to exchange ideas, meet with people, or be in situations that require versatility and quick thinking. Things begun now are easily changed by outside influences.

Moon in Cancer

Moon in Cancer is a good time to grow things. It stimulates emotional rapport between people and is a good time to build personal friendships, though people may be more emotional and moody than usual.

Moon in Leo

Moon in Leo is a good time for public appearances, showmanship, being seen, entertaining, drama, recreation, and happy pursuits. People may be overly concerned with praise and subject to flattery.

Moon in Virgo

Moon in Virgo is good for any task that requires close attention to detail and careful analysis of information. There is a focus on health, hygiene, and daily schedules. Watch for a tendency to overdo and overwork.

Moon in Libra

Moon in Libra is a good time to form partnerships of any kind and to negotiate. It discourages spontaneous initiative, so working with a partner is essential. Artistic work and teamwork are highlighted.

Moon in Scorpio

Moon in Scorpio increases awareness of psychic power and favors any activity that requires intensity and focus. This is a good time to conduct research and to end connections thoroughly. There is a tendency to manipulate.

Moon in Sagittarius

Moon in Sagittarius is good for any activity that requires honesty, candor, imagination, and confidence in the flow of life. This is a good time to tackle things that need improvement, but watch out for a tendency to proselytize.

Moon in Capricorn

Moon in Capricorn increases awareness of the need for structure, discipline, and patience. This is a good time to set goals and plan for the future. Those in authority may be insensitive at this time.

Moon in Aquarius

Moon in Aquarius favors activities that are unique and individualistic and that concern society as a whole. This is a good time to pursue humanitarian efforts and to identify improvements that can be made. People may be more intellectual than emotional under this influence.

Moon in Pisces

Moon in Pisces is a good time for any kind of introspective, philanthropic, meditative, psychic, or artistic work. At this time personal boundaries may be blurred, and people may be prone to seeing what they want to see rather than what is really there.

January Moon Table

Date	Sign	Element	Nature	Phase
1 Mon 3:10 am	Cancer	Water	Fruitful	Full 9:24 pm
2 Tue	Cancer	Water	Fruitful	3rd
3 Wed 2:23 am	Leo	Fire	Barren	3rd
4 Thu	Leo	Fire	Barren	3rd
5 Fri 3:12 am	Virgo	Earth	Barren	3rd
6 Sat	Virgo	Earth	Barren	3rd
7 Sun 7:15 am	Libra	Air	Semi-fruitful	3rd
8 Mon	Libra	Air	Semi-fruitful	4th 5:25 pm
9 Tue 3:05 pm	Scorpio	Water	Fruitful	4th
10 Wed	Scorpio	Water	Fruitful	4th
11 Thu	Scorpio	Water	Fruitful	4th
12 Fri 2:04 am	Sagittarius	Fire	Barren	4th
13 Sat	Sagittarius	Fire	Barren	4th
14 Sun 2:42 pm	Capricorn	Earth	Semi-fruitful	4th
15 Mon	Capricorn	Earth	Semi-fruitful	4th
16 Tue	Capricorn	Earth	Semi-fruitful	New 9:17 pm
17 Wed 3:32 am	Aquarius	Air	Barren	1st
18 Thu	Aquarius	Air	Barren	1st
19 Fri 3:26 pm	Pisces	Water	Fruitful	1st
20 Sat	Pisces	Water	Fruitful	1st
21 Sun	Pisces	Water	Fruitful	1st
22 Mon 1:27 am	Aries	Fire	Barren	1st
23 Tue	Aries	Fire	Barren	1st
24 Wed 8:39 am	Taurus	Earth	Semi-fruitful	2nd 5:20 pm
25 Thu	Taurus	Earth	Semi-fruitful	2nd
26 Fri 12:40 pm	Gemini	Air	Barren	2nd
27 Sat	Gemini	Air	Barren	2nd
28 Sun 1:57 pm	Cancer	Water	Fruitful	2nd
29 Mon	Cancer	Water	Fruitful	2nd
30 Tue 1:53 pm	Leo	Fire	Barren	2nd
31 Wed	Leo	Fire	Barren	Full 8:27 am

February Moon Table

Date	Sign	Element	Nature	Phase
1 Thu 2:13 pm	Virgo	Earth	Barren	3rd
2 Fri	Virgo	Earth	Barren	3rd
3 Sat 4:47 pm	Libra	Air	Semi-fruitful	3rd
4 Sun	Libra	Air	Semi-fruitful	3rd
5 Mon 10:56 pm	Scorpio	Water	Fruitful	3rd
6 Tue	Scorpio	Water	Fruitful	3rd
7 Wed	Scorpio	Water	Fruitful	4th 10:54 am
8 Thu 8:53 am	Sagittarius	Fire	Barren	4th
9 Fri	Sagittarius	Fire	Barren	4th
10 Sat 9:21 pm	Capricorn	Earth	Semi-fruitful	4th
11 Sun	Capricorn	Earth	Semi-fruitful	4th
12 Mon	Capricorn	Earth	Semi-fruitful	4th
13 Tue 10:11 am	Aquarius	Air	Barren	4th
14 Wed	Aquarius	Air	Barren	4th
15 Thu 9:42 pm	Pisces	Water	Fruitful	New 4:05 pm
16 Fri	Pisces	Water	Fruitful	1st
17 Sat	Pisces	Water	Fruitful	1st
18 Sun 7:05 am	Aries	Fire	Barren	1st
19 Mon	Aries	Fire	Barren	1st
20 Tue 2:12 pm	Taurus	Earth	Semi-fruitful	1st
21 Wed	Taurus	Earth	Semi-fruitful	1st
22 Thu 7:07 pm	Gemini	Air	Barren	1st
23 Fri	Gemini	Air	Barren	2nd 3:09 am
24 Sat 10:06 pm	Cancer	Water	Fruitful	2nd
25 Sun	Cancer	Water	Fruitful	2nd
26 Mon 11:42 pm	Leo	Fire	Barren	2nd
27 Tue	Leo	Fire	Barren	2nd
28 Wed	Leo	Fire	Barren	2nd

Times are in Eastern Time.

March Moon Table

Date	Sign	Element	Nature	Phase
1 Thu 12:57 am	Virgo	Earth	Barren	Full 7:51 pm
2 Fri	Virgo	Earth	Barren	3rd
3 Sat 3:20 am	Libra	Air	Semi-fruitful	3rd
4 Sun	Libra	Air	Semi-fruitful	3rd
5 Mon 8:23 am	Scorpio	Water	Fruitful	3rd
6 Tue	Scorpio	Water	Fruitful	3rd
7 Wed 5:03 pm	Sagittarius	Fire	Barren	3rd
8 Thu	Sagittarius	Fire	Barren	3rd
9 Fri	Sagittarius	Fire	Barren	4th 6:20 am
10 Sat 4:52 am	Capricorn	Earth	Semi-fruitful	4th
11 Sun	Capricorn	Earth	Semi-fruitful	4th
12 Mon 6:44 pm	Aquarius	Air	Barren	4th
13 Tue	Aquarius	Air	Barren	4th
14 Wed	Aquarius	Air	Barren	4th
15 Thu 6:12 am	Pisces	Water	Fruitful	4th
16 Fri	Pisces	Water	Fruitful	4th
17 Sat 2:57 pm	Aries	Fire	Barren	New 9:12 am
18 Sun	Aries	Fire	Barren	1st
19 Mon 9:07 pm	Taurus	Earth	Semi-fruitful	1st
20 Tue	Taurus	Earth	Semi-fruitful	1st
21 Wed	Taurus	Earth	Semi-fruitful	1st
22 Thu 1:30 am	Gemini	Air	Barren	1st
23 Fri	Gemini	Air	Barren	1st
24 Sat 4:53 am	Cancer	Water	Fruitful	2nd 11:35 am
25 Sun	Cancer	Water	Fruitful	2nd
26 Mon 7:45 am	Leo	Fire	Barren	2nd
27 Tue	Leo	Fire	Barren	2nd
28 Wed 10:30 am	Virgo	Earth	Barren	2nd
29 Thu	Virgo	Earth	Barren	2nd
30 Fri 1:52 pm	Libra	Air	Semi-fruitful	2nd
31 Sat	Libra	Air	Semi-fruitful	Full 8:37 am

April Moon Table

Date	Sign	Element	Nature	Phase
1 Sun 6:57 pm	Scorpio	Water	Fruitful	3rd
2 Mon	Scorpio	Water	Fruitful	3rd
3 Tue	Scorpio	Water	Fruitful	3rd
4 Wed 2:55 am	Sagittarius	Fire	Barren	3rd
5 Thu	Sagittarius	Fire	Barren	3rd
6 Fri 2:01 pm	Capricorn	Earth	Semi-fruitful	3rd
7 Sat	Capricorn	Earth	Semi-fruitful	3rd
8 Sun	Capricorn	Earth	Semi-fruitful	4th 3:18 am
9 Mon 2:50 am	Aquarius	Air	Barren	4th
10 Tue	Aquarius	Air	Barren	4th
11 Wed 2:40 pm	Pisces	Water	Fruitful	4th
12 Thu	Pisces	Water	Fruitful	4th
13 Fri 11:25 pm	Aries	Fire	Barren	4th
14 Sat	Aries	Fire	Barren	4th
15 Sun	Aries	Fire	Barren	New 9:57 pm
16 Mon 4:51 am	Taurus	Earth	Semi-fruitful	1st
17 Tue	Taurus	Earth	Semi-fruitful	1st
18 Wed 8:02 am	Gemini	Air	Barren	1st
19 Thu	Gemini	Air	Barren	1st
20 Fri 10:26 am	Cancer	Water	Fruitful	1st
21 Sat	Cancer	Water	Fruitful	1st
22 Sun 1:09 pm	Leo	Fire	Barren	2nd 5:46 pm
23 Mon	Leo	Fire	Barren	2nd
24 Tue 4:40 pm	Virgo	Earth	Barren	2nd
25 Wed	Virgo	Earth	Barren	2nd
26 Thu 9:13 pm	Libra	Air	Semi-fruitful	2nd
27 Fri	Libra	Air	Semi-fruitful	2nd
28 Sat	Libra	Air	Semi-fruitful	2nd
29 Sun 3:11 am	Scorpio	Water	Fruitful	Full 8:58 pm
30 Mon	Scorpio	Water	Fruitful	3rd

Times are in Eastern Time.

May Moon Table

Date	Sign	Element	Nature	Phase
1 Tue 11:20 am	Sagittarius	Fire	Barren	3rd
2 Wed	Sagittarius	Fire	Barren	3rd
3 Thu 10:06 pm	Capricorn	Earth	Semi-fruitful	3rd
4 Fri	Capricorn	Earth	Semi-fruitful	3rd
5 Sat	Capricorn	Earth	Semi-fruitful	3rd
6 Sun 10:48 am	Aquarius	Air	Barren	3rd
7 Mon	Aquarius	Air	Barren	4th 10:09 pm
8 Tue 11:11 pm	Pisces	Water	Fruitful	4th
9 Wed	Pisces	Water	Fruitful	4th
10 Thu	Pisces	Water	Fruitful	4th
11 Fri 8:40 am	Aries	Fire	Barren	4th
12 Sat	Aries	Fire	Barren	4th
13 Sun 2:15 pm	Taurus	Earth	Semi-fruitful	4th
14 Mon	Taurus	Earth	Semi-fruitful	4th
15 Tue 4:43 pm	Gemini	Air	Barren	New 7:48 am
16 Wed	Gemini	Air	Barren	1st
17 Thu 5:47 pm	Cancer	Water	Fruitful	1st
18 Fri	Cancer	Water	Fruitful	1st
19 Sat 7:11 pm	Leo	Fire	Barren	1st
20 Sun	Leo	Fire	Barren	1st
21 Mon 10:03 pm	Virgo	Earth	Barren	2nd 11:49 pm
22 Tue	Virgo	Earth	Barren	2nd
23 Wed	Virgo	Earth	Barren	2nd
24 Thu 2:52 am	Libra	Air	Semi-fruitful	2nd
25 Fri	Libra	Air	Semi-fruitful	2nd
26 Sat 9:39 am	Scorpio	Water	Fruitful	2nd
27 Sun	Scorpio	Water	Fruitful	2nd
28 Mon 6:29 pm	Sagittarius	Fire	Barren	2nd
29 Tue	Sagittarius	Fire	Barren	Full 10:20 am
30 Wed	Sagittarius	Fire	Barren	3rd
31 Thu 5:27 am	Capricorn	Earth	Semi-fruitful	3rd

June Moon Table

Date	Sign	Element	Nature	Phase
1 Fri	Capricorn	Earth	Semi-fruitful	3rd
2 Sat 6:06 pm	Aquarius	Air	Barren	3rd
3 Sun	Aquarius	Air	Barren	3rd
4 Mon	Aquarius	Air	Barren	3rd
5 Tue 6:53 am	Pisces	Water	Fruitful	3rd
6 Wed	Pisces	Water	Fruitful	4th 2:32 pm
7 Thu 5:26 pm	Aries	Fire	Barren	4th
8 Fri	Aries	Fire	Barren	4th
9 Sat	Aries	Fire	Barren	4th
10 Sun 12:04 am	Taurus	Earth	Semi-fruitful	4th
11 Mon	Taurus	Earth	Semi-fruitful	4th
12 Tue 2:53 am	Gemini	Air	Barren	4th
13 Wed	Gemini	Air	Barren	New 3:43 pm
14 Thu 3:20 am	Cancer	Water	Fruitful	1st
15 Fri	Cancer	Water	Fruitful	1st
16 Sat 3:21 am	Leo	Fire	Barren	1st
17 Sun	Leo	Fire	Barren	1st
18 Mon 4:41 am	Virgo	Earth	Barren	1st
19 Tue	Virgo	Earth	Barren	1st
20 Wed 8:29 am	Libra	Air	Semi-fruitful	2nd 6:51 am
21 Thu	Libra	Air	Semi-fruitful	2nd
22 Fri 3:11 pm	Scorpio	Water	Fruitful	2nd
23 Sat	Scorpio	Water	Fruitful	2nd
24 Sun	Scorpio	Water	Fruitful	2nd
25 Mon 12:29 am	Sagittarius	Fire	Barren	2nd
26 Tue	Sagittarius	Fire	Barren	2nd
27 Wed 11:52 am	Capricorn	Earth	Semi-fruitful	2nd
28 Thu	Capricorn	Earth	Semi-fruitful	Full 12:53 am
29 Fri	Capricorn	Earth	Semi-fruitful	3rd
30 Sat 12:37 am	Aquarius	Air	Barren	3rd

Times are in Eastern Time.

July Moon Table

Date	Sign	Element	Nature	Phase
1 Sun	Aquarius	Air	Barren	3rd
2 Mon 1:31 pm	Pisces	Water	Fruitful	3rd
3 Tue	Pisces	Water	Fruitful	3rd
4 Wed	Pisces	Water	Fruitful	3rd
5 Thu 12:50 am	Aries	Fire	Barren	3rd
6 Fri	Aries	Fire	Barren	4th 3:51 am
7 Sat 8:51 am	Taurus	Earth	Semi-fruitful	4th
8 Sun	Taurus	Earth	Semi-fruitful	4th
9 Mon 12:58 pm	Gemini	Air	Barren	4th
10 Tue	Gemini	Air	Barren	4th
11 Wed 1:59 pm	Cancer	Water	Fruitful	4th
12 Thu	Cancer	Water	Fruitful	New 10:48 pm
13 Fri 1:31 pm	Leo	Fire	Barren	1st
14 Sat	Leo	Fire	Barren	1st
15 Sun 1:31 pm	Virgo	Earth	Barren	1st
16 Mon	Virgo	Earth	Barren	1st
17 Tue 3:42 pm	Libra	Air	Semi-fruitful	1st
18 Wed	Libra	Air	Semi-fruitful	1st
19 Thu 9:13 pm	Scorpio	Water	Fruitful	2nd 3:52 pm
20 Fri	Scorpio	Water	Fruitful	2nd
21 Sat	Scorpio	Water	Fruitful	2nd
22 Sun 6:12 am	Sagittarius	Fire	Barren	2nd
23 Mon	Sagittarius	Fire	Barren	2nd
24 Tue 5:49 pm	Capricorn	Earth	Semi-fruitful	2nd
25 Wed	Capricorn	Earth	Semi-fruitful	2nd
26 Thu	Capricorn	Earth	Semi-fruitful	2nd
27 Fri 6:41 am	Aquarius	Air	Barren	Full 4:20 pm
28 Sat	Aquarius	Air	Barren	3rd
29 Sun 7:28 pm	Pisces	Water	Fruitful	3rd
30 Mon	Pisces	Water	Fruitful	3rd
31 Tue	Pisces	Water	Fruitful	3rd

August Moon Table

Date	Sign	Element	Nature	Phase
1 Wed 6:54 am	Aries	Fire	Barren	3rd
2 Thu	Aries	Fire	Barren	3rd
3 Fri 3:51 pm	Taurus	Earth	Semi-fruitful	3rd
4 Sat	Taurus	Earth	Semi-fruitful	4th 2:18 pm
5 Sun 9:32 pm	Gemini	Air	Barren	4th
6 Mon	Gemini	Air	Barren	4th
7 Tue	Gemini	Air	Barren	4th
8 Wed 12:01 am	Cancer	Water	Fruitful	4th
9 Thu	Cancer	Water	Fruitful	4th
10 Fri 12:18 am	Leo	Fire	Barren	4th
11 Sat 11:59 pm	Virgo	Earth	Barren	New 5:58 am
12 Sun	Virgo	Earth	Barren	1st
13 Mon	Virgo	Earth	Barren	1st
14 Tue 12:57 am	Libra	Air	Semi-fruitful	1st
15 Wed	Libra	Air	Semi-fruitful	1st
16 Thu 4:54 am	Scorpio	Water	Fruitful	1st
17 Fri	Scorpio	Water	Fruitful	1st
18 Sat 12:45 pm	Sagittarius	Fire	Barren	2nd 3:49 am
19 Sun	Sagittarius	Fire	Barren	2nd
20 Mon	Sagittarius	Fire	Barren	2nd
21 Tue 12:00 am	Capricorn	Earth	Semi-fruitful	2nd
22 Wed	Capricorn	Earth	Semi-fruitful	2nd
23 Thu 12:56 pm	Aquarius	Air	Barren	2nd
24 Fri	Aquarius	Air	Barren	2nd
25 Sat	Aquarius	Air	Barren	2nd
26 Sun 1:32 am	Pisces	Water	Fruitful	Full 7:56 am
27 Mon	Pisces	Water	Fruitful	3rd
28 Tue 12:35 pm	Aries	Fire	Barren	3rd
29 Wed	Aries	Fire	Barren	3rd
30 Thu 9:30 pm	Taurus	Earth	Semi-fruitful	3rd
31 Fri	Taurus	Earth	Semi-fruitful	3rd

Times are in Eastern Time.

September Moon Table

Date	Sign	Element	Nature	Phase
1 Sat	Taurus	Earth	Semi-fruitful	3rd
2 Sun 4:02 am	Gemini	Air	Barren	4th 10:37 pm
3 Mon	Gemini	Air	Barren	4th
4 Tue 8:03 am	Cancer	Water	Fruitful	4th
5 Wed	Cancer	Water	Fruitful	4th
6 Thu 9:54 am	Leo	Fire	Barren	4th
7 Fri	Leo	Fire	Barren	4th
8 Sat 10:29 am	Virgo	Earth	Barren	4th
9 Sun	Virgo	Earth	Barren	New 2:01 pm
10 Mon 11:20 am	Libra	Air	Semi-fruitful	1st
11 Tue	Libra	Air	Semi-fruitful	1st
12 Wed 2:15 pm	Scorpio	Water	Fruitful	1st
13 Thu	Scorpio	Water	Fruitful	1st
14 Fri 8:45 pm	Sagittarius	Fire	Barren	1st
15 Sat	Sagittarius	Fire	Barren	1st
16 Sun	Sagittarius	Fire	Barren	2nd 7:15 pm
17 Mon 7:07 am	Capricorn	Earth	Semi-fruitful	2nd
18 Tue	Capricorn	Earth	Semi-fruitful	2nd
19 Wed 7:52 pm	Aquarius	Air	Barren	2nd
20 Thu	Aquarius	Air	Barren	2nd
21 Fri	Aquarius	Air	Barren	2nd
22 Sat 8:27 am	Pisces	Water	Fruitful	2nd
23 Sun	Pisces	Water	Fruitful	2nd
24 Mon 7:04 pm	Aries	Fire	Barren	Full 10:52 pm
25 Tue	Aries	Fire	Barren	3rd
26 Wed	Aries	Fire	Barren	3rd
27 Thu 3:16 am	Taurus	Earth	Semi-fruitful	3rd
28 Fri	Taurus	Earth	Semi-fruitful	3rd
29 Sat 9:26 am	Gemini	Air	Barren	3rd
30 Sun	Gemini	Air	Barren	3rd

October Moon Table

Date	Sign	Element	Nature	Phase
1 Mon 2:00 pm	Cancer	Water	Fruitful	3rd
2 Tue	Cancer	Water	Fruitful	4th 5:45 am
3 Wed 5:12 pm	Leo	Fire	Barren	4th
4 Thu	Leo	Fire	Barren	4th
5 Fri 7:19 pm	Virgo	Earth	Barren	4th
6 Sat	Virgo	Earth	Barren	4th
7 Sun 9:10 pm	Libra	Air	Semi-fruitful	4th
8 Mon	Libra	Air	Semi-fruitful	New 11:47 pm
9 Tue	Libra	Air	Semi-fruitful	1st
10 Wed 12:09 am	Scorpio	Water	Fruitful	1st
11 Thu	Scorpio	Water	Fruitful	1st
12 Fri 5:53 am	Sagittarius	Fire	Barren	1st
13 Sat	Sagittarius	Fire	Barren	1st
14 Sun 3:17 pm	Capricorn	Earth	Semi-fruitful	1st
15 Mon	Capricorn	Earth	Semi-fruitful	1st
16 Tue	Capricorn	Earth	Semi-fruitful	2nd 2:02 pm
17 Wed 3:36 am	Aquarius	Air	Barren	2nd
18 Thu	Aquarius	Air	Barren	2nd
19 Fri 4:20 pm	Pisces	Water	Fruitful	2nd
20 Sat	Pisces	Water	Fruitful	2nd
21 Sun	Pisces	Water	Fruitful	2nd
22 Mon 2:58 am	Aries	Fire	Barren	2nd
23 Tue	Aries	Fire	Barren	2nd
24 Wed 10:33 am	Taurus	Earth	Semi-fruitful	Full 12:45 pm
25 Thu	Taurus	Earth	Semi-fruitful	3rd
26 Fri 3:41 pm	Gemini	Air	Barren	3rd
27 Sat	Gemini	Air	Barren	3rd
28 Sun 7:27 pm	Cancer	Water	Fruitful	3rd
29 Mon	Cancer	Water	Fruitful	3rd
30 Tue 10:42 pm	Leo	Fire	Barren	3rd
31 Wed	Leo	Fire	Barren	4th 12:40 pm

Times are in Eastern Time.

November Moon Table

Date	Sign	Element	Nature	Phase
1 Thu	Leo	Fire	Barren	4th
2 Fri 1:48 am	Virgo	Earth	Barren	4th
3 Sat	Virgo	Earth	Barren	4th
4 Sun 4:01 am	Libra	Air	Semi-fruitful	4th
5 Mon	Libra	Air	Semi-fruitful	4th
6 Tue 8:02 am	Scorpio	Water	Fruitful	4th
7 Wed	Scorpio	Water	Fruitful	New 11:02 am
8 Thu 1:59 pm	Sagittarius	Fire	Barren	1st
9 Fri	Sagittarius	Fire	Barren	1st
10 Sat 10:55 pm	Capricorn	Earth	Semi-fruitful	1st
11 Sun	Capricorn	Earth	Semi-fruitful	1st
12 Mon	Capricorn	Earth	Semi-fruitful	1st
13 Tue 10:45 am	Aquarius	Air	Barren	1st
14 Wed	Aquarius	Air	Barren	1st
15 Thu 11:41 pm	Pisces	Water	Fruitful	2nd 9:54 am
16 Fri	Pisces	Water	Fruitful	2nd
17 Sat	Pisces	Water	Fruitful	2nd
18 Sun 10:56 am	Aries	Fire	Barren	2nd
19 Mon	Aries	Fire	Barren	2nd
20 Tue 6:43 pm	Taurus	Earth	Semi-fruitful	2nd
21 Wed	Taurus	Earth	Semi-fruitful	2nd
22 Thu 11:10 pm	Gemini	Air	Barren	2nd
23 Fri	Gemini	Air	Barren	Full 12:39 am
24 Sat	Gemini	Air	Barren	3rd
25 Sun 1:38 am	Cancer	Water	Fruitful	3rd
26 Mon	Cancer	Water	Fruitful	3rd
27 Tue 3:35 am	Leo	Fire	Barren	3rd
28 Wed	Leo	Fire	Barren	3rd
29 Thu 6:08 am	Virgo	Earth	Barren	4th 7:19 pm
30 Fri	Virgo	Earth	Barren	4th

December Moon Table

Date	Sign	Element	Nature	Phase
1 Sat 9:49 am	Libra	Air	Semi-fruitful	4th
2 Sun	Libra	Air	Semi-fruitful	4th
3 Mon 2:55 pm	Scorpio	Water	Fruitful	4th
4 Tue	Scorpio	Water	Fruitful	4th
5 Wed 9:49 pm	Sagittarius	Fire	Barren	4th
6 Thu	Sagittarius	Fire	Barren	4th
7 Fri	Sagittarius	Fire	Barren	New 2:20 am
8 Sat 7:01 am	Capricorn	Earth	Semi-fruitful	1st
9 Sun	Capricorn	Earth	Semi-fruitful	1st
10 Mon 6:39 pm	Aquarius	Air	Barren	1st
11 Tue	Aquarius	Air	Barren	1st
12 Wed	Aquarius	Air	Barren	1st
13 Thu 7:40 am	Pisces	Water	Fruitful	1st
14 Fri	Pisces	Water	Fruitful	1st
15 Sat 7:44 pm	Aries	Fire	Barren	2nd 6:49 am
16 Sun	Aries	Fire	Barren	2nd
17 Mon	Aries	Fire	Barren	2nd
18 Tue 4:37 am	Taurus	Earth	Semi-fruitful	2nd
19 Wed	Taurus	Earth	Semi-fruitful	2nd
20 Thu 9:34 am	Gemini	Air	Barren	2nd
21 Fri	Gemini	Air	Barren	2nd
22 Sat 11:28 am	Cancer	Water	Fruitful	Full 12:49 pm
23 Sun	Cancer	Water	Fruitful	3rd
24 Mon 11:59 am	Leo	Fire	Barren	3rd
25 Tue	Leo	Fire	Barren	3rd
26 Wed 12:50 pm	Virgo	Earth	Barren	3rd
27 Thu	Virgo	Earth	Barren	3rd
28 Fri 3:23 pm	Libra	Air	Semi-fruitful	3rd
29 Sat	Libra	Air	Semi-fruitful	4th 4:34 am
30 Sun 8:23 pm	Scorpio	Water	Fruitful	4th
31 Mon	Scorpio	Water	Fruitful	4th

Times are in Eastern Time.

Dates to Destroy Weeds and Pests

Dates	Sign	Quarter
Jan 3 2:23 am–Jan 5 3:12 am	Leo	3rd
Jan 5 3:12 am–Jan 7 7:15 am	Virgo	3rd
Jan 12 2:04 am–Jan 14 2:42 pm	Sagittarius	4th
Jan 31 8:27 am–Feb 1 2:13 pm	Leo	3rd
Feb 1 2:13 pm–Feb 3 4:47 pm	Virgo	3rd
Feb 8 8:53 am–Feb 10 9:21 pm	Sagittarius	4th
Feb 13 10:11 am–Feb 15 4:05 pm	Aquarius	4th
Mar 1 7:51 pm–Mar 3 3:20 am	Virgo	3rd
Mar 7 5:03 am–Mar 9 6:20 am	Sagittarius	3rd
Mar 9 6:20 am–Mar 10 4:52 am	Sagittarius	4th
Mar 12 6:44 pm–Mar 15 6:12 am	Aquarius	4th
Apr 4 2:55 am–Apr 6 2:01 pm	Sagittarius	3rd
Apr 9 2:50 am–Apr 11 2:40 pm	Aquarius	4th
Apr 13 11:25 pm–Apr 15 9:57 pm	Aries	4th
May 1 11:20 am–May 3 10:06 pm	Sagittarius	3rd
May 6 10:48 am–May 7 10:09 pm	Aquarius	3rd
May 7 10:09 pm–May 8 11:11 pm	Aquarius	4th
May 11 8:40 am–May 13 2:15 pm	Aries	4th
May 29 10:20 am–May 31 5:27 am	Sagittarius	3rd
Jun 2 6:06 pm–Jun 5 6:53 am	Aquarius	3rd
Jun 7 5:26 pm–Jun 10 12:04 am	Aries	4th
Jun 12 2:53 am–Jun 13 3:43 pm	Gemini	4th
Jun 30 12:37 am–Jul 2 1:31 pm	Aquarius	3rd
Jul 5 12:50 am–Jul 6 3:51 am	Aries	3rd
Jul 6 3:51 am–Jul 7 8:51 am	Aries	4th
Jul 9 12:58 pm–Jul 11 1:59 pm	Gemini	4th
Jul 27 4:20 pm–Jul 29 7:28 pm	Aquarius	3rd

Dates to Destroy Weeds and Pests

Dates	Sign	Quarter
Aug 1 6:54 am–Aug 3 3:51 pm	Aries	3rd
Aug 5 9:32 pm–Aug 8 12:01 am	Gemini	4th
Aug 10 12:18 am–Aug 11 5:58 am	Leo	4th
Aug 28 12:35 pm–Aug 30 9:30 pm	Aries	3rd
Sep 2 4:02 am–Sep 2 10:37 pm	Gemini	3rd
Sep 2 10:37 pm–Sep 4 8:03 am	Gemini	4th
Sep 6 9:54 am–Sep 8 10:29 am	Leo	4th
Sep 8 10:29 am–Sep 9 2:01 pm	Virgo	4th
Sep 24 10:52 pm–Sep 27 3:16 am	Aries	3rd
Sep 29 9:26 am–Oct 1 2:00 pm	Gemini	3rd
Oct 3 5:12 pm–Oct 5 7:19 pm	Leo	4th
Oct 5 7:19 pm–Oct 7 9:10 pm	Virgo	4th
Oct 26 3:41 pm–Oct 28 7:27 pm	Gemini	3rd
Oct 30 10:42 pm–Oct 31 12:40 pm	Leo	3rd
Oct 31 12:40 pm–Nov 2 1:48 am	Leo	4th
Nov 2 1:48 am–Nov 4 4:01 am	Virgo	4th
Nov 23 12:39 am–Nov 25 1:38 am	Gemini	3rd
Nov 27 3:35 am–Nov 29 6:08 am	Leo	3rd
Nov 29 6:08 am–Nov 29 7:19 pm	Virgo	3rd
Nov 29 7:19 pm–Dec 1 9:49 am	Virgo	4th
Dec 5 9:49 pm–Dec 7 2:20 am	Sagittarius	4th
Dec 24 11:59 am–Dec 26 12:50 pm	Leo	3rd
Dec 26 12:50 pm–Dec 28 3:23 pm	Virgo	3rd

Times are in Eastern Time.